The Origins of
English Individualism

The Origins of English Individualism

THE FAMILY, PROPERTY
AND
SOCIAL TRANSITION

Alan Macfarlane

CAMBRIDGE UNIVERSITY PRESS

NEW YORK

Published in the USA and Canada by
The Syndics of the Cambridge University Press
32 East 57th Street, New York, NY 10022, USA

© Basil Blackwell 1978

First published by Basil Blackwell 1978
First published by Cambridge University Press 1979

Printed in the United States of America
Typeset by Preface Ltd., Salisbury, Wiltshire
Printed and bound by Vail-Ballou Press, Inc., Binghamton, New York

Library of Congress Catalog Card Number: 78-73956
ISBN 0 521 22587 6   hard covers
ISBN 0 521 29570 X   paperback

To the memory of

**Donald Kennedy Macfarlane
of Locheport**

1916 — 1977

Contents

Apologies and
Acknowledgements

It is always difficult to write a book which appears to attack the work of
friends. If one apologizes one adds insult to injury. All that I can say to
those from whom I have learnt so much, but with whose views I have
disagreed here, is that I myself have long been misled, as the preface will
make clear. Many of the criticisms I make could be made against my
own earlier work.

On the other hand it is a pleasant task to thank those who have helped
to make this book possible. It would never have been written without
the advice and inspiration of Teodor Shanin. He not only acted as a
catalyst in suggesting that I should write about the English peasantry,
but has subsequently given me much good advice on peasantry in
general. The inspiration of the work of the S.S.R.C. Cambridge Group
for the History of Population and Social Structure, particularly Peter
Laslett, Roger Schofield and Tony Wrigley, was also essential in many
ways and I am most grateful to them. One member of the Group who
not only provided general support and stimulus but also particular
information and encouragement was Richard Smith. His enthusiasm
and detailed findings were absolutely essential. It is impossible to
express my gratitude for his generosity except by saying that this book
is, particularly in relation to the medieval section, largely the book
which he could and might have written, though his conclusions might
have been different from mine. It is a lonely business being a heretic,
especially when trespassing out of one's own time period as a historian.
Without Richard Smith's encouragement I would never have turned a
short article into a book. It is furthermore a book which will either be
confirmed or refuted by the work which he is currently engaged on. The
other medievalist who was sufficiently encouraging to enable me to
proceed was my first teacher, James Campbell. He kindly read an early
draft of the section on medieval society and warned me against some of
its excesses. Keith Thomas read the whole draft and not only suggested

ways of improving the argument but also gave me a number of valuable references. The section on Marx and Weber was read by Geoffrey Hawthorn, who confirmed my interpretation of their work and gave me indispensable moral support in relation to the general argument. The whole text was read for style and content by Jessica Styles and the proofs were checked by Charles Jardine. Piers Videbsky helped check the notes, read and commented on the whole text, and made invaluable suggestions on how to improve the presentation. Mary Wraith typed the manuscript with speed and efficiency and Polly Steele guided it through the press. Members of the Department of Social Anthropology at Cambridge, and particularly Jack Goody, have been a source of ideas and support, as have my students. The Research Centre at King's College, Cambridge and the Social Science Research Council have provided financial support for the detailed work on the sample villages which is referred to in the text. I am grateful to all these individuals and corporate bodies. I am also grateful to the archivists at the County Record Offices at Carlisle, Chelmsford, and Kendal and the Public Record Office, London, for help in finding local records. My final debt is the greatest. It is to Sarah Harrison who has helped in too many ways to enumerate. Her work on the local records is the basis for the sections on Earls Colne and Kirkby Lonsdale, her knowledge of manorial law and manorial documents was indispensable. I have discussed each chapter with her and many of the ideas have been changed as a result of such discussions. She has read the draft through several times and also checked the proofs. Without her encouragement the book would not have been written; without her unrivalled knowledge of early modern land records it would have been much the worse.

Abbreviations and Conventions

Place of publication of all books is London, unless otherwise specified.
Spelling and punctuation in quotations has been modernized.
The following abbreviations are used:

Ec.H.R.	Economic History Review
E.R.O.	Essex Record Office, County Hall, Chelmsford, Essex
n.	note
n.s.	new series
P & P	Past and Present
P.R.O.	Public Record Office, Chancery Lane, London
soc.	society
trans.	translated by
T.C.W.A.A.S.	Transactions of the Cumberland and Westmorland Archaeological and Antiquarian Society

Books which are frequently cited, or cited in several chapters, are listed in the following list of abbreviated titles. If a work is cited by a shortened title in a footnote, but is not in this list, it will have been given a full title in a footnote earlier in that chapter.

List of Abbreviated Titles

Bendix, *Weber*

R. Bendix, *Max Weber: An Intellectual Portrait* (Paperback edn, London, 1966).

Bennett, *Manor*

H. S. Bennett, *Life on the English Manor* (1937; Paperback edn, Cambridge, 1960).

Blackstone, *Commentaries*

Commentaries on the Laws of England (18th edn, 1829).

Bloch, *Land*

Land and Work in Medieval Europe (1967), trans. J. E. Anderson.

Bracton, *Laws*

On the Laws and Customs of England (Cambridge, Massachusetts, 1968), ed. George Woodbine, trans. Samuel E. Thorne, vol. 2.

DeWindt, *Land*

E. B. DeWindt, *Land and People in Holywell-cum-Needleworth* (Toronto, 1972).

Galeski, *Rural*

Boguslaw Galeski, *Basic Concepts of Rural Sociology* (Manchester, 1972).

Goody, *Family*

Jack Goody, Joan Thirsk and E. P. Thompson (eds.), *Family and Inheritance: Rural Society in Western Europe 1200–1800* (Cambridge, 1976).

Hajnal, *European Marriage*	'European marriage in perspective' in D. V. Glass and D. E. C. Eversley (eds.) *Population in History* (1965).
Hexter, *Reappraisals*	J. H. Hexter, *Reappraisals in History* (1961).
Hilton, *Bond Men*	Rodney Hilton, *Bond Men Made Free: Medieval Peasant Movements and the English Rising of 1381* (1973).
Hilton, *Peasantry*	R. H. Hilton, *The English Peasantry in the Later Middle Ages* (Oxford, 1975).
Homans, *Villagers*	G. C. Homans, *English Villagers of the Thirteenth Century* (1940; New York, 1960).
Hoskins, *Midland Peasant*	W. G. Hoskins, *The Midland Peasant: The Economic and Social History of a Leicestershire Village* (1957: paper edn, 1965).
Howell, *Peasant Inheritance*	Cicely Howell, 'Peasant inheritance customs in the Midlands, 1280–1700' in Goody, *Family* (see above).
Kamenka, *Feudalism*	Eugene Kamenka and R. S. Neale (eds), *Feudalism, Capitalism and Beyond* (1975).
Kosminsky, *Studies*	E. A. Kosminsky, *Studies in the Agrarian History of England in the Thirteenth Century* (Oxford, 1956), ed. R. H. Hilton.
Laslett, *Household*	Peter Laslett (ed.), *Household and Family in Past Time* (Cambridge, 1972).
Lofgren, *Family and Household*	Orvar Lofgren, 'Family and Household among Scandinavian Peasants', *Ethnologia Scandinavica* (1974).
Maitland, *English Law*	Sir F. Pollock and F. W. Maitland, *History of English Law before the Time of Edward I*

	(2nd edn, Cambridge, 1968), 2 vols.
Marx, *Capital*	Karl Marx, *Capital* (1887; Lawrence and Wishart edn, 1954), 3 vols.
Montesquieu, *Spirit*	Baron de Montesquieu, *The Spirit of the Laws* (1748; Hafner edn, New York, 1975), trans. by Thomas Nugent.
Macfarlane, *Reconstructing*	Alan Macfarlane, Sarah Harrison and Charles Jardine, *Reconstructing Historical Communities* (Cambridge, 1977).
Plucknett, *Common Law*	T. Plucknett, *A Concise History of the Common Law* (5th edn, 1956).
Pocock, *Ancient Constitution*	J. G. A. Pocock, *The Ancient Constitution and the Feudal Law* (Cambridge, 1957).
Postan, *England*	'England' in *The Cambridge Economic History of Europe,* vol. i, *The Agrarian Life of the Middle Ages,* ed. M. M. Postan (2nd edn, Cambridge, 1966).
Postan, *Essays*	M. M. Postan, *Essays on Medieval Agriculture and General Problems of the Medieval Economy* (Cambridge, 1973).
Postan, *Medieval*	M. M. Postan, *The Medieval Economy and Society* (Penguin edn, 1975).
Raftis, *Tenure*	J. A. Raftis, *Tenure and Mobility: Studies in the Social History of the Medieval English Village* (Toronto, 1964).
Redfield, *Peasant*	Robert Redfield, *Peasant Society and Culture* (Chicago, 1960).
Rogers, *Six Centuries*	J. E. Thorold Rogers, *Six Centuries of Work and Wages* (12th edn, 1917), p. 44.

Searle, *Lordship* Eleanor Searle, *Lordship and Community: Battle Abbey and its Banlieu 1066–1538* (Toronto, 1974).

Shanin, *Peasants* Teodor Shanin (ed.), *Peasants and Peasant Societies* (Penguin, 1971).

Shanin, *Awkward Class* Teodor Shanin, *The Awkward Class* (Oxford 1972).

Shanin, *Peasant Economy*, i Teodor Shanin, 'The Nature and Logic of the Peasant Economy', *Jnl. Peasant Studies*, vol. 1, No. 1 (Oct. 1973).

Shanin, *Peasant Economy*, ii The same, vol. 1, No. 2 (Jan. 1974).

Smith, *Life Cycles* R. M. Smith, 'English Peasant Life-cycles and Socio-Economic Network: A quantitative geographical case study' (Cambridge Univ. Ph.D. thesis, 1974).

Spufford, *Communities* Margaret Spufford, *Contrasting Communities: English Villagers in the Sixteenth and Seventeenth Centuries* (Cambridge, 1974).

Thomas, *Polish Peasant* W. I. Thomas and F. Znaniecki, *The Polish Peasant in Europe and America* (1918; 2nd edn, reprinted by Dover Books, New York, 1958).

Thorner, *Peasantry* Daniel Thorner, 'Peasantry' in the *International Encyclopaedia of the Social Sciences*.

Tocqueville, *Ancien* Alexis De Tocqueville, *L'Ancien Regime* (Oxford, 1956) trans. M. W. Patterson.

Titow, *Rural Society* J. Z. Titow, *English Rural Society 1200–1350* (1969).

Weber, *Protestant* Max Weber, *The Protestant Ethic and the Spirit of Capitalism* (Unwin University Books edn, 1930), trans. Talcott Parsons.

Weber, *Theory* Max Weber, *The Theory of Social and Economic Organization*

Weber, *General*

(Free Press Paperback edn, New York, 1964), ed. Talcott Parsons. Max Weber, *General Economic History* (Collier Books edn, New York, 1961), trans. Frank H. Knight.

Since Robinson Crusoe's experiences are a favourite theme with political economists, let us take a look at him on his island. Moderate though he be, yet some few wants he has to satisfy, and must therefore do a little useful work of various sorts, such as making tools and furniture, taming goats, fishing and hunting ... Necessity itself compels him to apportion his time accurately between his different kinds of work. Whether one kind occupies a greater space in his general activity than another, depends on the difficulties, greater or less as the case may be, to be overcome in attaining the useful effect aimed at. This our friend Robinson soon learns by experience, and having rescued a watch, ledger, and pen and ink from the wreck, commences, like a true-born Briton, to keep a set of books .... Let us now transport ourselves from Robinson's island bathed in light to the European middle ages shrouded in darkness.

(Karl Marx, *Capital* (Lawrence and Wishart edn., 1974), vol. i, p. 81)

The alternative solution — the shrinking of the ego to a hard ultimate kernel which provides the basis, or at least the touchstone, for everything — is worthy of consideration. It might suitably be called the Crusoe tradition: Marx already observed that Robinson was a favourite character with the economists, but he is present even more in the backs of the minds of philosophers, even if they did not so frequently invoke him by name. The fittingness of the Crusoe myth to an individualistic age need hardly be stressed.

(Ernest Gellner, *Thought and Change* (1964), p. 104)

Introduction

This is a book that wrote itself. I had intended to spend a precious sabbatical term drawing together a large amount of material I had already collected on a very different subject. But I found that before it was possible to commence that study, I needed to get clear in my mind what sort of society England was over the centuries leading up to the industrial revolution. I intended to write two short articles and then to move on. The articles were written,[1] but I became gripped and intrigued by what I was finding. Now, at the end of the process, it is easier to see some of the reasons why I should have felt it necessary to range so widely.

When I first undertook research and wrote about witchcraft in Tudor and Stuart England I did so within the conventional framework provided by a degree in history at Oxford.[2] Despite some warnings from my first tutor, an acquaintance with medieval and early modern history and historians had led me to accept a general picture of English history which saw a slow but steady economic growth, a transition from a small-scale 'peasant' society, which gradually broke apart in the sixteenth century and out of whose ruin emerged the first industrial nation. I therefore interpreted witchcraft accusations as the spiritual and social concomitants of the changes which Tawney and Weber had charted. They were the result of the new economic and social individualism which was undermining the communal, village-based, society. As the market and cash penetrated into the once face-to-face, subsistence, society, economic forces and traditional ethical demands clashed. Out of this arose the guilt and anxiety which we manifestly find in the witch-

[1] They are both to be published in 1978; 'The Peasantry in England before the Industrial Revolution. A Mythical Model?' in David Green, Colin Haselgrove and Matthew Spriggs (eds.), *Social Organisation and Settlement*, and 'The myth of peasantry: family and economy in a northern parish' in Richard Smith (ed.), *Land, Kinship and Life Cycle*. I am grateful to the editors of these collections for comments on these early articles.
[2] *Witchcraft in Tudor and Stuart England: A Regional and Comparative Study* (1970).

craft trials. The explanation worked reasonably well it seemed, and I was happy to accept the medievalist's account of the largely 'traditional' society up to the fifteenth century. There were, however, two rather large unresolved problems which this account could not deal with and which I was consequently forced to brush aside as impossible to solve.

One of these problems was the reason for the decline of witchcraft prosecutions; the second was the peculiarity of English witchcraft within Europe. In relation to the second, it became clear that if one looked at Scottish or Continental witchcraft beliefs they were fundamentally different from those in England and highlighted what was absent in England. At a very general level, there was a notable absence of a sexual motif in England; the *incubus* and *succubus*, the sexual orgies with the Devil and other witches, were absent. English witchcraft was very decorous. Secondly, there was the absence of a food and hunger motif in England. The nearest we get to the cannibalistic orgies described outside England is the roast beef picnics of the Lancashire witches. Thirdly, English witchcraft beliefs made the suspects very individualistic. The covens and group meetings ascribed to witches elsewhere were absent; in England they tended to act alone, even if they sometimes knew the names of other suspects. Fourthly, there was an absence of attack on the *nouveaux riches*, against those who were marginally gaining on their neighbours and acquiring an unfairly large slice of the local resources. In England, witchcraft was directed against the slightly poorer who made demands on their neighbours. It was not used, as it is in many societies, to prevent economic differentiation, but rather to allow it to occur. These and other differences could not be satisfactorily explained within the framework which I had inherited.

Although one could ascribe the peculiarities to differences of legal systems within Europe, for instance England's system of Common Law and juries, as opposed to the use of torture and Roman Law elsewhere, this only seemed to explain a little of the difference. Since I was firmly convinced by my general reading that the Continent, despite differences such as language or political system, was basically similar to England in culture, economy and social system. I was unable to understand why witchcraft should have been so different. It could clearly not reflect any deeper differences, since I was led to believe that there were none. This is the first block which I encountered.

After witchcraft I turned to the study of sexual and marital relations in England in the same period.[3] My supervisor, the anthropologist Isaac

---

[3]'The Regulation of Marital and Sexual Relationships in Seventeenth Century England' (Unpublished M.Phil.thesis, University of London, 1968).

Schapera, pointed out that a horror of incest was, according to Malinowski and Radcliffe-Brown, a universal human fear. He suggested that I should look at the historical material to see how such horror was manifested in England. I found that such revulsion was hardly present at all. The English from early times seemed singularly unconcerned about incest. This led me to an examination of the general sexual and marital pattern, which again did not seem to conform to what anthropologists had found in other peasant societies. Kinship seemed relatively unimportant, marriage seemed to be little controlled by parents, the relations between the sexes seemed unusually relaxed, even when one compared England with the contemporary Mediterranean region. Once again, what one would have expected if England had been the sort of country historians portrayed did not fit; but since no other model was available I was unable to go further.

While working on witchcraft and sexual behaviour I had come across a number of interesting seventeenth century diaries, outstanding among them the diary of an Essex clergyman, Ralph Josselin.[4] My training led me to expect that, living before the watershed of the industrial revolution, his social and mental and economic life would appear very remote, very different from my own. It would still carry many of the overtones of the earlier medieval period from which the country was just emerging. I was startled to find, on the contrary, how 'modern' his world was; his family life, attitudes to children, economic anxieties, and the very structure of his thought was very familiar indeed. His sophistication and wide knowledge were impressively obvious and his feelings were instantly recognizable. Of course there were features that were different; a constant background of chronic sickness, a marked interest in the Day of Judgement, certain political and religious beliefs. Yet it was his similarity rather than the difference which was striking. I felt, as those who have read Pepys' diary must have felt, that the diary reveals a man whose motives and actions are almost totally familiar. Neither of these or the many other diaries of the period fitted at all well with my general picture of pre-industrial England. Nor was I able to account for the widespread keeping of personal diaries at such an early date in England.

I then turned to an anthropological study of a contemporary Himalayan society.[5] Two things especially struck me when comparing it to England in the past. The first was the very great difference in *per capita* wealth in the two societies. Historians kept talking about

[4]*The Family Life of Ralph Josselin, A Seventeenth-Century Clergyman; An Essay in Historical Anthropology* (Cambridge, 1970); Alan Macfarlane (ed.), *The Diary of Ralph Josselin 1616-1683* (1976), Records of Social and Economic History, new series, 3.
[5]*Resources and Population; A study of the Gurungs of Nepal* (Cambridge, 1976).

England in the pre-industrial period as a 'subsistence' economy, with people on the verge of starvation, technologically backward, economically unsophisticated. But when I compared the technology, the inventories of possessions and the budgets of a contemporary Asian society with those for English sixteenth-century villagers, I found that there was already an enormous gap. The English were, on the whole, an immeasurably wealthier people, with a far higher investment in tools and other productive forces. To think of India or China in the early twentieth century as directly comparable to England just before the industrial revolution appeared to be a serious mistake. This raised the question of how and when England had accumulated wealth at the village level. This was clearly related to another major difference, the demographic one. It appears that almost all peasant and tribal societies follow what has been termed a 'crisis' pattern, with rapid population build-up, then a crisis of some kind, usually engendered by war, famine or epidemic disease. Population drops to a low level and then starts to build up again. This pattern characterized much of western Europe up to the eighteenth century, disappearing in the eighteenth century in Norway and France, for example. The curious fact is that, from at least the middle of the fourteenth-century, such a pattern has been absent in England. I could find nothing in the literature on economic or social life to explain why England should have escaped from such a cycle three centuries or more before any other large nation, or on how this was related to its affluence.

Finally, I have been engaged during the last fourteen years in an intensive study of two English parishes from the fourteenth to the eighteenth centuries.[6] After collecting together every piece of surviving information about each place and processing it by hand and computer, it will be necessary to analyse the results within a general theoretical framework. As I worked on these documents and compared the results with general historical accounts of change in England there was again a very considerable gap between what I was discovering and what I *should* have been finding. Instead of relatively 'closed' and integrated 'communities' at the start, which gradually broke apart with the growing penetration of the market, increasing geographical mobility, the break-down of kinship groups and other changes, it began to appear that there was no long secular trend. There were, it is true, considerable fluctuations and certain major changes in the distribution of wealth, the demographic structure and technology. Yet it was just not possible to use the models of community-based societies which historians and

---

[6]Alan Macfarlane, Sarah Harrison and Charles Jardine, *Reconstructing Historical Communities* (Cambridge, 1977).

anthropologists had devised in relation to many parts of the world. I was fairly certain that, however one defined 'Community,' there was relatively little of it in the villages we were studying, as far back as the sixteenth century. Yet I was uncertain whether this was something new or old at that date; whether an older closeness had recently broken down and whether England was generally exceptional within Europe in this respect. In other words, I was once again dissatisfied with the general framework within which I was working, but did not know precisely why, or where I should look for an alternative model. This book is an attempt to sketch out an alternative history of England which would resolve some of these difficulties.

The title needs some explanation, for it is designedly doubly ambiguous. Marc Bloch has pointed out in the 'Idol of Origins,' that the word 'origins' means both 'beginnings' and also 'causes' and that there is 'frequent cross-contamination of the two meanings.'[7] I am here using both these meanings, enquiring into both when English individualism began, and what caused it. But the problem is compounded by the ambiguity of the word 'individualism.' This is also used in two different senses in this book. Both the meanings can be read into a remark by F. W. Maitland when he wrote, concerning the highly developed property rights of women, that England 'long ago' had chosen her 'individualistic path.'[8] The first meaning is the argument that England as a whole was different from the rest of Europe, and even from Scotland, thus acting 'individually' or separately. In this sense, England stood alone. The second meaning is at the level of the single person. It is that a central and basic feature of English social structure has for long been the stress on the rights and privileges of the individual as against the wider group or the State. This is the more general meaning of individualism as used, for example, by Macpherson in relation to economics and political philosophy, or Riesman in relation to culture.[9] It is the view that society is constituted of autonomous, equal, units, namely separate individuals, and that such individuals are more important, ultimately, than any larger constituent group. It is reflected in the concept of individual private property, in the political and legal liberty of the individual, in the idea of the individual's direct communication with God. The argument below concentrates on the economic aspects of individualism, but other features will also be alluded to. This work is thus a search not only for a revised framework

[7]Marc Bloch, *Historian's Craft* (Manchester, 1954), pp. 29-30.
[8]Maitland, *English Law*, p. 433.
[9]A lucid discussion of the various meanings of individualism is Steven Lukes, *Individualism* (1973). The author distinguishes eleven different constituents of the term, but argues that they tend to be very closely interrelated.

which would make some of my own previously unsolved theoretical problems soluble, but one which would help to explain whether and when England became different from other parts of Europe and the nature of the social structure which we have inherited.

January, 1978   Ivy Farm Barn,
                                                 Lode,
                                                 Nr. Cambridge.

1

The Nature of a Peasant Society

There are practical, emotional and intellectual reasons for wanting to understand English history between the thirteenth and eighteenth centuries. One practical reason is that since England was the first country to industrialize, it is considered to be a good guide to those Third World countries also wishing to do so. It is hoped that lessons may be learnt so that the widespread poverty and malnutrition which currently characterize up to two thirds of the globe may be alleviated. This motive is widely acknowledged;[1] if we could understand why the 'industrial revolution' occurred first in England and what *caused* it, we might be able to encourage economic growth elsewhere, while avoiding the worst excesses of the process. England is a test case, a model, perhaps the best documented case study that we possess of the way a basically agricultural society turned into an urban and industrial nation. An emotional reason is that we wish to understand ourselves in time; we recognize that much of what we now are is explained by the past and that even the differences make it possible to hold up a mirror to ourselves. Since much of American culture stemmed from the Anglo-Saxon migration in the seventeenth century, this quest for 'roots' is common to much of the world. This is all the more so since the effects of first English and later American imperialism have spread throughout much of the globe: a great deal of modern India, Africa or South America cannot be understood without some comprehension of what happened on a small island with only a few million inhabitants between the thirteenth and eighteenth centuries. Put in another way, as Keith Thomas wrote some years ago. 'The justification of all historical study must ultimately be that it enhances our self-consciousness, enables us to see ourselves in perspective and helps us towards that greater free-

---

[1]For example, George Dalton, 'Peasantries in Anthropology and History,' *Current Anthropology*, 13, No. 3-4 (June-Oct. 1972), p. 385.

dom which comes from self-knowledge.'[2] A study of English history is not just a means to self-knowledge for modern Englishmen but for all those who have suffered from English oppression or benefited from English 'civilization,' whether in the Highlands of Scotland, New England or Bengal. For all these people, it is of interest to know what England was like compared to other agricultural nations and other civilizations.

That England was the first to industrialize and seemed precocious in other ways are among the reasons that its history attracted the great sociologists of the eighteenth and nineteenth centuries. Much of the material upon which Karl Marx rested his theories was drawn from English history, as was that for Weber's speculations on the link between protestantism and capitalism. Sir Henry Maine and Ferdinand Tönnies were two other major thinkers who drew on English evidence.[3] Another reason for their attraction and ours, is that England is perhaps the best documented of all nations in the world over the last six hundred years. A combination of large-scale bureaucracy and literacy, the manorial system, peace, and a reasonable climate for the preservation of records means that from the middle of the thirteenth century onwards we can examine in very considerable detail the history of ordinary people. It is possible, for example, to follow the history of a village year by year for five or six centuries. From the sixteenth century numerous sources overlap and make it possible to examine up to ninety-five per cent of the population for at least part of their lives.[4] A number of recent developments, including the re-discovery of large quantities of records, have opened up the past in a new way during the last twenty years. The history of ordinary people in England over a number of centuries is thus not only important but discoverable.

There are four central and related problems which will lie behind this book. Why did the industrial revolution occur first in England? When did England start to be different from other parts of Europe? In what, principally, did that difference consist? How far is the history of the English transformation a useful analogy for contemporary Third World societies? These are broad questions, and only a start on the road

---

[2]Keith Thomas, 'History and Anthropology,' *P & P*, 24 (1963), p. 18.
[3]Maine's work is cited at the end of Chapter 7 below: Ferdinand Tönnies, *Community and Association* (1887; 1955), trans. Charles P. Loomis.
[4]Rogers, *Six Centuries* pp. 17-8, claimed that 'That archives of English history are more copious and more continuous than those of any other people ... No other country possesses such a wealth of public records.' Whether this is a view that is still tenable with the discovery of superb records in Japan may be disputed, but certainly it is one of the two or three best documented nations. There is a discussion of the sources for various nations in Macfarlane *Reconstructing*, pp. 27-31. A discussion of the 'visibility' of the poorer part of the population and a method for using the records is contained in the same work.

to answering them can be made here. Since the direction we set off in will determine the result of the journey, it is necessary to consider the alternatives before we proceed. Many people have already written on the subject; it is therefore as well to consult them first.

Those who have speculated most broadly are comparative sociologists and anthropologists. Their views on England before the industrial revolution are also a guide to historical thought, since they naturally place much reliance on historians. Looking at a cross-section of recent works on the sociology of large-scale agrarian civilizations, it appears that observers are agreed that England between the Norman invasion and the industrial revolution of the eighteenth century was a 'peasant' society. For instance, Barrington Moore assumes the presence of an English peasantry, as does Robert Redfield.[5] George Dalton lumps together the whole of 'Europe,' including England, as a 'peasant' area up to the nineteenth century.[6] The map of the 'major peasant regions of the world' in Eric Wolf's authoritative text-book includes England, and Thorner regards the feudal monarchies of thirteenth century Europe, presumably including England, as 'peasant.'[7] All these authors are experts on 'peasantry' and do not use the term merely in its loose general meaning of 'rural dweller'; they use it to describe a particular form of social and economic and ideological structure, a system of interrelated features, with almost the same degree of speciality as 'capitalist,' 'industrialist' or 'feudal.' When they write about the 'pattern transformation of the peasantry' which is 'clearly seen in most parts of North-Western Europe,' they are referring to a massive change from one system to another.[8] Their more precise meaning can be investigated by looking first at the meaning and definition of the word 'peasant' and then by proceeding behind the word to see the set of features which are believed to be usefully represented by it.

It is clear that using 'peasant' in its commonsense meaning, or even in the way that it is often employed by anthropologists, England was indeed a 'peasant' society from the thirteenth to eighteenth centuries. The Oxford English Dictionary defines a 'peasant' as 'one who lives in the country and works on the land, either as a small farmer or as a labourer; the name is also applied to any rustic of the working class; a countryman, a rustic.' It is probable that some historians who use the term mean nothing more than this and are using it as synonymous with 'non-industrial'; hence the great contrast is between 'industrial' and

[5]Barrington Moore, *Social Origins of Dictatorship and Democracy* (1966), pp. 20-9; Redfield, *Peasant*, pp. 66-7.
[6]Dalton, 'Peasantries'.
[7]Eric Wolf, *Peasants* (New Jersey, 1966), p. 2; Thorner in Shanin, *Peasants*, p. 204.
[8]Shanin in Shanin, *Peasants*, p. 250.

'peasant' nations. This dichotomy can be elaborated and quantified if necessary. Daniel Thorner suggests that two of the five criteria which a society must fulfil to be called 'peasant' are that 'half the population must be agricultural' and 'more than half of the working population must be engaged in agriculture.'[9] By these criteria, England was clearly a 'peasant' society until the middle of the nineteenth century. It also fits well into the definition of peasantry given by Firth:

By a peasant economy one means a system of small-scale producers, with a simple technology and equipment often relying primarily for their subsistence on what they themselves produce. The primary means of livelihood of the peasant is cultivation of the soil.[10]

The most common meaning of the word when used by historians of England makes the criterion of size of landholding units, sometimes combined with a suggestion concerning the nature of ownership, central to the definition. Keith Thomas states that when he talks of English peasants he means 'farmers whose unit of operation was not large enough to support more than the farmer's own family'; H. J. Habakkuk equates peasants with 'owner-cultivators'; G. E. Mingay defines them as 'small owner-occupiers' and believes that the word is synonymous with 'small farmer'; Hobsbawm and Rudé describe a peasant society as one where the bulk of the population consists of families 'owning or occupying their own small plot of land'; M. M. Postan defines a peasant as 'an occupying owner or a tenant of a holding capable, but only just capable, of providing his family with a "subsistence income."'[11] It will be seen that common to all the definitions are the smallness of the unit of ownership or tenancy and the fact that the owner or tenant lives and works on the land. Thus, feudal copyholders or modern small tenant-farmers could both, in theory, be 'peasants.'

This definition is useful when investigating the changing distribution of land ownership in a society. It has been particularly employed in attempts to solve a puzzle that emerged forcefully during the nineteenth century, namely the fact that the agrarian structure of England had apparently become very different from that of the rest of Europe. We are told that 'Agricultural England in the nineteenth century presented a unique and amazing spectacle to the enquiring foreigner, it had no peasants.'[12] Whereas in other countries in Europe

[9]In ibid., p. 203.
[10]Quoted in Dalton, 'Peasantries,' p. 386.
[11]I am grateful to Keith Thomas for raising this issue, for references, and for the definition quoted; H. J. Habakkuk, 'La disparition du paysan anglais,' *Annales*, 20 no. 4 (July-Aug. 1965), p. 659; G. E. Mingay, *Enclosure and the Small Farmer in the Age of the Industrial Revolution* (Economic Hist. Soc., 1968), pp. 9-10; E. J. Hobsbawm and George Rudé, *Captain Swing* (Penguin edn., 1973), p. 3: Postan, *England*, p. 620.
[12]Hobsbawm, *Captain Swing*, p. 3.

and even in the Celtic fringe of Britain, families still made their living on little plots of land they owned or occupied, this was not the case in England: England had a structure of landlords and hired men. As Mingay has put it,

Towards the end of the nineteenth century . . . there was a growing public concern with the decline of the English peasantry. The realization grew that the English agrarian structure had become markedly different from that of the Continent. . . . the lost peasantry became a main theme of agrarian history. . . .[13]

Since the main difference was presumed to be in the size of the units of agricultural production, historians set themselves the task of establishing when landed property became concentrated into fewer hands and tried to explain why such a change should have occurred. Some argued that the main 'decline' occurred in the period between 1660 and 1750, others that much of the change had occurred in the sixteenth century with a final 'disappearance' in the later seventeenth century.[14]

Without a great deal of space, it is impossible to give any precise impression of the changes in distribution of land in England from the thirteenth to nineteenth centuries. The way in which ownership is described is very different in medieval, early modern and nineteenth century documents; and consequently a five-hundred year survey and comparison of the distribution of landholding is very difficult. Furthermore, detailed work on certain parishes leads us to believe that landholding records are particularly treacherous, giving false impressions concerning occupancy and residence. Nevertheless, we may hazard a guess that by the end of the nineteenth century about ten per cent of English land was in the hands of owner-occupiers, while at the start of the century between ten and fifteen per cent had been held by this group. This was a considerable drop from the end of the seventeenth-century when about thirty per cent was probably in their hands.[15] Although it is possible that at the end of the sixteenth century the proportion had reached as high as a half of all land, it is dangerous to infer that this apparently linear progression upwards can be pushed back further with a larger and larger proportion in the hands of 'small farmers.' It is quite possible, and even likely, that it had reached a peak in the fifteenth and sixteenth centuries and that before that the proportion had been lower. For example, Postan provides figures at the village level which suggest that 'middle-rank' tenants, that is, those

[13]Mingay, *Enclosure and the Small Farmer*, p. 9; see also p. 32.
[14]Ibid., p. 31; Habakkuk, 'La disparition . . . ,' pp. 650ff.
[15]Mingay, *Enclosure and the Small Farmer*, pp. 14-5.

whom he believed lived on plots large enough to support them but not too large to be worked by themselves, only constituted a third of the population at the end of the thirteenth century.[16] It is thus quite possible that the 'small-farmer' category fluctuated between a third and a half between the twelfth and the seventeenth centuries and that England was no more 'peasant' in this sense at the start of that period than at the end. It is not worth pursuing this matter much further, however, since such a definition of 'peasant' is only a preliminary and fairly unsatisfactory one.

While the definition is useful for some economic historians, it is far too blunt for social historians. Furthermore, it is not the one which most anthropologists and sociologists have in mind when they talk about 'peasants,' nor is it in the definition which is behind the work of Marx and Weber or a number of modern medieval historians. It is not precise enough because it only deals with one of the features of agrarian structure, size of holding, and says nothing about the actual operational unit of production and consumption. Nor does it say anything about the nature of ownership. Though it is easy to fall into the assumption that ownership, production and consumption will necessarily be dictated in a uniform way by farm size, this is not necessarily the case. We will be misled if we believe that two agricultural societies, say England and France, will necessarily be similar, 'peasant,' merely because they are divided into landholding units of a similar size. Therefore, to proceed further, and even to answer the question as to the differences visible in the nineteenth century, we need a more sophisticated definition.

During the years after the Second World War anthropologists were also searching for a better analytical definition than that based on technology and the means of production. In order to differentiate their objects of study not only from industrial nations but also from societies at the other end of the continuum of complexity, they could no longer be satisfied with a crude dichotomy which would encompass New Guinea, Africa, India and Latin America as well as pre-industrial England. In order to separate what are often lumped as 'tribal' societies from peasant societies, a new set of criteria were added to the old ones, principally by Kroeber and Redfield. They stated that peasants formed a 'part society':

the culture of a peasant community, on the other hand is not autonomous. It is an aspect or dimension of the civilization of which it is a part. As the peasant society is a half-society, so the peasant culture is a half-culture.[17]

---

[16]Postan, *Medieval*, p. 145.
[17]Redfield, *Peasant*, p. 40.

This is elaborated by Thorner in the form of two further criteria. One is that a peasantry can exist only where there is a State; in other words, a ruling hierarchy, an external political power sovereign over the particular community of 'peasants.' The second is that there are almost inevitably towns with markets, the culture of which is quite different from that of the countryside.'[18] Wolf summarizes the position when he writes that 'the State is the decisive criterion of civilization . . . which marks the threshold of transition between food gatherers in general and peasants.'[19] Yet here again, even taking these more practical definitions, it is clear that England would fall into the category 'peasant' from the twelfth century onwards, for it was noted for its powerful centralized State and the growth of important towns.

If we wish to indicate that England was neither a 'tribal' nor an 'industrialized' society between the thirteenth and eighteenth centuries, the use of the term 'peasant' is often useful and acceptable. It is important to be aware, however, that the word is used in a more specific analytical sense to denote a particular type of social and economic structure. Used in this second sense, the word is no longer in itself important, but behind it there stands a whole set of features which are believed to be correlated. It would be possible to abandon the word 'peasant' here and call this set of characteristics the 'domestic mode of production.'[20] But for the sake of brevity we will continue to use the word 'peasant.' Turning our attention to the set of supposedly inter-related variables, the 'system' which is merely given such a label, we find that it is from this that Dalton, Redfield, Wolf and others, basing their work on English historians' findings, believed England to be evolving when it industrialized.

It is clearly necessary to have criteria by which we can differentiate between rural nation states which under the commonsense and earlier anthropological definitions would all be lumped together as 'peasant.' It is plain that, for example, Russia, India, China and Western Europe in the Middle Ages exhibited very different demographic, economic and social patterns. We need to elaborate a set of indices by which these differences can be measured. A number of writers have therefore argued that while the preceding features of peasantry are *necessary* pre-requisites of a peasant society, they are not *sufficient* in themselves to

---

[18] In Shanin, *Peasants*, pp. 203-4.
[19] Wolf, *Peasants*, p. 11.
[20] A term employed, though with a somewhat wider meaning, by M. Sahlins, *Stone Age Economics* (1974), chs. 2, 3. There are implications that this 'mode' is of the same nature as Marx's other modes, feudal, capitalist, Asian, for example, which leads into another debate. This is a further reason for using 'peasant' in this present work, where we do not have space to pursue that argument.

allow us to speak of a real peasant society. It is contended that one further criterion is required, a feature which has immense consequences for many other aspects of the social, economic and ideological orders. This central feature is the nature of the basic unit of ownership, production and consumption.

On the basis of extensive acquaintance with the literature on peasant societies throughout the world, Daniel Thorner added a final touch to his definition of peasantry:

> Our fifth and final criterion, the most fundamental, is that of the unit of production. In our concept of peasant economy the typical and most representative units of production are the peasant family households. We define a peasant family household as a socio-economic unit which grows crops primarily by the physical efforts of the members of the family. The primary activity of the peasant households is the cultivation of their own lands, strips or allotments.[21]

This central feature has been described by all those who have written recently about peasants. Manning Nash stresses that 'the social units involved in production and consumption are households, not in combination. The economy is household-organized.'[22] Marshall Sahlins describes how in the 'domestic mode of production,'

> the domestic groups of primitive society have not yet suffered demotion to a mere consumption status, their labour power detached from the familial circle. . . . The household is as such charged with production, with the deployment and use of labour power. . . . Production is geared to the family's customary requirements. Production is for the benefit of the producers.'[23]

Teodor Shanin stresses that there is no division between the social and economic spheres: 'the peasant family farm forms the primary and basic unit of both peasant society and economy.'[24] He expands this when he writes that:

> Peasant households form the nuclei of peasant society. . . . A peasant household is characterized by the nearly total integration of the peasant family's life with its farming enterprise. The family provides the work team for the farm, while the farm's activities are geared mainly to production of the basic consumption needs of the families and the dues enforced by the holders of political and economic power . . . The household was the basic unit of production, consumption, property holding, socialization, sociability, moral support and mutual economic help.[25]

[21] In Shanin, *Peasants*, p. 205.
[22] M. Nash, *Primitive and Peasant Economic Systems* (Pennsylvania, 1966), p. 40.
[23] Sahlins, *Stone Age Economics*, pp. 76-7.
[24] Shanin, *Peasant Economy*, p. 67.
[25] Shanin, *Awkward Class*, pp. 28-9.

Elsewhere the same author writes that 'the family farm is the basic unit of peasant ownership, production, consumption and social life. The individual, the family and the farm, appear as an indivisible whole.'[26] B. Galeski, who has worked extensively on Polish rural social structure, emphasizes the same point. He argues that the 'basic characteristic' of peasantry is 'the fusion or (more exactly) the identification of the enterprise (i.e. the commodity-producing establishment) with the domestic economy of the family household.'[27] 'This fusion has major consequences for the whole of village life' and it is essential to realize that 'peasant husbandry is both enterprise and domestic economy.'[28] Along the same lines Rodney Hilton defines a peasant economy as 'one in which the large majority of the population consists of families who cultivate crops and rear animals on their individual holdings. The primary function of production in the family holding is to provide the subsistence needs of the family itself.'[29] This is further elaborated when he states that a central defining characteristic of peasants is that 'they work their holdings essentially as a family unit, primarily with family labour.'[30] The nature of such a system becomes apparent when we contrast it with a 'capitalist' economy where the social and demographic unit, the basic unit of reproduction and consumption, is often the household, but the basic unit of production is the firm or 'enterprise' which employs individuals. This identification of social and economic spheres is, of course, recognized in the derivation of the very word 'economy,' coming from the Greek for 'household.'[31]

It is especially interesting that there appear to be a number of features which are necessarily and causally interconnected with this basic blending of the unit of production, reproduction and consumption. This has led several observers to argue that 'peasantry' is a particular type of social formation, 'a specific mode of production on a par with

---

[26]Shanin, *Peasants*, p. 241.

[27]Galeski, *Rural*, pp. 10-11.

[28]Ibid., pp. 11, 45.

[29]Hilton, *Bond Men*, p. 25.

[30]Hilton, *Peasantry*, p. 13. An early discussion which stressed the identification of social and economic units is that by Sorokin *et al.*, part of which is reprinted in George Dalton (ed.), *Economic Development and Social Change* (New York, 1971) p. 412.

[31]For the origins, see K. Polanyi, C. Arensberg and H. W. Pearson (eds.), *Trade and Market in the Early Empires*, (Illinois, 1957), pp. 3-11, 64-93. A number of Russian scholars, the best known of them being A. V. Chayanov, have contributed very significantly to the general discussion of the domestic economy of the peasantry. I have decided to omit any direct reference to their work since I do not wish to complicate the argument here by becoming involved in the heated debate between Populists and Marxists. I am grateful to Teodor Shanin for advice on this point.

feudalism and capitalism.'[32] Whether we go as far as this, it is possible to agree with Shanin that 'comparative studies have consistently pointed to some startling similarities between peasant societies — startling in view of the diversity in history, political structure, production technology and so on.'[33] Redfield had made the same point earlier when he wrote that 'Peasant society and culture has something generic about it. It is a kind of arrangement of humanity with similarities all over the world.'[34] There are two reasons why this is especially important for the study of the English past. If it is indeed the case that England had a 'peasant' social structure, then analogies between England and the other major peasantries of India, China, Southern and Eastern Europe, and Latin America, are likely to be both legitimate and fruitful. Not only are such analogies helpful for understanding the English past, but English history will provide a map for the future development of such peasantries. A second consequence is that since there is a set of inter-related features, a 'system,' it may be possible, once it is established that England had some of the features of the system, to deduce the likely presence of others. This is particularly important for certain periods or topics where the material is especially thin. In other words, we would have a 'model' which would help us to comprehend and explore the past.

In order to make this a useful tool, we need to specify more exactly what are the general features that seem to go together in 'peasantry.' What would we expect to find if we looked at any particular peasant society? It is clear that attempting to compress the major characteristics of a society into part of a chapter, when whole books have been devoted to the subject, will not only mean leaving out a great deal, particularly concerning the religious and ideological level, but will lead to the creation of a very simplified 'ideal-type' model in Weber's sense. It is likely that no particular society will fit exactly, at any time, all the features to be enumerated. Nevertheless, it is essential to have a more precise notion of what we would expect to find when we talk of England's being a 'peasant' society in an analytical sense, and what it would be likely to share with other peasantries.

There is now a wide and rich literature not only on 'peasantry' in

---

[32]Shanin, *Peasant Economy*, i, p. 78 is here citing the opinion of Chayanov. For a recent criticism from a Marxist viewpoint see Judith Ennew, Paul Hirst and Keith Tribe, '"Peasantry" as an Economic Category,' in *Jnl. of Peasant Studies*, 4, no. 4 (July, 1977), pp. 295-322.
[33]Shanin, *Peasant Economy*, i, p. 67.
[34]Redfield, *Peasant*, p. 17; for further specification of this 'sameness' see pp. 60-1.

general but on specific peasantries.[35] The following account is based on general reading on peasant societies in the Mediterranean,[36] in Asia[37] and in northern Europe,[38] as well as the general works referred to above. But to construct a general description from all these sources would, given the space limitation, produce an unsatisfactory rag-bag. It therefore seems best to concentrate on one particular area, and on three authorities. The area I have chosen is eastern Europe. There are four main justifications for this choice. The first detailed analaysis of 'peasantry' was undertaken in this area by Thomas and Znaniecki in their work on the *Polish Peasant* published in 1918. This pioneering book has been complemented by a recent theoretical analysis, also stemming from Poland, by Galeski. Simultaneously, very interesting work was being undertaken in Russia, and some of the results of this have recently been discussed in a book and several articles by Teodor Shanin. In both Poland and Russia the confrontation of intelligentsia and 'peasants' was particularly sharp, and the desire for political and economic revolution led to an uncommonly sustained effort to understand the basic nature of 'peasantry.' This resulted in unusually original work, and it constitutes the second justification for building our description on work from this area.

The third reason for the choice is that eastern Europe is at exactly the right distance from England. It is close enough, within a general 'European' culture area and permeated by Christianity, to make it

[35]General work includes the works by Dalton, Galeski, Barrington-Moore, Nash, Redfield, Shanin, Wolf, already cited. A useful brief introduction is Thorner, *Peasantry*. A number of good articles have appeared recently in the *Journal of Peasant Studies* and *Peasant Studies Newsletter* (now *Peasant Studies*).

[36]J. Davis, *Land and Family in Pisticci* (1973); Ernestine Friedl, *Vasilika: A Village in Modern Greece* (New York, 1962); Joel M. Halpern, *A Serbian Village* (Columbia, 1956); Peter Loizos, *The Greek Gift; Politics in a Cypriot Village* (Oxford, 1975); Julian Pitt-Rivers (ed.), *Mediterranean Countrymen* (Paris, 1963); Julian Pitt-Rivers, *The People of the Sierra*, (1954; 2nd edn., Chicago, 1971), Paul Stirling, *Turkish Village* (1965); a recent survey is J. Davis, *People of the Mediterranean* (1977).

[37]F. G. Bailey, *Tribe, Caste and Nation* (Manchester, 1960); S. C. Dube, *Indian Village* (reprint New York, 1967); T. Scarlett Epstein, *Economic Development and Social Change in South India* (Manchester, 1962); B. Gallin, *Hsin Hsing, Taiwan: A Chinese Village in Change* (Berkeley, 1966); Clifford Geertz, *Agricultural Involution* (Berkeley, 1968); T. G.Kessinger, *Vilyatpur 1848-1968: Social and Economic Change in a North Indian Village* (Berkeley, 1974); E. R. Leach, *Pul Eliya: A Village in Ceylon* (Cambridge, 1961); Mahmood Mamdani, *The Myth of Population Control: Family, Caste and Class in an Indian Village* (New York, 1972); Harold H. Mann, *The Social Framework of Agriculture* (1968); McKim Marriott (ed.), *Village India: Studies in the Little Community* (1955, Phoenix edn., Chicago, 1969); G Obeyesekere, *Land Tenure in Village Ceylon* (Cambridge, 1967); G. W. Skinner, 'Marketing and Social Structure in Rural China,' 3 pts., *Jnl. Asian Studies*, 24, Nov. 1964, Feb., May, 1965); R. H. Tawney, *Land and Labour in China* (1932).

[38]C. Arensberg, *The Irish Countryman* (1937); Goody, *Family*; Lofgren, *Family and Household*.

reasonable and acceptable to compare England with this region. There are many who may recoil at comparison of England and, for example, Asia, alleging that there are too many other cultural and historical variables to make it worthwhile. On the other hand, being outside Western Europe places Eastern Europe outside the area of immediate concern. If we are trying to discuss why industrialization occurred first in England and the degree to which England is different from, say France or Italy, it is clearly inappropriate to construct the indexes by which to measure the societies from one of the nations we are trying to compare.

The final justification is as follows. Our search for the roots of English differences will take us back to the thirteenth century. This century and the medieval period in general in England has been dominated by the work of scholars of East European origin, particularly E. A. Kosminsky, Sir Paul Vinogradoff and M. M. Postan.[39] It is clear from their writing that they were consciously comparing medieval England with traditional Russia. To understand what they meant when they talked about 'peasants' in medieval England we need to have some idea of what the term means in Eastern Europe.

The central feature of traditional East European peasantry was that ownership was not individualized. It was not the single individual who exclusively owned the productive resources, but rather the household. 'Property' therefore meant something different from its present sense in the West. The general distinction is made by Nash when writing of primitive and peasant economics: 'rights are a reflection of a person's or social unit's place in the social structure' and therefore 'they are not rights to property in the same sense as tenure in the laws and economics of the Western world. Part of being a member in a tribe or community, in the family or the lineage, in the clan or the phratry is to have access to specified pieces of land.'[40] Galeski writes about the Polish family farm that 'the children are both the heirs of, and workers on, the farm. As heirs they are also co-owners.'[41] 'The farm is handed down from generation to generation, while the family — the successive usufructuries — carries a responsibility to its own children (and to village opinion) for the property in its charge.'[42] Thus it is not merely the particular household, but the family through time, who are the

[39]Professor Shanin pointed out that, at the opposite end, the 'most important Eastern scholars of their own societies used England as a major model for consideration, e.g. Preobrazhenski's centrally influential piece, on *Ways of Capital Accumulation*' (personal communication).
[40]Nash, *Primitive and Peasant*, p. 34.
[41]Galeski, *Rural*, p. 63.
[42]Ibid., p. 62.

owners. The heirs have as much right as the present 'owners.' This traditional situation is expanded by Thomas and Znaniecki. Since the topic is central to the ensuing analysis of England, it is necessary to quote their descriptions at some length. We are told that in traditional Poland

the parents are morally obliged to endow their children as well as they can, simply because they are not full and exclusive proprietors but rather managers of their inherited property . . . being a manager rather than a proprietor, the father naturally has to retire when his son . . . becomes more able than he to manage the main bulk of the property — the farm.[43]

The authors then elaborate on this: 'Land property is essentially familial; the individual is its temporary manager. Who manages it is therefore not essential provided he does it well; it may be the father, the oldest son, the youngest son, the son-in-law.'[44] But because property is familial, it does not follow that this is a system of communal ownership by a group of wider kin, nor can it be deduced that a whole set of people has individual shares.

This familial character of the farm should not be interpreted as if the family were an association holding a common property. The members of the family have essentially no economic share in the farm; they share only the social character of members of the group, and from this result their social right to be supported by the group and their social obligation to contribute to the existence of the group.[45]

It was only with the greatest difficulty, we are told, that the idea that the property could be divided between all the 'heirs' was later introduced. Originally 'the individual had no claim to the property at all.'[46] The authors see the roots of the destruction of the peasant system in the growth of the concept that an individual has rights to property as against other individuals.

The more intense the desire to advance and the more rapid the progress itself, the more difficult it was to retain the familial form of the property. The individuals began by claiming the products of their own activity; then the principle of individual ownership became extended to the hereditary familial land. . . .[47]

They describe many features of the traditional economy and society, and note that 'all this was changed as soon as property became

[43]Thomas, *Polish Peasant*, p. 92.
[44]Ibid., p. 158.
[45]Ibid., p. 159.
[46]Ibid., p. 194.
[47]Ibid., p. 195.

individual.'[48] The central point is clear; the individual held no ultimate and exclusive property rights, even the ownership of movables was temporary.[49] The group dominated the individual in terms of ownership.

The same situation has been described for late nineteenth century Russia by Shanin. On 'the peasant customary understanding of property rights,' he writes: 'Even though land, cattle and equipment may be formally defined as belonging to the man who heads the household, in actual fact he acts rather as a holder and manager of the common family property with the right to sell it or give it away heavily restricted, or made altogether absent, by peasant custom. . . .'[50] In other words,

Family property was the major legal reflection of the character of the Russian peasant household. Unlike private property, family property limited the rights of the formal owner (khozyain); he acted as the head administrator of the property (bol'shak) rather than as a property-owner in the sense current outside peasant society. An extreme expression of this feature was the legal possibility and actual practice of removing the head of a household from his position in some cases of 'mismanagement' or 'wastefulness' and appointing another member of the household instead.[51]

A further discussion of this family ownership shows that 'common ownership by the peasant family' is a feature upon which all commentators agree. As the Court of Appeal ruled, the allotted lands 'are regarded as the property not of the person legally registered as the proprietor, but of all the members of the family, the head of the household being only the household representative.'[52] This being the case, and 'formal membership of a family household' being conferred by birth or adoption,[53] it is clear that inheritance, and particularly the practice of making a written will, were excluded. Shanin writes that

the very notion of inheritance as developed in non-peasant societies failed by definition to appear. The passing of property from generation to generation did not necessarily involve the death of a parent and was approached legally as a partitioning of family property between its members.'[54]

Of necessity, 'Inheritance by will did not exist as far as land and agricultural equipment were concerned and, in other cases, was extremely

[48]*Idem.*
[49]Ibid., p. 163.
[50]Shanin, *Peasant Economy*, i, p. 68.
[51]Shanin, *Awkward Class*, pp. 30-1.
[52]Quoted in *ibid.*, p. 220
[53]Ibid., p. 221.
[54]Ibid., p. 31; there is a more detailed discussion on pp. 222-4.

limited and open to challenge as unjust before the peasant courts.'[55] Thus, there was a birth-right in the estate but a single individual had little or no right to claim a specific share as 'his' or 'hers' and to do what he or she willed with it. Exclusive, individual ownership with the possibility of disposing of the rights in an object was absent. This explains to a very considerable extent the identification of farm and family; the household was the basic unit of production and consumption because it was also the basic unit of ownership. Yet the fact that it was the unit of ownership does not necessarily imply that it was also the unit of production. That it was indeed so is the second central feature of peasantry.

In general it has been observed that in primitive and peasant economies 'farm labour is family labour.' Nash writes that 'contract for labour is rare . . . in short, a labour market does not exist, and when people are hired the occasion is special and wage levels are customary . . . .'[56] In order to qualify as a 'peasantry' Thorner argued that 'the total contribution of . . . nonfamily members to actual crop production must be much less than that of the family members.'[57] Shanin also notes that family labour is far more important than hired labour.[58] This is specified to be the case in Poland even up to the present. Galeski estimates that farms based on family labour alone 'constitute slightly more than eighty per cent of the total of individual farms in Poland.'[59] As a result 'the family are the farm's production team.'[60] Thomas and Znaniecki describe how the very idea of wage labour was abhorrent to the peasant and almost totally absent in traditional Poland.[61] Indeed it is suggested by Galeski that the presence of 'hired labour' paid for by wages is 'a definite indicator of an enterprise, and of a capitalist type of enterprise at that.'[62] The presence of a considerable number of servants or day-labourers paid for by wages is therefore fundamentally inconsistent with peasant social structure and it is noticeable that such a phenomenon was absent in traditional peasant societies. The growth of a labour market signals the end of peasantry. Co-producers are co-owners and they are also joint consumers, for the same unit consumes most of what it produces.

Production in a peasant society, apart from that portion paid in rent or taxes, is almost wholly for direct consumption, for use, rather than

[55] Ibid., p. 223.
[56] Nash, *Primitive and Peasant*, p. 24.
[57] Thorner, *Peasantry*, p. 508.
[58] Shanin, *Peasant Economy*, i, p. 71.
[59] Galeski, *Rural*, p. 17.
[60] Ibid., p. 165.
[61] *Polish Peasant*, p. 170.
[62] Galeski, *Rural*, p. 18.

exchange in the market. This can be seen in a number of ways. Thomas and Znaniecki argue that the 'concept of income itself which we use here is originally strange to the peasant . . . . The products of the farm are not destined to be sold and not evaluated quantitatively.'[63] Galeski states that 'until comparatively recently the peasant family produced almost everything it needed for its existence.'[64] It bought very little from other households or in the open market, nor did it put much of its own produce in the market. In fact a high level of products sent to the market — Galeski suggests sixty per cent of the total product — is a sure indicator of the capitalistic enterprise.[65] One consequence of the fact that each household produces all that it needs is that there is little division of labour at the local level. Galeski describes how 'in the majority of villages in Poland, the simple amenities of church, school, shops, handicrafts, do not exist.[66] Specialist craftsmen and rural industries are very little developed. Each household can not only provide its own foodstuffs but has most of the skills to maintain the farm.

Directly related to the foregoing identification of ownership, production and consumption unit are several other basic features. One is the absence of cash, local exchange and markets. Shanin points out that the use of money at the local level is extremely limited since it is not needed to purchase consumables or labour.[67] The peasant has a relative independence from general market forces.[68] Commercial life and agricultural life co-exist as separate systems, as Redfield observed.[69] A good picture of such a situation at the start of this century is provided in the *Polish Peasant:* 'There was originally no commerce between members of a community, no buying and selling at all . . . .'[70] When money was introduced it was treated not as a new exchange medium, but as just another form of property. 'Money is a relatively new kind of property . . . For the peasant, money property has originally not the character of capital . . . He does not at first even think of making money produce; he simply keeps it at home.'[71] The authors provide an account of how money is at first kept in different spheres, for instance that paid

[63]*Polish Peasant*, p. 166.
[64]*Rural*, p. 37.
[65]Ibid., pp. 17-8. Shanin pointed out that this percentage, while true of Poland, is not necessarily an accurate indicator in other societies, for example India (personal communication).
[66]Ibid., p. 80.
[67]Shanin, *Peasant Economy*, i, p. 75.
[68]Shanin in Shanin, *Peasants*, p. 240.
[69]Redfield, *Peasant*, p. 29.
[70]*Polish Peasant*, p. 184.
[71]Ibid., p. 164.

in dowry must be used to purchase land and for nothing else.[72] Put in more general terms, this is still largely a 'natural' economy, where it is not possible to translate all objects into one scale, where it is not feasible to purchase everything, since not everything has a price. Again the extensive use of money and the setting of prices to objects indicates a shift away from such a system to a market, capitalist one.

The object which is least likely to come on the market is land. Although small pieces of land may be bought and sold to even out demographic differences between households or in crises, it is very clear that an extensive and open market in land, which treats land as just another commodity, is absent in traditional peasantries. As Redfield put it generally, citing the work of Wolf in support, 'those agriculturalists who carry on agriculture for reinvestment and business, looking on the land as capital and commodity, are not peasants but farmers.'[73] Not only is it the case that individual households are extremely unwilling to sell land, but the community as a whole will often not allow it to go to an outsider.[74] Furthermore, peasants are usually very loath even to mortgage land: Thomas and Znaniecki observe that 'mortgaging the farm, in view of the half-sacred character of land property, is hated by the peasant . . . sale, division or mortgaging of the farm means a lowering of the social standing of the family.'[75] 'Land should never be mortgaged, except to a member of the family . . . mortgaged property becomes a purely economic category and loses its whole symbolic value.'[76] If this is the case with mortgaging, the sale of land is an even greater disaster and even less likely to occur. This is related to the nature of ownership, described above, which is based on the premise that a particular generation is only the temporary manager of an ancestral estate that must, if at all possible, be handed down intact to descendants. The frequent purchase and sale of land is clearly incompatible with such a system, nor is it easily to be achieved where no single individual can take the decision to sell. If we discover a very active land market it is clear that we are dealing with a different system.

When the authors of the *Polish Peasant* spoke of the 'symbolic value' of land, they were alluding to yet another fundamental feature of peasantry, namely the widely observed attachment to land and desire to 'keep the name on the land.' It is not difficult to see this as closely connected to the preceding pattern of ownership and production, but it

[72]Ibid., p. 165.
[73]*Peasant*, pp. 18-19.
[74]An example is a Mexican community cited by Nash, *Primitive and Peasant*, p. 72.
[75]*Polish Peasant*, p. 118.
[76]Ibid., pp. 161-2.

is such a striking characteristic that it is worth documenting briefly. Those who have studied peasants in general comment on the attachment to the land. Wolf describes how 'A piece of land, a house, are not merely factors of production; they are also loaded with symbolic values.'[77] Redfield writes that 'one sees a peasant as a man who is in effective control of a piece of land to which he has long been attached by ties of tradition and sentiment. The land and he are parts of one thing, one old-established body of relationships.'[78] 'Land is a unique value, and no sum of money can be too large to pay for it,' for it is a 'social rather than an economic value.'[79] This is intimately related to the fact that a particular piece of land is associated with a particular family; it is not merely a matter of 'keeping the name on the land' in general, on any old land, but a specific association with parcels in a certain place. Thomas and Znaniecki describe how 'a farm upon which many generations of the same family have worked is quite naturally associated with this particular family and often even bears its name . . . .'[80] Galeski confirms that 'the farm is the basis of the family's maintenance, its insurance for the future and the basis of its prestige. It is the common good of the family, a heritage passed down from generation to generation.'[81] Of course, in practice, families die out and migrate, but the ideals are strong and in a considerable number of instances it is possible to find the same family owning the same land over a number of generations. A busy land market not only destroys such ideals, but is logically incompatible with them.

Clearly, the pattern of geographical mobility is closely connected to these ideals. Although there may be some outward migration, for instance of women at marriage or of younger children, on the whole peasant societies are geographically relatively immobile. In the context of Poland, for example, this is taken for granted, our authors only alluding to it in asides. Thomas and Znaniecki suggest that one reason for the absence of romantic love is that it is psychologically impossible because 'in most cases . . . all the possible partners are known from childhood.'[82] Galeski refers to the 'marked spatial stability' of the inhabitants of villages, stating that it is 'a characteristic of the village community that the persons living in it are connected primarily by social, but also by territorial origin. They were usually born in the

---

[77]Wolf, *Peasants*, p. 15.
[78]Redfield, *Peasant*, p. 19.
[79]Thomas, *Polish Peasant*, pp. 190, 161.
[80]Ibid., p. 161.
[81]*Rural*, p. 164.
[82]*Polish Peasant*, pp. 125-6. The quotation is given to show geographical immobility; that familiarity always inhibits romantic attachment is very doubtful.

village or in a neighbouring village ....'[83] If there is geographical mobility, it takes a particular form, namely from the countryside to the towns, for 'one never, or hardly ever, meets people from the towns in the villages.'[84] The idea that people should spend their lives in half a dozen villages, or move from village to town and then back to the village is largely absent. Most of those who live in a community pass through all the major phases of their life in one area among a group of people they know from cradle to grave. Many of those around them are neighbours, but many are also kin, for one consequence of limited geographical immobility and an association between land and family is that territories fill up with kin.

The importance of real and fictive kinship in peasant societies is widely accepted and hardly needs documenting. To illustrate it from the Polish context, we find Galeski referring to the 'strong ties of kinship among the families which make up the community.'[85] This is reinforced by the frequent intra-village marriages and results in the fact that 'there are usually only a few family names in the village community. The village consists of several interrelated large families (or clans). For this reason, a village is sometimes defined as a family neighbour group.'[86] It is very often these kin who act as political, religious and social support for the households. The 'familistic' atmosphere and idiom of peasantries, from Sicily to Mexico, from India to Russia, is very clear. But not only is there a stress on wider kinship and a proliferation of relatives in the vicinity, there appears to be some correlation with the size and structure of the household.

It is well known that even in peasant societies most households are usually composed only of the nuclear family, parents and children. This is especially likely to be the case in the households with less land. A household consisting of more than one married couple (for example groups of married brothers as in the Indian joint family household) or grandparents and married children (as in some parts of southern and eastern Europe) may merely be a strong ideal, to which only a small fraction of the families attain. Nevertheless, it does seem possible to argue that where ownership is by a group rather than an individual, and where family labour is important in production, this is often reflected in residential arrangements. Even if it does not always result in complex and extended households, it will often mean that households will be larger since male children, co-owners with their parents, stay at home for longer than in societies where they are early shed onto the labour

[83]*Rural*, pp. 81-2.
[84]Ibid., p. 82.
[85]Ibid., p. 60.
[86]Ibid., p. 82.

market. It would appear that in the nineteenth century the residential unit in Eastern Europe was often composed of more than merely the nuclear family. Thus we are told that 'the traditional peasant family is generally a three-generation one' but that 'the peasant family in its multi-generation form is becoming a thing of the past,' and that we are seeing 'the decay of the multi-generation family.'[87] Work on the demography of Russia in the nineteenth century confirms that households including several married couples were fairly common.[88] It could therefore be stated that in traditional peasantries at least a quarter of the households will contain more than one married couple. In some cases, as in the famous Serbian 'zadruga,' there may be four or five married couples and their children.[89]

Within these households there is commonly a particular authority pattern which may broadly be termed 'patriarchal'. Since the acting head of the household is not merely the head of a social unit, the family, but also simultaneously the head of a small firm, in other words the work boss, he can appeal to two systems of authority. The absence of geographical mobility, alternative-occupations and private property of the members weakens the power of those who would oppose him. As a result it has been noted that the acting male head has unusual power. He has such power in relation to the children. Shanin noted that the unity of the family and the farm implied a 'patriarchal head.'[90] The nature of the family farm and the division of labour meant that 'Vast patriarchal authority was in the hands of the head of the household. Children were under the absolute authority of their seniors.'[91] The same feature was noted by Galeski, who speaks of the 'distinctly patriarchal features' which still exist in Poland and which correspond to the functions of the family.[92] This has also been noted earlier by Thomas and Znaniecki, who stated that 'The parental authority is complex . . . naturally the control is unusually strong . . . the power of authority is really great; a rebellious child finds nowhere any help, not even in the younger generation.'[93] In a sense there is a paradox here, for the children are by birth co-owners of the property with their parents and their productive labour may be as important as their parents'. Yet the fact that once they leave the home they are without occupation and support

[87]Ibid., pp. 58, 166-7.
[88]This work is being undertaken by Peter Czap: for example see his paper on 'Marriage and the Peasant Joint Family in Russia in the Era of Serfdom' in D. Ransel (ed.), *The Family in Imperial Russia* (Illinois, 1978).
[89]E. A. Hammel, 'The zadruga as process' in Laslett, *Household.*
[90]*Awkward Class*, pp. 28-9.
[91]Ibid. p. 175.
[92]*Rural*, p. 58; see also pp. 47, 64.
[93]*Polish Peasant*, p. 91.

places them in a very vulnerable position. As the authors noted, one of the central conflicts between the parental generation and their children in America was between an authoritarian, patriarchal structure and the more egalitarian system of the United States.[94] The growth of individual property rights and of wages for cash are among the factors that give the children some resources with which to withstand their father's commands.

The other aspect of this patriarchalism lies in the relation of males to females. It is well known that in most peasant societies women make an important contribution to the economics of the domestic unit. Yet it is characteristic of such systems that their status and rights are low. A wife is in relation to her husband something like a child in relation to his or her father; they are largely without separate property and separate rights. This low status of women has again been widely noted, for example by all of the three sources upon which this discussion has mainly been based. Shanin states that though a peasant woman 'shouldered a heavy burden of labour and responsibility ... yet her social position remained low. Authority over and representation of the household was given to the man ... '[95] This was directly related to the system of ownership and production. We are told that 'Peasant law did not consider women, strictly speaking members of a household, "because they cannot perpetuate a family." Therefore a woman did not hold property-rights over the household if male members of the family lived.'[96] Galeski notes that it is only with the destruction of 'peasantry' that women obtain economic independence.[97] The subordinate position of women in other peasant societies, for example in traditional India or China, has received much attention.[98] It appears that it is not merely a result of a particular technology, plough cultivation, but related to a particular form of socio-economic organization.

Another area of social relations which appears to be intimately connected to the peasant social structure is marriage. Three features of the pattern may be singled out, the first being the age at marriage. It has been observed that in almost all the great peasant nations, for example in Asia and eastern Europe, first marriage for women is at an early age, soon after puberty, in the late teens. This contrasts strongly with the late age at marriage, twenty-five or later, found in parts of north-western

[94]Ibid., pp. 103-4.
[95]*Awkward Class*, p. 175.
[96]Ibid., p. 222.
[97]*Rural*, p. 69.
[98]For example, see E. Boserup, *Woman's Role in Economic Development* (1970), pt. 1, Jack Goody, *Production and Reproduction* (Cambridge, 1976), ch. 4.

Europe from at least the sixteenth century.[99] No satisfactory explanation has been given for this fact, but it may not be a coincidence that in societies where family labour is at a premium, and hence the reproductive power of women is likely to be encouraged, there should be a pattern of early marriage. The fact that females, both as children and later as wives, are always in subordination to males also helps to make such a pattern feasible. It is also made possible by a second feature of the pattern, namely the fact that marriages are usually 'arranged' rather than made on the basis of 'romantic love' and individual choice. Galeski describes a traditional situation where parents and kin take the initiative in finding a mate.[100] This author goes on to argue that the idea of individual choice and love marriages is in direct antithesis to the very nature of peasantry.[101] Why this should be so is well described by Thomas and Znaniecki. They show the power of arranged marriage and the matchmaker in traditional Poland and the fact that it is parents who choose their child's partner.[102] The reason is again related to the fact that marriage is not merely a social relationship, it is not just a contract between two individuals, but is overlaid with the fact that two economic enterprises are also affected. Each marriage thus crucially affects the personal interests of all the kin, and they are naturally involved in the decision. Again the authors emphasized that marriage based on romantic attraction and private choice is diametrically opposed to such a social system and is a good index that a traditional peasantry is dissolving.

The third feature of marriage in peasant societies also supports the contention that young age at marriage is related to the need to increase family labour, for it is the complementary fact that in peasant societies marriage is an almost universal phenomenon. This statistical fact, namely that almost one hundred per cent of the women who reach the age of 45 have been married, was again noted as characteristic of eastern Europe, Asia and elsewhere by John Hajnal. It contrasts with the 'unique' north-west European pattern of selective marriage, in which between ten and twenty per cent of the women never get married.[103] But again no satisfactory explanation has been suggested. It is not difficult to see how it is related to a peasant or domestic mode of production. Where the basic and only unit in the society is the family, within which the marital pair is the core, all must marry who wish to have a full role in the society. Furthermore, marriage is necessary to produce labour.

[99]Hajnal, *European Marriage.*
[100]Galeski, *Rural,* p. 61.
[101]*Ibid.,* p. 68.
[102]*Polish Peasant,* p. 91.
[103]Hajnal, *European Marriage.*

The economic and social necessity of marriage in such a system, as well as the way in which pressure upon a person to marry works, are again excellently described in the *Polish Peasant:*

> The whole familial system of attitudes involves absolutely the postulate of marriage for every member of the young generation ... A person who does not marry within a certain time ... provokes in the family-group an attitude of unfavourable astonishment; they seem to have stopped in the midst of a continuous movement, and they are passed by and left alone.[104]

The authors admit that there are exceptions, for example those with physical or intellectual defects. Yet all others, except potential priests, were 'required to marry.' Those who did not do so were regarded as defective and unstable.

> The community demands from its members a steadiness of life which is necessary for its interior harmony; but a peasant individual can acquire this steadiness only after his marriage ... A single person, ... cannot remain indefinitely with his family, for the latter is organized in view of the marriage of all of its members. He cannot carry on normal occupational activity alone — cannot farm or keep a small shop — he can be either only a hired labourer, living with strangers, or a servant ... A single person does not take an equal share with married couples in the life of the community ... He cannot even keep a house, receive, give entertainments, etc.[105]

The authors proceed to describe how weddings are important social events and emphasize the value of marriage. After marriage the young couple are addressed as 'you,' while their unmarried siblings continue to be addressed as 'thou.' The unmarried tend to become paupers, vagabonds, isolates or rebels. Marriage again is not merely a matter of individual decision, a possibility; it is a matter of family and community concern, almost as inevitable as death.

The combination of the economic and social features which have been outlined above tends to give peasant society structures certain outstanding characteristics. One of these is that they appear to be characterized by a particular pattern of social mobility. One aspect of this is that great extremes of wealth and poverty 'are peculiar to the capitalist town. In the village community class differences are relatively small.'[106] The predicted growth of differentiation, with the creation of a landless proletariat, does not appear to happen. As the author notes in the Polish context, a study of family farms suggests that 'the existing differentiation ... is not increasing. This means that so far tendencies towards

[104]*Polish Peasant*, p. 107.
[105]Ibid., p. 113.
[106]Galeski, *Rural*, p. 84.

polarization are not being realized.'[107] The most detailed analysis of the
pressures towards equalization and a pattern whereby families fluctuate
over time, and there is no growing differentiation, is by Shanin. He
points out that there is a *tendency* towards what he terms 'multi-direc-
tional' and 'cyclical' mobility, and describes in detail the biological,
demographic and other determinants of this pattern.[108] Shanin also
writes that such a tendency has been noted in many peasant societies. [109]
He summarizes some of the factors involved as follows:

> In a number of major peasant societies powerful cyclical mobility operates with
> peasant family farms continually changing their economic position as a result
> of the simultaneous yet opposite processes of the cumulation of economic
> advantages versus the levelling trends reflecting the higher rate of partitioning
> of wealthier households, the impact of nature, selective extinction, and so on
> reported from peasant societies separated by thousands of miles and polarised
> historical, political, cultural and geographical conditions ... All these
> processes make for a powerful levelling impact and reinforce communal
> homogeneity and stability.[110]

The result is that a village tends to be composed not of one or two rich
men who own the whole land, but a large number of smaller landholders, each independent. The absence of wage labour also makes the
development of a rural proletariat unlikely.

Yet while there is some equality within the peasant strata, the gap
between the peasantry and other social groups is very pronounced, for
there is little, if any, mobility between them. This can be seen in the gap
between the peasantry and the nobility, who have very little in common.
Likewise, there is only slight contact between town and country culture,
again related to the one-way movement into the towns. The only
representatives of the 'intelligentsia/town/nobility' who penetrate into
the countryside are the clergy and the teachers. They are characteristically very isolated. Thus in Poland, we are told, 'The priest and the
teacher, representatives of non-agricultural occupations, remain not
only outside the peasant stratum but also outside or above the village
community.'[111] The 'intelligentsia' in traditional Russia lived on little
islands of their own among the peasantry, their dress, language, ideas
totally opposed to those of the peasants.[112] The town and country were

[107]Ibid., p. 125.
[108]*Awkward Class, passim,* especially pp. 74, 81 ff, 102. Shanin has pointed out that 'the
tendency may still result in polarization but via a process which is more complex than
usually expected' (personal communication).
[109]Ibid., p. 76.
[110]Shanin, *Peasant Economy,* ii, p. 193.
[111]Galeski, *Rural,* p. 84.
[112]Shanin, *Awkward Class,* p. 182.

different worlds. 'The old class-organization presents two independent and partly parallel hierarchies — that of the country, and that of the town population.'[113] 'In the city the peasant is an onlooker; he talks chiefly with other peasants.'[114] This system of rigid separation, an absence of easy backwards and forwards mobility, lies behind the discussion, particularly developed in relation to India but applicable elsewhere, of the difference between the 'Great Tradition,' that is, the pan-national, general, religious and political and legal order, and the 'Little Tradition' of the local community. The original analysis was made by Redfield.[115] The national laws are opposed to the local customs; the national religion is opposed to the local religion.[116] Again, it is not difficult to see how this is intimately related to low geographical mobility, strong kinship ties, a desire to retain the family holding, the absence of localized cash, and the other features. The opposition between the 'Little' and the 'Great' can also be stated in another way by citing the very considerable literature which shows the strength of the 'local community' as the basic constituent element of peasant societies.

The strength of a local community, the peasant village or hamlet, has been stressed in both the general and the specific literature on peasantry. Redfield describes how in the Mexican countryside, "The local communities tend to be endogamous, each has a more or less homogenous culture, and the sense of local community loyalty is strong.'[117] Stirling writes of a Turkish village that 'People belong to their village in a way in which they belong to no other social group. On any definition of community the village is a community — a social group with many functions, not all of them explicit, and to which people are committed by birth or marriage, and bound by many ties.'[118] Turning to our specific area, the same self-sufficiency and strength of community bonds is constantly alluded to. Shanin observes that 'the village community operates to a great extent as an autonomous society ....'[119] This author speaks in many places of this community-based society, of the hostility to outsiders, the satisfaction of all wants within the community, and other features.[120] The same phenomenon is noted by Galeski for Poland, where he argues that the local community acts as

---

[113]Thomas, *Polish Peasant*, p. 128.
[114]Redfield, *Peasant*, p. 29.
[115]Ibid., ch. 3; for another discussion see Wolf, *Peasants*, p. 102-5.
[116]An excellent account of the relations is McKim Marriott, 'Little Communities in an Indigenous Civilization' in Marriott (ed.) *Village India* (Chicago, 1969).
[117]Redfield, *Peasant*, p. 33.
[118]Stirling, *Turkish Village*, p. 29.
[119]Shanin, *Peasant Economy*, i, p. 67.
[120]*Awkward Class*, pp. 32-3, 39, 141.

the central economic, ritual, cultural and social control unit: the 'village community is a primary group. Relationships among the inhabitants are based on personal contacts.'[121] The result of this is that a peasant society is made up of a host of largely identical, but mutually antagonistic and bounded territorial groups. This is put in other words by Shanin when he states that the primacy of household and community lead to a tendency 'towards segmentation into units of high similarity and low mutual interaction.'[122] This is a feature of such societies, a vertical segmentation, which this author notes was observed by both Marx and Durkheim, and, we may add, De Tocqueville.[123] Although it is clear that peasant societies will vary in strength of community boundaries, it appears to be generally true that such nations could be called 'particularist' rather than 'universalist.' Differences of dialect, clothing, cooking, folklore and other features are highly developed as one moves from one 'community' to another, even though the socio-economic structure may be remarkably similar in each. There is, above all, a strong sense of 'our place' as opposed to the outside world.

Other indices such as kinship reckoning and terminology, adoption and fostering, will be discussed in chapter six. It would be possible to elaborate further associated features of this pattern, particularly in the sphere of belief and ideology. Yet for the present purpose, since we will be concentrating in this work on the economic, social and demographic, the set of interlocked features elaborated above is sufficient. It should again be stressed that the description above is a model, a simplified abstraction from reality. As a result it would be absurd to expect any particular society to fit all the features exactly; nor would we expect any specific feature to be entirely 'pure.' There are always some who marry late, there is almost always some marketing, some cash, some wage labour, some geographical mobility. Yet it is useful to have a strong model of the basic socio-economic nature of peasantry with which to confront a particular historical reality. If it is the case that when the confrontation takes place *some* of the features are missing, we need not abandon the whole model. But if in looking at a majority of the variables the situation is totally opposed to the characteristics described above, then we are entitled to ask whether we are dealing with a 'peasantry' which has any analogy with the peasantries studied by anthropologists and comparative sociologists.

One further qualification is necessary. The system we have described is very roughly that found before the twentieth century in parts of Asia

[121]*Rural*, p. 81 and ch. 4, *passim*.
[122]*Awkward Class*, p. 39.
[123]Ibid., p. 177; Tocqueveille, *Ancien*, pp. 83, 102-3.

and Eastern Europe. It may be termed a 'classical' peasantry. It cannot be observed in its pure form for even by the time when it began to be systematically recorded, at the start of the twentieth century, it had changed considerably. In western Europe the changes occurred much earlier and there may also have been perennial and basic differences. For this reason it is necessary to be aware that the later nineteenth century 'peasantry' as encountered in, for example, western Ireland or southern France, was already different in form. In relation to the presence of cash and markets, land sales, rural specialization, age at marriage and all the other features, ethnographic accounts suggest that west European peasantries had moved a long way away from the 'classical' peasantry described above. In relation to the present work, the difference is most important in relation to the unit of ownership. The nature of the contrast between 'classical' and 'west European' peasant ownership is most easily illustrated by a diagram. In the former, all the members of the family are joint-owners; in areas of single-heir inheritance in western Europe, only one son is a joint-holder with his father.

A. Classical peasantry [124]

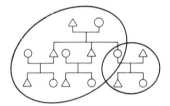

B. West European peasantry.

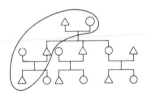

Key   △ = male   ○ = female   ⌐⌐ = descent   ⌊⌋ = marriage
○ = boundary of co-ownership

In the following chapters it may be assumed that we are speaking about 'classical' peasantry, unless it is specifically stated to the contrary.

[124]It is assumed in this model that inheritance is primarily through males. This is an over-simplification since societies where inheritance and descent is through females (matrilineal/uterine) may also, presumably, form a classical peasantry though the implications would be different. I am grateful to Jessica Styles for this caution.

2

When England Ceased to be a Peasant Society: Marx, Weber and the Historians

We have seen that modern sociologists and anthropologists have been prepared to classify England as a 'peasant' social structure up to the urban and industrial revolution. They think in terms of a transition from a basically 'feudal/peasant' system, through a 'capitalist/peasant' phase, to a 'capitalist/modern' one. These are clumsy labels and an attempt to date the changes is equally awkward, but it is probably reasonable to see the turning points as follows:[1]

feudal/peasant ⟶ capitalist/peasant ⟶ capitalist/modern

    1066   1450-1650   1750-1850

Thus, the argument would go on, the last two stages were similar to, but happened several centuries earlier than, the changes which occurred in most of the rest of Europe and is occurring or will occur in the Third World.[2]

We may wonder to what extent this chronology and this characterization accurately reflect the consensus of views of those who have worked intensively on the period up to the eighteenth century. Again it should be stressed that we are not concerned with labels or with the simple definition of peasantry, which makes it synonymous with 'agrarian.' At issue is firstly the degree to which experts believe that the specific set of features which may be analysed as lying behind the term 'peasantry' once existed in England. The second question is whether, and when, England changed from a particular type of rural society that manifested most of these features to the present system, where they appear to be totally absent.

[1]Thus the major watersheds are the sixteenth and eighteenth centuries, with the whole period from 1450-1800 as 'transitional,' a mixture of the two poles.
[2]For a diagram which sets out the progress of Europe and the Third World into the 'capitalist/modern' phases, with each nation 'taking off' from the well-ordered runway of pre-industrial life, see W. W. Rostow, *Stages of Economic Growth*, (Cambridge, 1960), p. 1.

Given our lack of interest in the word in the looser meaning, it is unnecessary to discuss the fact that many historians of England continue to talk about the 'peasants,' or use the word in the title of their works, even when writing of the later seventeenth century or the early eighteenth.[3] This may have helped to convince sociologists, but they had stronger grounds than this for believing, on the evidence presented to them, in the developmental sequence elaborated above. This can be seen from a necessarily brief survey of historical work during the last century and a half. Throughout this summary it should be remembered that the examples chosen are not meant to be extreme cases, nor can they represent the complexity of the work of the authors cited. Yet such a survey is necessary, always bearing in mind our previous characterization of peasantry, in order to establish what will appear to be the general shape of the changes which have occurred in England. Since the works surveyed contain a cross-section of work in this field, it seems fair to conclude that it is not merely anthropologists and sociologists who will be affected by their views. All those who pass through the British educational system, or are affected by the media, imbibe many of the views described below. There may, on occasion, be feelings of dissatisfaction with the general picture, but any specific individual is likely to be finally convinced that the general description of changes must be correct since almost all the experts appear to be agreed on the subject.

The roots of present views could be traced back to many authors and to an early period. But in order to prevent this book from turning into a historiographical work we will arbitrarily commence at the middle of the nineteenth century. Furthermore we will isolate three major thinkers who have done more than most to lay down the theoretical framework upon which contemporary work is based. These three writers were Macaulay, Marx and Weber.

Macaulay's views are most clearly expressed in the famous third chapter of his *History of England* published in 1848, and, although they were much criticized, we shall see that much of the philosophy behind them is with us still. He paints a picture of a world in 1685 which is enormously different from that of 1848 and hardly recognizable.[4] The world north of the Trent was savage and barbarous, a wilderness of heath inhabited by robbers,[5] and agriculture generally 'was in what would now be considered as a very rude and imperfect state.'[6] Even the

---

[3] For example, Hoskins, *Midland Peasant*; Joan Thirsk, *English Peasant Farming* (1957).
[4] Thomas Babington Macaulay, *History of England* (Everyman edn., 1906) pp. 209-11. All extracts are from vol. 1.
[5] Ibid., pp. 213ff.
[6] ibid., p. 233.

aristocracy and gentry lived like drunken boors, disgusting in their language and sensuality;[7] it was 'very seldom that the country gentleman caught glimpses of the great world; and what he saw of it tended rather to confuse than to enlighten his understanding.'[8] The clergy were as ignorant and beastly. The yeomanry were, however, 'an eminently manly and truehearted race,' they were the 'petty proprietors who cultivated their own fields with their own hands, and enjoyed a modest competence.'[9] There were few towns and cities, and places which were populous in the nineteenth century were then 'hamlets without a parish church, or desolate moors, inhabited only by grouse and wild deer.'[10] There was consequently a vast gap between the sophisticated Londoner and the rest of the ignorant and savage inhabitants. The Londoner was 'indeed, a different being from the rustic Englishman. There was not then the intercourse which now exists between the two classes . . . A cockney, in a rural village, was stared at as much as if he had intruded into a Kraal of Hottentots . . .'[11] The chief reason for the barbarity and isolation was the 'extreme difficulty which our ancestors faced in passing from place to place.'[12] To prove this point, Macaulay then describes for fifteen pages the appalling state of the highways, physically impassable and infested with highwaymen.[13] Beyond these muddy tracks, in the rural desolation, there lived ninety percent of the population in one extended rural slum. But they could not be described: 'Nothing has yet been said of the great body of the people . . . Nor can very much be said. The most numerous class is precisely the class respecting which we have the most meagre information . . . History was too much occupied with courts and camps to spare a line for the hut of the peasant or for the garret of the mechanic. . . .'[14] Yet Macaulay felt he knew enough to believe that not only was there physical degradation and poverty in a landscape that sounds like a description of a particularly impoverished part of the Third World today, but that the inhabitants were cruel and inhumane.

It is pleasing to reflect that the public mind of England has softened while it has ripened, and that we have, in the course of ages, become, not only a wiser, but also a kinder people . . . our ancestors were less humane than their posterity . . . Masters, well born and bred, were in the habit of beating their servants.

[7]Ibid., p. 240.
[8]Ibid., p. 241.
[9]Ibid., p. 251.
[10]Ibid., p. 258.
[11]Ibid., p. 278.
[12]Ibid., p. 279.
[13]Ibid., pp. 280ff.
[14]Ibid., p. 311.

Pedagogues knew no way of imparting knowledge but by beating their pupils. Husbands, of decent station, were not ashamed to beat their wives . . .[15]

It was a world from which Macaulay felt it was good to have escaped. He was concerned with the period after 1685 and therefore did not speculate much about the earlier centuries. But with such a sharp downward gradient in the quality of life from 1848 to 1685 it is dreadful to contemplate the world in which medieval country folk must have lived. If dirt, disease and poverty surrounded the isolated peasants in their 'huts' at the end of the seventeenth century, if they lived from hand to mouth in a coarse and cruel way, we can dismiss the five centuries up to the glorious revolution of 1688 as a period of almost unmitigated horror. The view of the gradual rise from barbarism is well illustrated by a famous passage in his *Essays.*

The history of England is emphatically the history of progress. It is the history of a constant movement of the public mind, of a constant change in the institutions of a great society. We see that society, at the beginning of the twelfth century, in a state more miserable than the state in which the most degraded nations of the East now are. . . . We see the most debasing and cruel superstition exercising boundless dominion over the most elevated and benevolent minds. We see the multitude sunk in brutal ignorance, and the studious few engaged in acquiring what did not deserve the name of knowledge. In the course of seven centuries the wretched and degraded race have become the greatest and most highly civilised people that ever the world saw, have spread their dominion over every quarter of the globe . . . .[16]

The values which lie behind Macaulay's work would appear to have been discredited, yet we will find that even in the 1970s there are some curious echoes of his philosophy of history.[17]

In total contrast to Macaulay's confident view of progressive advance is the general theory of Karl Marx. Marx chose England because it was the best documented and the earliest example of what he saw as a change from one 'mode of production,' feudalism, to another, capitalism. Writing of the countries within the capitalist mode of production, he explained that 'up to the present time, their classic ground is England. That is the reason why England is used as the chief illustration in the development of my theoretical ideas . . . .'[18] England had the best statistics and for many features 'furnishes the classical example' from

---

[15]Ibid., pp. 318-9.
[16]*Lord Macaulay's Essays* (Popular edn., 1906), p. 325, essay on 'Sir James Mackintosh's History of the Revolution.'
[17]It should not be necessary to stress that the world he portrays fits in most respects very neatly into the model of peasantry presented in the previous chapter; Macaulay clearly believed he was describing a vanished rural peasant society.
[18]Marx, *Capital*, i, p. 19.

which other nations should learn.[19] For instance, in considering the dissolution of the medieval property system, 'England in this respect (is) the model country for the other continental countries.'[20] The great shift from one type of society and economy to another occurred in England in the last third of the fifteenth century and in the sixteenth century. In the later fourteenth century, he writes, 'the mode of production itself had as yet no specific capitalistic character.'[21] He continues that

the prelude of the revolution that laid the foundation of the capitalist mode of production, was played in the last third of the fifteenth century and the first decade of the sixteenth century . . . (in) the forcible driving of the peasantry from the land.'[22]

This was part of the 'agricultural revolution which commenced in the last third of the fifteenth century, and continued during almost the whole of the sixteenth.'[23] More generally, 'the capitalist era dates from the sixteenth century,'[24] for 'the circulation of commodities is the starting-point of capital,' and so 'the modern history of capital dates from the creation in the sixteenth century of a world-embracing commerce and a world-embracing market:'[25] this is the 'manufacturing period' which lasts from 'the middle of the sixteenth to the last third of the eighteenth.'[26] England was seen as the first European nation to take an economic path that others would follow.

Although he was not primarily interested in the pre-capitalist mode in England and Europe, Marx did devote some time to sketching in several of its features, for he believed that 'the economic structure of capitalistic society has grown out of the economic structure of feudal society. The dissolution of the latter set free the elements of the former.'[27] Since this was the case, and since historically capitalism had developed 'in opposition to peasant agriculture,'[28] it was important to establish the general nature of a system of feudal or 'small-peasant' agriculture which was in many respects the opposite of capitalism.[29] We

---

[19]*Capital*, i, pp. 19, 607, 20.
[20]Karl Marx, *Grundrisse: Foundations of the Critique of Political Economy* (Penguin edn., 1973), trans. Martin Nicolaus, p. 277.
[21]*Capital*, i, p. 689.
[22]Ibid., i, p. 672.
[23]Ibid., i, p. 694.
[24]Ibid., i, p. 669.
[25]Ibid., i, p. 145.
[26]Ibid., i, p. 318.
[27]Ibid., i, p. 668.
[28]Ibid., i, p. 316.
[29]Ibid., iii, pp. 614-5.

may briefly and somewhat over-simply sketch in Marx's view of the difference of the two modes.

Marx believed that absolute private property was an essential element of capitalism and that it did not develop until capitalism prevailed. He argues that

the legal view . . . that the landowner can do with the land what every owner of commodities can do with his commodities . . . this view . . . arises . . . in the modern world only with the development of capitalist production.[30]

Private property is a 'modern' phenomenon, an essential feature of capitalist production.[31] Capitalism as a system 'transforms' the 'feudal landed property, clan property, small-peasant property' into modern, individualistic ownership.[32] He argues that 'feudal titles' were very different from the rights of modern private property in estates.[33] The introduction of absolute individual rights, with a purely economic interest, 'discarding all its former political and social embellishments and associations' were 'the great achievement(s) of the capitalist mode of production.'[34] Marx thus considered that there was a tenurial revolution centering on the late fifteenth to the end of the sixteenth centuries. No longer was land held by lords and peasants on conditional tenures that prevented them from doing what they wished to do with it and hence to exploit it in an economically 'rational' way. Economic activities were torn away from social life and modern individualistic property law, as it was to be observed in the eighteenth century, was gradually developed. The basic unit of ownership in medieval society was not the individual but the household. This can be seen in Marx's treatment of the Germanic 'mode of production' which Marx believed, as Hobsbawm points out, 'forms the socio-economic formation of feudalism in conjunction with the medieval town.'[35]

He describes how, in the Germanic system, 'the economic totality is, at bottom, contained in each individual household, which forms an independent centre of production for itself (manufactures purely as domestic secondary task for women etc.)' This is in contrast to the 'world of antiquity' where 'the city with its territory is the economic totality,' for 'in the Germanic world, the totality is the individual residence, which itself appears as only a small dot on the land belonging

---

[30]Ibid., iii, p. 616.
[31]*Idem.*
[32]Ibid., iii, p. 617.
[33]Ibid., i, p. 676.
[34]Ibid., iii, p. 618.
[35]Eric Hobsbawm in the introduction to Karl Marx, *Pre-Capitalist Economic Formations* (1964), trans. Jack Cohen, p. 38.

to it, and which is not a concentration of many proprietors, but the family as independent unit.' He continues that in the Germanic system the basis of society is not the citizen of a state but 'rather the isolated, independent family residence.'[36] It is clear from the whole passage that Marx thought of the lowest, basic unit of society as being the household, parents and children, who own, produce and consume as a group and enter into relations of association with other free and independent households. Though modified by feudal relations, this 'domestic mode of production' with the household as a joint labour-pool, with family and farm inextricably intertwined, continued in medieval feudal society. In peasant society, which had characterized England in the middle ages, we find

the patriarchal industries of a peasant family, that produces corn, cattle, yarn, linen and clothing for home use. These different articles are, as regards the family, so many products of its labour, but as between themselves, they are not commodities.

Both consumption and production are shared: 'the labour-power of each individual, by its very nature, operates in this case merely as a definite portion of the whole labour-power of the family.'[37] In sum, the unit of ownership, production and consumption is the household, which acts as a joint or corporate group. Among the consequences of this is the fact that 'there was little division of labour in the heyday of feudalism' since each household produced almost all it needed to consume.[38]

There are a number of correlates of this pattern, inextricably connected to it. One is that medieval England is basically what Marx calls a 'natural economy'; that is to say, money and markets play little part, production is mainly for direct use rather than for exchange. Thus he remarks that rent in kind 'has been dragged over into modern times from the natural economy of the Middle Ages,'[39] and speaks of the contrast between modern capitalism and the 'natural agricultural economy' of medieval Europe.[40] Even on large estates 'self-sufficient economy'[41] prevailed, while in ordinary households 'the peasant family produced the means of subsistence and the raw materials, which they themselves, for the most part, consumed . . . .'[42] In fact, feudalism could be defined as a system in which production was mainly for direct use;

[36]*Grundrisse*, p. 484.
[37]*Capital*, i, p. 82.
[38]T. B. Bottomore and Maximilien Rubel (eds.), *Karl Marx: Selected Writings in Sociology and Social Philosophy* (Penguin edn., 1963), p. 129.
[39]*Capital*, iii, p. 787.
[40]Ibid., iii, p. 334.
[41]Ibid., iii, p. 884.
[42]Ibid., i, p. 699.

capitalism was one in which commodities are produced for exchange.[43] Marx provides a clear description of this basically subsistence, non-monetized society where a 'peasant family' produces for its own use, not 'commodities.' Services and payment, when they were made to the lords, were in kind.[44] It was the sixteenth century expropriation which thinned out the 'independent, self-supporting peasantry.'[45]

The widespread use of money and evaluation of objects in monetary terms was entirely foreign to this 'natural' medieval economy. When money rents began to be paid, 'the character of the entire mode of production is thus more or less changed; for the peasant family is drawn into a market economy and loses its 'independence.'[46] Money in the medieval period was used by the 'peasant' only in situations of 'accident' or 'extraordinary upheavals.'[47] England was a barter, subsistence economy. It was not until the sixteenth-century that monetary relationships helped to erode the old structure, for Marx believed that 'the payment of money rent was a development which is only possible generally when the world-market, commerce and manufacture have reached a certain relatively high level . . . .'[48] This was a late phase. Thus it was that the old hand-to-mouth, 'immediate consumption' society of the Middle Ages, turns into the accumulative, producing, society of bourgeois capitalism.[49] Just as the history of landed property and change in the tenurial law provides a 'mirror' in which we can see the growth of capitalism,[50] so the development of markets and a cash nexus in everyday life is another mirror.

The fact that money was almost totally absent, combined with the fact that the basic unit of ownership and consumption was the household, meant that wage-labour was unimportant in medieval society. Marx believed that the 'transformation of rent in kind into money-rent' both anticipated and was inevitably correlated to 'the formation of a class of propertyless day-labourers.'[51] It was on this 'new class,' which arose mainly in the sixteenth century in England,[52] that capitalism was based: the 'capitalist mode of production in general is based on the expropriation of the conditions of labour from the labourers.'[53] It is a pre-condition of capitalism that the peasant 'had ceased to be attached

---

[43]*Pre-Capitalist Economic Formations*, p. 46, as elaborated by Sweezy.
[44]*Capital*, i, p. 82.
[45]Ibid., i, p. 697.
[46]Ibid., iii, p. 797.
[47]Ibid., iii, p. 598.
[48]Ibid., iii, p. 799; see also 797.
[49]Ibid., i, pp. 552, 558.
[50]*Grundrisse*, p. 252.
[51]*Capital*, iii, p. 798.
[52]Ibid., iii, p. 799.
[53]Ibid., iii, p. 614.

to the soil' so that changes in the society and the economy of the sixteenth century 'gave rise to the wage-labourer as well as the capitalist.'[54]
Marx argued that 'capital therefore presupposes wage-labour; wage-
labour presupposes capital. They condition each other; each brings the
other into existence.'[55] In England we can study 'the events that
transformed the small peasants into wage-labourers,'[56] for 'in England
alone . . . has it the classic form.'[57] Marx was aware that there were some
wage-labourers in 'the latter half of the fourteenth century,' but they
'formed then and in the following century only a very small part of the
population' who were 'well protected in its position by the independent
peasant proprietary in the country.'[58] What Marx meant by this is
shown elsewhere. He explains that the immense majority of the
population consisted then, and to a still larger extent, in the fifteenth
century, of free peasant proprietors.' But there was also wage-labour:

The wage-labourers of agriculture consisted partly of peasants, who utilized
their leisure time by working on the large estates, partly in an independent
special class of wage-labourers, relatively and absolutely few in numbers. The
latter also were practically at the same time peasant farmers, since, besides their
wages, they had allotted to them arable land to the extent of four or more acres,
together with their cottages. Besides they, with the rest of the peasants, enjoyed
the usufruct of the common land, which gave pasture to their cattle . . . .[59]

There were, therefore, very few, if any, landless labourers, according to
Marx. England was a country 'bestrewn with small peasant
properties.'[60]

Then came the massive changes associated with the rise of a money
economy, modern individualistic ownership and the decline of an
independent peasantry. The 'progressive destruction of the peasantry'
started in the last third of the fifteenth century when 'great masses of
men are suddenly and forcibly torn from the means of subsistence and
hurled . . . on the labour market.'[61] The whole foundation, the 'basis of
the whole process,' was laid by the 'expropriation of the agricultural
producer, of the peasant, from the soil.'[62] The Henrician and
Elizabethan concern with vagabonds and the introduction of a national
poor law is both evidence of the expropriation and a desperate attempt
to control the rootless, landless, 'free,' labourers who for the first time

[54] Ibid., i. p. 669.
[55] Bottomore and Rubel (eds.), *Writings*, p. 156.
[56] *Capital*, i, p. 699.
[57] Ibid., i, p. 670.
[58] Ibid., i, p. 689.
[59] Ibid., i, p. 671.
[60] Ibid., i, p. 672.
[61] Ibid., i, pp. 700, 669.
[62] Ibid., i, p. 669.

swarmed the land. The 'peasantry' did not altogether vanish in the six-teenth century, Marx argued, for 'even in the last decade of the seven-teenth century, the yeomanry, the class of independent peasants, were more numerous than the class of farmers.' They were finally eliminated in the first half of the eighteenth century.[63] Marx suggested reasons why this peasantry, which existed not only in England but throughout Europe in the sixteenth and seventeenth centuries, finally collapsed.[64] But as commentators have frequently pointed out, it is in his accounts of why one 'mode of production' should change into another, that Marx is least convincing, giving only a few vague hints as to the internal contradictions which lead to the collapse.[65] What he is certain of is that between the Norman Conquest and the last third of the fifteenth century, England was a 'peasant' society: 'peasant agriculture on a small scale, and the carrying on of independent handicrafts, which together form the basis of a feudal mode of production,' were present.[66] When the strictly feudal relationship of lord to peasant faded away, a stage of semi-peasant, semi-capitalist production succeeded. It was a period of transition, with money, wage-labour, growing markets and individual ownership, finally culminating in the industrial revolution of the eighteenth century. Thus, the non-feudal peasant society was a transitional phase through which all European societies would pass between the pure feudal and the 'capitalist' stages.[67]

Marx mentioned other associated features of the medieval pattern. He remarked that 'in the Middle Ages the population was purely agricultural. Under such a government as was the feudal system there can be but little traffic and hence but little profit. . .';[68] The 'production and the circulation of commodities are the general prerequisites of the capitalist mode of production.'[69] In the Middle Ages the merchant was merely one who 'transferred' the goods produced by guilds or peasants,[70] though later the merchant and the towns would be the nuclei from which the new capitalist mode would emerge. Land was treated as valuable in itself, not as a commodity to be freely bought and

---

[63]Ibid., i, p. 676. As Michael Duggett points out ('Marx on Peasants,' *Jnl. Peasant Studies*, vol. 2, no. 2 (Jan. 1975), p. 168, the 'disappearing of the English peasantry has since prompted immense controversy as to its cause, its duration and its consequences,' nevertheless, for Marx, 'It was the Civil War and the "Glorious Revolution" of the seventeenth century that were the crucial period'.

[64]*Ibid.*, iii, p. 807.

[65]Hobsbawm in the introduction to *Pre-Capitalist Economic Formations*, p. 43; *Capital*, i, p. 714.

[66]*Capital*, i, p. 316, n. 3.

[67]Ibid., iii, p. 807.

[68]Ibid., iii, p. 610.

[69]Ibid., i, p. 333.

[70]Ibid., iii, p. 336.

sold: in peasant society land is considered a good in itself, while in contrast 'the circulation of land as a commodity . . . is practically the result of the development of the capitalist mode of production . . . .'[71]

Marx's views have been elaborated in some detail because they have been enormously influential. Engels made no real changes to the chronology or the basic argument, though he added a few other features to the pattern and elaborated what he thought Marx meant. He accepted Marx's idea of a long 'period of peasant natural economy' which was changed 'the moment money penetrated into this mode of economy,'[72] a change which started to occur in the fifteenth century.[73] He accepted the idea of a medieval society based on households as the basic unit of production and consumption. He describes how, after the decline of tribal society, 'the exchanging family heads remain working peasants, who produce almost all they require with the aid of their families on their own farmsteads.'[74] He accepted the idea that there was a basic change in the nature of property law and relations both to land and other individuals. Capitalist production, 'by changing all things into commodities, (it) dissolved all inherited and traditional relations and replaced time hallowed custom and historical right by purchase and sale, by the "free contract."'[75] He thus claimed that Marx had anticipated Maine's contrast between 'status' and 'contract' and had seen the change as centred in the sixteenth century. Furthermore, Engels added some of the social correlates of the change, for instance from a system of arranged marriage to one of free marriage choice under capitalism.[76]

It is just as difficult to summarize the complex and interrelated set of ideas of Max Weber in a few paragraphs as it was in the case of Marx. Weber accepted the broad general outline of a major shift between two major systems in parts of Europe in the sixteenth century which Marx has described. He also accepted very broadly the fact that a system which might be termed 'peasant' or 'feudal' gave way to one which could be termed 'capitalist.' Furthermore, he agreed with most of the major features of the two polar types as described by Marx.[77] His major task was to explain why this had occurred only in parts of Europe,

[71] Ibid., iii, p. 811.
[72] Engels in *Capital*, iii, p. 898.
[73] *Capital*, iii, p. 900.
[74] Ibid., iii, p. 897.
[75] Frederick Engels, *The Origin of the Family, Private Property and the State* (Chicago, 1902), trans. E. Untermann, p. 96.
[76] Engels, *Origin of the Family*, pp. 92, 95, 98.
[77] For the similarity of the analyses by Marx and Weber in relation to the transition to be explained, see Geoffrey Hawthorn, *Enlightenment and Despair; A History of Sociology* (Cambridge, 1977), p. 158.

particularly the north-west, and not in the rest of the world, and here his emphasis was very different from Marx's. Before we proceed to his attempted explanation, we may briefly examine his picture of the pre-capitalist society out of which capitalism erupted, and his dating of the change.

Weber argued that Europe in the middle ages was fundamentally similar to other agrarian civilizations in that the basic unit of production and consumption was the small peasant household where farm and family were not separated. He spoke of the 'fundamental basis of the extraordinary importance of small units in agriculture,' which could be found in China and India, and is 'very important in all parts of Asia and also in Europe in the Middle Ages.' This 'existence of the small peasant in a sense depends directly on the absence of capital accounting and on retaining the unity of household and enterprise.'[78] He seems to have envisaged the household as a joint community of ownership, production and consumption, as did Marx, writing, for instance, that 'in the Middle Ages the household community was retained through many generations, for example in the commercial houses of the cities . . . Cousins, sisters-in-law, and mothers-in-law ate and lived together . . . .'[79] He argues that in later centuries the original medieval household where ownership, production and consumption were all united has been stripped of all but its consumption aspect: 'the household has . . . undergone an extensive internal transformation . . . its function has become restricted to the field of consumption, and its management placed on an accounting basis.'[80] Furthermore, he argues that this separation of the social and the economic, of landownership and the household, was central to the development of a 'rational' capitalist system,[81] for it allowed the 'separation of business from the household, which completely dominates modern economic life . . . .'[82] As Marx had argued, one reason for this was the 'dissolution of the manors' so that 'private property in land has been completely established.'[83] 'Manorial law reached its highest development in the thirteenth century,'[84] and private absolute property was largely absent. The emergence of modern individual property, part of a general movement from a subsistence, 'natural' economy, destroyed the medieval peasant. Thus 'in England, the mere fact of the development of a market, as such

[78]Weber, *Theory*, p. 263.
[79]Quoted Bendix, *Weber*, p. 41.
[80]Weber, *General*, p. 94.
[81]*Theory*, p. 277.
[82]Weber, *Protestant*, pp. 21-2.
[83]*General*, p. 94.
[84]Ibid., p. 65.

and alone, destroyed the manorial system from within . . . ,'[85] for it introduced profit, money and production for exchange rather than use, as Marx had also argued. Of course, there had been some 'free peasants outside the community circle of the lord's estate . . . essentially private owners,' especially in England,[86] but their economy was also based on the household and was a subsistence one. Medieval peasants produced for their own consumption and hence 'had no interest in making the soil yield more than was necessary for their own maintenance.'[87] They were attached to the soil, particularly those on the lord's estate: 'the peasant could withdraw from the community only by forfeiting his land and by securing another man to take his place.'[88] Thus Weber poses a strong antithesis between the accumulative, monetized economy and ethic of capitalism and the 'hand-to-mouth existence of the peasant.'[89]

The turning point for Weber was the sixteenth century. It could be seen in two central changes, as well as the separation between family and business already alluded to. One was the creation of a class of landless, 'free' labourers. Weber followed Marx in believing that pure wage-labour was absent in the medieval period, but that a free labour supply was an essential pre-requisite and component of the later factory system. The mass of labour 'was created in England, the classical land of later factory capitalism, by the eviction of the peasants.'[90] Weber saw the 'free labour market' and the manorial system as diametrically opposed;[91] it is only with the decline of feudalism that 'the peasantry are freed from the land and the land from the peasantry.'[92] The 'expropriation of labour has developed since the sixteenth century in an economy characterized by a progressive development of the market system . . . .'[93] This was essential for capitalism, for 'it is in contradiction to the essence of capitalism, and the development of capitalism is impossible, if such a propertyless stratum is absent . . . .'[94] Like Marx, he believed that the sixteenth century Poor Law had been enacted because of the large number of persons 'who had been rendered destitute by the revolution in the agricultural system,' and that it was the development of the market

[85]Ibid., p. 86.
[86]Ibid., p. 66.
[87]Ibid., p. 67.
[88]*Idem.*
[89]*Protestant*, p. 76.
[90]*General*, p. 129.
[91]Ibid., p. 83.
[92]Ibid., p. 92.
[93]*Theory*, p. 247.
[94]*General*, p. 208.

which meant that 'the peasants were expropriated in favour of the proprietors.'[95]

The other major shift was in the attitude towards accumulation. Weber recognized that capital accumulation 'existed in China, India, Babylon, in the classic world, and in the Middle Ages,'[96] but the peculiar 'ethic' which stressed untiring, never-ending, acquisition was absent and only developed, Weber argued, in certain parts of Protestant Europe in the sixteenth century. It was only then that parts of north-west Europe became different in kind from every other known world civilization; 'in modern times the Occident has developed . . . . very different form of Capitalism which has appeared nowhere else.'[97] Unlimited acquisitiveness was the central feature of this unique form of capitalism,[98] which was 'to a large extent peculiar to the modern Western World.'[99] It is well known that Weber believed that this ethic was somehow associated with Calvinism, though not in any simple system of cause and effect. As Bendix puts it, Weber's studies show that 'this religious development of the Reformation was one late element in the century-long emergence of certain unique features of Western Civilization'; thus 'Puritanism was a late development that reinforced tendencies that had distinguished European society for a long time past.'[100] It is clear that the great change occurred at exactly the time Marx suggested, namely the late fifteenth and sixteenth centuries, and that even if it was not the cause, Puritanism 'stood at the cradle of the modern economic man.'[101] For Calvinism stressed the individual, the 'individualistic motives of rational legal acquisition by virtue of one's own ability and initiative.'[102] Thus, though modern western capitalism 'was derived from the peculiarities of the social structure of the Occident,' it was inconceivable without Calvinism,[103] for Protestantism 'had the psychological effect of freeing the acquisition of goods from the inhibitions of traditionalistic ethics.'[104]

It is thus clear that even though he was partly setting up two 'ideal type' models, Weber saw two systems, one which existed throughout all large agrarian civilizations up to the fifteenth century, and a peculiar one which emerged in a corner of north-western Europe at the end of the

[95] Ibid., pp. 227, 86.
[96] *Protestant*, p. 52.
[97] Ibid., p. 21.
[98] Ibid., p. 53.
[99] *Theory*, pp. 278-9.
[100] Bendix, *Weber*, pp. 280, 71-2.
[101] *Protestant*, p. 174.
[102] Ibid., p. 179.
[103] Ibid., p. 25.
[104] Ibid., p. 171.

fifteenth century, and which gradually developed into industrialization. He realized, as did Marx, that England was a particularly good
example since it was the first to move from one system to the other.
England was 'the home of capitalism,'[105] and consequently 'the English
development' was very important, since it 'determined the character of
the evolution of capitalism.'[106] Weber believed that this difference grew
up in the sixteenth century, as England became the first country to
change from 'peasant' to 'capitalist.' By the seventeenth century it had a
special form of aristocracy dependent purely on money rents;[107]
England and parts of Germany by the sixteenth century saw the expropriation of the peasantry, while 'France, in contrast with England,
became a land of small and medium sized farms,' as did much of
Germany and Denmark.[108] The inheritance system of England with its
stress on primogeniture also separated it from much of the
Continent.[109]

Weber gives several major reasons why England appeared to
become different in the fifteenth century so that, for example, 'while in
England shop industry arose, so to speak, of itself, on the Continent
it had to be deliberately cultivated by the state.'[110] One was the fact that
it was an island: 'thanks to its insular position England was not
dependent on a great national army . . . hence the policy of peasant
protection was unknown in England and it became the classical land of
peasant eviction . . .'[111] The difference from the rest of Europe was 'by
no means fortuitous, but is the outcome of a continuous development
over centuries' and 'was the result of the insular position.'[112] A
contributory factor was the 'special position of the English city.'[113]
Another was the effect of the Norman Conquest, which led to a
powerful centralized state and a firm framework for the development of
rational law and the market.[114] Finally, there was religion, for it was 'the
power of religious influence, not alone, but more than anything else,
which created the differences' between England and the Continent.[115]
Weber argued forcibly that there was no 'fundamental difference
between the English and German characters at the end of the Middle
Ages, which cannot easily be explained by the differences of their

[105]*General*, p. 251.
[106]Ibid., p. 225.
[107]Ibid., p. 94.
[108]Ibid., p. 86.
[109]Ibid., p. 92.
[110]Ibid., pp. 129-30.
[111]Ibid., p. 129; see also *Theory*, p. 277.
[112]*Theory*, p. 277.
[113]*General*, p. 246.
[114]Bendix, *Weber*, p. 377.
[115]*Protestant*, p. 89.

political history,' it was only after the fifteenth century that major economic and religious changes set England apart and made her 'the home of capitalism.'[116] The general framework which Weber seems to have in the back of his mind is that all agrarian societies were in essence similar up to the fifteenth century, then England became different, (along with some areas on the Continent, such as Holland), to be followed several centuries later by the rest of Europe. It was no coincidence that this economic difference appeared just where Calvinism took hold.

We have seen that Marx gave no very convincing account of why feudalism should dissolve into capitalism in the later sixteenth century. Weber's main effort was to explain why this should be the case, and why other great agrarian civilizations, which appeared to be at the same stage as Europe in the fifteenth century, did not follow the same route. Two of his major reasons concerned the removal of impediments to single-minded, 'rational,' economic accumulation. One of these impediments was what he called 'magic,' which he saw as the polar opposite to 'rationality;' the rise of the Protestant ethic was merely one aspect of that 'emancipation from magic, that "disenchantment of the world" that Weber regarded as the distinguishing peculiarity of Western culture.'[117] Weber argued that 'western civilization is further distinguished from every other by the presence of men with a rational ethic for the conduct of life . . . .'[118] The destruction of 'magic,' by which Weber meant a whole bundle of attitudes and feelings towards the external world, was inherent in the abstract, ascetic, religion of Christianity itself.[119] But whereas medieval Catholicism with its heavy emphasis on ritual, on good works, on saints and festivals, had incorporated much of the 'magic' of pre-Christian systems, Weber argued that the Puritans 'rejected all trust in magical manipulation.'[120] The Quakers, Baptists and others especially argued for the 'radical elimination of magic from the world.'[121] Thus Weber combined a long-term feature, Christianity, with a particular trend, Protestantism. He made no sustained attempt to explain why Christianity should have been accepted or maintained, or why Protestantism should have developed where and when it did; he was content to argue that it helped to separate economics from social and religious relations. Again, the turning point came during the fifteenth and sixteenth centuries.

The second major change was in social life, which could be termed

[116]Ibid., pp. 88-9.
[117]Bendix, *Weber*, p. 69.
[118]*General*, p. 233.
[119]Ibid., p. 265.
[120]Bendix, *Weber*, p. 135.
[121]*Protestant*, p. 149; see also p. 105.

the 'defamilization of society' to parallel the 'disenchantment.' Behind Weber's work there is a general evolutionary model that sees societies originating in a stage at which kinship dominates all life and large 'clans' absorb the individual, moving through an intermediate phase in which the larger groupings have been broken down by various pressures, to modern society where the family and kinship no longer dominate economic and social life.[122] In China and India such a movement has never occurred. In China 'the fetters of the kinship group were never shattered,' every individual was completely submerged in the clan system,[123] and any nascent move towards individualistic capitalism was crushed by the power of kinship groups, by the intimate link between family and land.[124] In Europe, however, a number of factors worked together to break the original 'clan' system, according to Weber. One was Christianity, which encouraged an abstract, non-familistic attitude, stressed the individual believer; 'every Christian community was basically a confessional association of individual believers, not a ritual association of kinship groups.'[125] This 'all-important destruction of the extended family by the Christian communities ...' was the foundation upon which an autonomous bourgeoisie developed in the cities of western Europe.'[126] But while Christianity in general was a dissolvent of the earlier state, Protestantism was especially powerful in its attack on the earlier kinship 'fetters.' Weber argued that

the great achievment of ethical religions, above all of the ethical and asceticist sects of Protestantism, was to shatter the fetters of the kinship group. These religions established the superior community of faith and a common ethical way of life in opposition to the community of blood, even to a large extent in opposition to the family.[127]

In addition to Christianity and Protestantism, there were other pressures. The growth of towns in the middle ages also put a stress on the individual rather than the wider kinship group.[128] Furthermore, the political system of feudalism was incompatible with extended kinship ties; 'the land is divided by the feudal lord, in independence of clan and kinship.'[129] As a part of this process the growth of a centralized government and bureaucracy was both a consequence and a further cause of the decline of kinship.[130] As with all of Weber, the complexity of the

[122]*General*, pp. 54ff.
[123]Bendix, *Weber*, pp. 78-9; *General*, p. 50.
[124]Bendix, *Weber*, pp. 114-5.
[125]Ibid., p. 74.
[126]Ibid., p. 417.
[127]Quoted in Bendix, *Weber*, p. 139.
[128]Bendix, *Weber*, pp. 74, 77.
[129]*General*, p. 50.
[130]Ibid., pp. 50-1.

argument makes it difficult to pin him down. What seems to lie behind his writing is an idea that already in feudal societies, particularly 'in the north, where the large family community was unknown,'[131] the widespread clan grouping which owned property as a unit had largely been undermined. Vestiges remained, so that he could write, 'in the middle ages the church strove to abolish the rights of the clan in inheritance.' There were still powerful kinship constraints in the later fifteenth century,[132] for it was only in the sixteenth century that the final separation of business affairs from family affairs occurred. It was then and during the next century that, as Bendix puts it, 'the Puritan divines brought about a profound depersonalization of family and neighbourhood life' which was linked to a 'decline in kinship loyalties and a separation of business affairs from family affairs.'[133] We may simplify Weber's ideas into the argument that there had been three stages in the evolution of modern society. First was 'clan' society, where kinship was paramount and the basic economic, social and religious unit was a wide group of kin; this had disappeared in north-western Europe by at least the thirteenth century, although traces remained. This was replaced by a second, intermediate, phase in which the basic unit was the household of parents and children. They might not live in the same house, but parents and married children formed a co owning 'peasant' unit. This configuration was finally destroyed, Weber argues, first in England from the later fifteenth century, and later elsewhere, allowing for the third stage — the separation between family and business and the economic isolation of the individual. It had many other correlates, which Weber also discusses or alludes to. In medieval society, as befitted a society based on the household, the acting head of the household ruled the rest in a powerful and 'patriarchal' way, his children never escaping his power until his death.[134] Women would also be subject to the patriarchal power of the head of the household. Weber thus finds that women's status in medieval England, for example, was very low: 'In ancient England the seduction of the wife was regarded as a mere property damage . . . The woman was a field slave . . . .'[135]

In a final discussion of the reasons why parts of north-western Europe became different from any other agrarian civilization which he had studied, Weber rejected a number of simple explanations such as the profits from colonialism, the growth of population, the inflow of precious metals. Instead he suggested as major factors the communi-

[131]Ibid., p. 173.
[132]Ibid., p. 51.
[133]Bendix, *Weber*, pp. 70-1.
[134]Ibid., p. 330.
[135]*General*, p. 98.

cations in north-western Europe, the military situation, the demand for luxury goods, the rationalization of economic life and the development of a new ethical system related to the general characteristics of Christianity and the particular features of Protestantism.[136] But he argued that it was not his job to show in detail how the major transformation from a feudal, patriarchal, peasant economy and society to a highly mobile 'capitalist' one occurred. That was a task for historians.[137] He believed that he had established both the nature of the two different systems and the date at which one had been transformed into another, and also pointed towards some of the reasons for the change. In combination with Marx's work, a framework of questions and discussion had been established which we shall find has altered very little in its more basic contour since Marx and Weber established it.

Thus from these figures, Macaulay, Marx and Weber, modern historians and sociologists derived a picture of the major shifts in European and particularly English society and economy over the period from the thirteenth century. They could combine the structure provided by Marx and Weber with the colourful picture of pre-industrial England painted by Macaulay. Though they might prefer the gloomy invective of Marx to the Victorian optimism of Macaulay, they could be left in no doubt that the further into the past they went the more different from themselves Englishmen became. Those inhabiting medieval England, before the 'revolutions' of the sixteenth century, lived in an entirely different economic, social and mental world from ourselves. For instance, 'early societies were made up of groups rather than individuals. A man on his own accounted for very little.'[138] The historian's task consisted of showing how this very different society turned into the one we now inhabit. What had been established, it appeared, was, 'that the affairs of the eleventh to thirteenth centuries were the affairs of a remote period with a social structure all its own . . . which . . . corresponded to nothing in Stuart England.'[139] We may now turn to specifically English historians in order to see the ways in which they have elaborated and modified the nineteenth century views.

With some notable exceptions, particularly the work of F. W. Maitland,[140] the historians writing in the next generation made no

[136]Ibid., pp. 258-60.
[137]Bendix, *Weber*, p. 382.
[138]Marc Bloch, *French Rural History: An Essay on its Basic Characteristics* (1966), trans. J. Sondheimer, p. 150. Or, as Marx put it, 'The further back we go into history, the more the individual . . . . seems to depend on and constitute a part of a larger whole' (*Introduction to the Critique of Political Economy*, quoted in S. Lukes *Individualism* (Oxford, 1973), p. 76).
[139]Pocock, *Ancient Constitution*, p. 210.
[140]In particular in his *English Law*. Sir F. Polock was co-author, though all except one chapter is the work of Maitland.

substantial change to these general theories. Medievalists still portrayed the middle ages as a closed, rural, small-scale world inhabited by great lords and simple peasants. Salzman wrote that 'Medieval society was built upon the basis of Land . . . a landless man was, at the time of the Norman Conquest, and for some centuries afterwards, a strange being, rarely to be found except in a few of the bigger towns.'[141] Eileen Power described the society as follows.

The hurrying, scattering generation of today can hardly imagine the immovable stability of the village of past centuries, when generation after generation grew from cradle to grave in the same houses, on the same cobbled streets, and folk of the same name were still friends, as their fathers and grand-fathers had been before them.[142]

G. G. Coulton was of the opinion that a prohibition against marrying people nearer than third cousins must have been impossible to observe in medieval villages since 'scarcely any peasant, in those small communities, can have been so unrelated to the rest as to keep within the code.'[143] Coulton's pupil H. S. Bennett wrote that

We must remember how circumscribed was the world in which the majority of these people lived. Their village was their world: beyond, some ten or twenty miles led to the local shrine or the great fair, and there, perhaps, once or twice a year they made their way; but, for the most part, their lives were ground out in a perpetual round from one field to another, and so to the next . . .[144]

Bennett later confirms Coulton's picture concerning marriage partners by arguing that a slow population growth rate makes it 'easy to see how static conditions were in the village, and what a limited number of young people there were in any of them at any given time, and how limited the potential list of marriageable men and women must have been.'[145] Not only did medievalists agree with each other, but they found support in the views of those writing on a slightly later period. Thus Coulton cited with approval, and with application to the medieval period, R. H. Tawney's observation concerning the sixteenth century that 'most men have never seen more than a hundred separate

[141]L. F. Salzman, *English Life in the Middle Ages* (Oxford, 1926), p. 36.
[142]E. Power, *Medieval People* (1924; University paperback edn., 1963), p. 160.
[143]G. G. Coulton, *Medieval Village, Manor and Monastery* (1925; Harper Torchbook edn., 1960), pp. 471-2.
[144]Bennett, *Manor*, p. 34.
[145]*Manor*, p. 240. This generation of medievalists also drew on the influential work of J. E. Thorold Rogers, a man with immense experience of medieval records, who wrote that 'the villagers frequented the same ale-houses as that at which their forefathers had caroused for generations,' and painted a picture of 'community,' monotony and physical hardship in a society where a 'landless man was an outlaw, a stranger; one registered in no manor, a thief . . .' (Rogers, *Six Centuries*, pp. 86, 97-9, 52).

individuals in the course of their whole lives, where most households live by tilling their great-grandfather's fields with their great-grandfather's plough';[146] Tawney's work helped to confirm the image of a change-over from a basically subsistence economy to a market one, from a distributive Catholic ethic to an accumulative Protestant one, from an integrated and hierarchical society to a ruthless and competitive one. Tawney's famous *Religion and the Rise of Capitalism* documented this change. It is clear that he believed that society was originally based on the household as the basic unit of production and consumption. Thus he wrote,

the household does not merely imply what we mean by 'the family,' a group of persons connected by blood but pursuing often quite separate occupations, and ... possessing quite separate economic interests. It is, on the contrary a miniature co-operative society, housed under one roof, dependent upon one industry, and including not only man and wife and children, but servants and labourers, ploughmen and threshers, cowherds and milkmaids, who live together, work together, and play together, just as one can see them doing in parts of Norway and Switzerland at the present day. When the economic foundations of their small organism are swept away by a change in the method of farming, the effect is not merely to ruin a family, it is to break up a business.'[147]

Much of what Macaulay had written about the seventeenth century was merely pushed back a couple of centuries, to the period after the Black Death. The views of Power, Tawney and the rest were given expression in Trevelyan's successful *English Social History* which described the gradual evolution of society from one where, for example, marriages were arranged and loveless, children were lashed and severely disciplined and physical conditions were harsh in the fifteenth century,[148] through the 'slow and long contested evolution' towards modern and more humane conditions.[149] Although much of what was written by these and other writers was exceptionally good, it was difficult for them to break out of the evolutionary framework that is behind all the nineteenth century writers. Put in a sentence, history is a progression from small, isolated communities inhabited by 'peasants,' very similar to the communities then being described by anthropologists in Asia and Africa, towards the market, monetized, 'open' social structure of the eighteenth century. It is a convincing story, and very difficult for any of us to abandon. Nor have historians shown a great

[146]R. H. Tawney, *The Agrarian Problem of the Sixteenth Century* (1912; Harper Torchbook edn., 1967), p. 264; cited in Coulton, *Medieval Village*, p. 393.
[147]Tawney, *Agrarian Problem*, p. 233.
[148]G. M. Trevelyan, *English Social History* (1944; 1948 edn.), pp. 65-7.
[149]Ibid., p. 70.

desire to do so, as we may see by looking at the final generation to be considered, those between about 1950 and the present.

The view of medievalists may be represented by two recent works by leading scholars. Both of these confirm the view that medieval England was basically a 'peasant' society, similar in many ways to the peasantries of contemporary developing societies. M. M. Postan writes that

> Needless to say, even in the Middle Ages the 'ideal type' of peasants would seldom be found complete and pure. Yet historians will not fail to recognize in the physiognomy of the medieval villager most of the traits of a true peasantry ... most villagers possessed family holdings of modest size, while many others occupied holdings not markedly greater or smaller than that. Similarly, even though many villagers employed hired labour, that labour was as a rule additional to the work of the holder himself and his family ... there is no doubt that the average household largely depended on its own output for food and fodder. As for attitudes to land, they seem to have been equally typical.[150]

In his recently published Ford lectures, Hilton defends the use of the term and concept 'peasant' to describe the inhabitants of late fourteenth-century England and describes many features of the society which would put it on a par with other 'peasantries.' For example, marriage was probably at an early age, and the household went through a stage of co-residence of two married couples. Villages were little closed worlds, 'jealous of the intrusion of strangers within the boundaries of concern' of what was still an 'interlocked community.'[151] As we shall see, there is now a good deal of disagreement among medievalists, but it is probably true to say that there is no general alternative picture to that which Power, Coulton and Bennett painted, and Postan and Hilton have elaborated.

As in the preceding decades, medieval historians have drawn comfort from the fact that their picture seemed to be confirmed by those who write about the sixteenth to eighteenth centuries. These later historians, in turn, broadly accept the picture of small-scale peasant society, of organic, tight-knit, communities gradually breaking apart. By the start of the eighteenth century we witness the law 'tearing down the remnants of the threadbare communal grid.'[152] Under the influence of new discoveries, new wealth, new mobility, with the major turning

---

[150]Postan, *Essays*, p. 280.
[151]Hilton, *Peasantry*, pp. 28-9, 56, 54.
[152]E. P. Thompson in Goody, *Family*, p. 339. Other modern historians present the same picture. Thus Hobsbawm and Rudé argue that whereas in Ireland 'the traditional system of mutual aid and collectivity' lasted until the twentieth century, by the middle of the eighteenth century England 'was no longer that kind of society. It was moving rapidly away from what it had maintained of such a society from the past' (E. J. Hobsbawm and George Rudé, *Captain Swing* (Penguin edn., 1973), p. 17).

point being the sixteenth to eighteenth centuries, England was transformed from a rural backwater into the leading nation of the world.
This view lies behind perhaps the most impressive contribution to the
study of social change in the period, namely in the work of Tawney's
successor, Christopher Hill. He characterizes the two and a half
centuries leading up to the industrial revolution as follows:

In 1530 the majority of English men and women lived in rural households
(mostly mud huts) which were almost economically self-sufficient: they wore
leather clothes, and ate black bread from wooden trenchers: they used no forks
or pocket-handkerchiefs. By 1780 England was being transformed by the factory
system: brick houses, cotton clothes, white bread, plates and cutlery were
becoming accessible even to the lower classes.[153]

Yet, despite the massive change, England remained throughout the
period in many ways similar to a modern Third World society,
especially in its regionalism and emphasis on household production:

throughout there are some permanent features of what today we should call a
'backward economy . . .' Bad communications made for an intense regionalism
. . . Inadequate communications slowed down the development of a national
market, and protected small household production . . .[154]

Thus, while there were political, agricultural and commercial revolutions in the seventeenth century, this was still basically a non-industrial
'peasant' society. The picture is a blend of Tawney, Weber and Marx.
The most recent attempts by economic historians to describe the whole
social order follow roughly the same lines. Phyllis Deane writes:

In sum, therefore, it is evident that the British economy of the mid-eighteenth
century displayed (though to a limited extent) a number of the features which
we now recognize as characteristic of a pre-industrial economy. It was poor
though not without some economic surplus; it was relatively stagnant . . . The
mass of the people lived close to economic disaster . . . Most of the community's
economic decisions were taken by family-based units of production, whose
output per member of the work force depended largely on the extent of their
holdings in land, ships or stocks of consumer goods. It might be described as a
'traditional society' in the sense defined by Rostow as the first of his stages of
economic growth.[155]

Charles Wilson describes the sixteenth century as a period of
cataclysmic change along the lines mapped out by Tawney,[156] in which

---

[153]Christopher Hill, *Reformation to Industrial Revolution: British Economy and Society
1530-1780* (1967), p. 9.
[154]*Idem.*
[155]Phyllis Deane, *The First Industrial Revolution* (Cambridge, 1965), p. 18.
[156]Charles Wilson, *England's Apprenticeship* (1965), pp. 4-9.

the 'peasants' were gradually declining.[157] Recently, Donald Coleman has provided another summary which confirms the picture again. The basic unit of production and ownership throughout the period was the household and hence family and kinship were far more important than later.

Much, probably most, of the country's work was carried on in family units: apprentices became part of a family; the family home — the cottage of the poor weaver; the house-cum-shop of the urban craftsman or retailer, even the country mansion of the landed gentleman — was also the place of work ... for most people the modern distinction between dwelling-places and work-places was unknown.[158]

It was a society in which the small local unit was important and custom was king, though all this was beginning to break up under the impact of trade, bullion, intellectual innovations and other factors. The picture put forward by nineteenth and early twentieth-century historians is confirmed.

Finally, it is worth considering just how far the social force of the small, local unit — farm and village — reinforced poor transport to ensure a high degree of conformity to local norms of behaviour, thus helping to perpetuate limited economic horizons. As the horizons began to widen so new aspirations began, slowly, to find themselves at variance with the forces of ritual and of customary behaviour which provided so much of the cement of social cohesion.[159]

From closed to open, from subsistence to cash, from stability to movement, the country moved along a course similar to that described by Marx and Weber.

This general view of the gradual evolution from a closed peasant society, through a mixed but still basically 'pre-industrial' pattern has been able to incorporate and find support from the work of those historians who have been concerned with the concept of property. This is an area which attracts both political philosophers and social historians. The major contrast they make is between a 'feudal,' non-individualistic idea of ownership, and a modern, absolute, idea of individual property. One summary of the change is suggested by Harold Perkin. He writes that the 'peculiarly English concept of absolute property' was 'bequeathed' to the late seventeenth century by the landed aristocracy which had 'fought for three centuries and more to establish it.'[160] The major change is thus alleged to have occurred

[157] Ibid., p. 250.
[158] D. C. Coleman, *The Economy of England 1450-1750* (Oxford, 1977), p. 8.
[159] Ibid., p. 11.
[160] H. J. Perkin, 'The Social Causes of the British Industrial Revolution', *Trans. Roy. Hist. Soc.*, 5th ser., 18 (1968), p. 134.

between the fifteenth and seventeenth centuries. In 'feudal societies,' Perkin writes, 'property, especially in land, was both something more and something less than ownership ... it was also contingent, conditional and circumscribed by the claims of God, the Church, the King, the inferior tenants and occupiers, and the poor.' This all underwent a massive change 'By a process lasting three centuries, from the commutation of labour services, through the enclosures and engrossing of Tawney's century to the abolition of feudal tenures at the Civil War.' This turned 'lordship into absolute ownership.' Here 'was the decisive change in English history which made it different from that of the Continent. From it every other difference in English society stemmed.'[161] It is clear that this follows the Marx-Weber-Tawney chronology and implies that if we wish to explore why England differed from the Continent and why it industrialized, we should look to the period between 1400-1700.

A similar view of the modern origins of individual ownership is taken by two influential historians of political theory. C. B. Macpherson has written a monograph which argues that the 'theory of possessive individualism' arose in the middle of the seventeenth century in the work of Harrington and Hobbes and was later expressed by Locke. Before this, presumably, a non-capitalist attitude to ownership prevailed. This new ethic was a reflection and justification of the emerging market economy.[162] These views have been repeated and expanded in a recent paper which again argues that modern 'capitalist' individual property in England was totally different from 'feudal' or 'pre-capitalist' property. The sixteenth and seventeenth centuries witnessed the major change.[163] J. G. A. Pocock dates the change even later, arguing that Harrington in the middle of the seventeenth century still had a pre-market view of property which conformed with the Greek view of 'oikonomia.' He states that it is impossible to find 'a classical bourgeois ideology and a market theory of personality' dominating political theory even by the end of the seventeenth century.[164] Leaving aside the dispute over the precise dating, what is clear is that there is believed to have been a shift, in England, between two different socio-economic systems, from communal, limited and conditional ownership, to modern individual and absolute ownership. As Marc Bloch observed, this was the 'one really striking transformation' in the

---

[161] Ibid., p. 135.
[162] *The Political Theory of Possessive Individualism* (Oxford, 1962).
[163] 'Capitalism and the Changing Concept of Property' in Kamenka, *Feudalism*, esp. pp. 109-10.
[164] 'Early Modern Capitalism: the Augustan Perception' in Kamenka, *Feudalism*, pp. 68, 83.

whole agrarian history of Europe. To him it seemed to have taken place 'from about the beginning of the fifteenth century up to the early years of the nineteenth,' and to have occurred in England, but not elsewhere in Europe.[165]

If we look at a small sample of the recent work in social and economic history we will find that it is all ultimately based on the same premise of a change from a 'peasant' system to another, non-peasant, one. For example, those who are interested in the history of witchcraft and magic have suggested that one of the major reasons for the rise of witchcraft accusations in the sixteenth century was the tension caused by a conflict between a traditional ethic of mutual responsibility and charity, the norms of self-contained and subsistence villagers, and the new acquisitive and individualistic spirit of capitalism and protestantism.[166] They accept a picture of England as a pre-industrial society alongside other pre-industrial societies, but one in which 'the decline of the English peasantry was already under way.'[167] We are told that in the seventeenth century there was a 'decline of . . . the household as a unit of production . . . ,' which undermined the family, 'the lowest unit of English society.'[168] The conflict over magic and witchcraft is one dimension of the change which Weber and Tawney had suggested.

Another major interest has been in local and regional history. Workers in this area have also tended to assume that despite considerable mobility and growing wealth, England was throughout most of the sixteenth and seventeenth centuries still a 'peasant' society, much like other pre-industrial societies. Local and regional studies support by their conclusions, if not necessarily by their contents, the views of national historians, depicting, as does Mervyn James for instance, regional society moving from 'lineage society' to 'civil society.'[169] Another school which bolsters up this theory of evolution is that of family history. The recent works of Edward Shorter, Lawrence Stone and Lloyd de Mause fit perfectly with the general picture, showing a gradual movement from wide family ties, arranged and loveless marriages, callous brutality to children, through to the modern,

[165]Bloch, *Land*, p. 49.
[166]Alan Macfarlane, *Witchcraft in Tudor and Stuart England* (1970), pp. 204-6. See also Keith Thomas, *Religion and the Decline of Magic* (1971), ch. 17, for an analogous though slightly different account of the new conditions of the sixteenth century, for example the new attitude to the poor and the destruction of the ritual protections against witchcraft.
[167]Thomas, *Religion and the Decline of Magic*, p. 4; for general analogies see Macfarlane, *Witchcraft*, chs. 17-19.
[168]Keith Thomas, 'Women and the Civil War Sects' reprinted in T. Aston (ed.) *The European Crisis 1560-1660* (1964), pp. 319, 338.
[169]Mervyn James, *Family, Lineage and Civil Society: A Study of Society, Politics, and Mentality in the Durham Region 1500-1640* (Oxford, 1974).

individualistic, family system, based on the nuclear family and love between the married pair.[170] Even demographic historians, whose individual findings do not always fit this scheme very well, have managed to adapt them to the general idea of change from medieval to modern. John Hajnal's work on 'the unique marriage pattern' suggests that it originated sometime in the later fifteenth or sixteenth centuries and that therefore there was a massive change at the end of the medieval period.[171] Peter Laslett's *The World we have Lost* and his more recent work rejects some of his predecessors conclusions, but still paints a picture of a society based on the household, on patriarchal power, a world very different from our own.[172]

This brief survey of the historical scene has not done full justice to the works mentioned. Nor has it referred to the dissenters: K. B. McFarlane spoke with suspicion of the 'so-called peasantry' of the later middle ages, and reprimanded J. E. Neale for trying to diminish the achievements of the later medieval period because Neale had found that 'the prologue, as it were, anticipated too much of his play.'[173] J. H. Hexter showed in a brilliant essay that 'the rise of the middle class' in the sixteenth century, and much of the supposed economic ruthlessness and rationality, could be found equally clearly as far back as records would allow one to go.[174] E. A. Wrigley has shown on several occasions that the geographical mobility, family limitation and demographic pattern of the seventeenth century do not fit the picture at all.[175] Furthermore, most of those who use the general framework inherited from the nineteenth century find it unsatisfactory in one way or another and

---

[170]Edward Shorter, *The Making of the Modern Family* (1976); Lawrence Stone, *The Family, Sex and Marriage in England 1500-1800* (1977); Lloyd de Mause (ed.), *The History of Childhood* (1976), ch. 1.

[171]Hajnal, *European Marriage*.

[172]Peter Laslett, *World we have lost* (1965; 2nd edn. 1971); *Family Life and Illicit Love in Earlier Generations* (Cambridge, 1977).

[173]K. B. McFarlane, *The Nobility of Later Medieval England* (1973), p. 215; 'Parliament and Bastard Feudalism' reprinted in R. W. Southern (ed.), *Essays in Medieval History* (Royal Historical Society, 1968), p. 240. This scepticism may have been passed to me not by blood, but through the teaching of McFarlane's pupil, James Campbell, at Worcester College, Oxford. An unpublished paper on 'Was the England of Chaucer the same as that of Shakespeare?' (Oxford, 1963), anticipates, on the political and administrative side, a good deal of the argument of this book. Recently Gimpel and Hallam have argued that medieval Europe was far more technologically advanced and 'capitalist' in its ethic than historians had previously assumed (Jean Gimpel, *The Medieval Machine: The Industrial Revolution of the Middle Ages* (1977); Hallam 'The Medieval Social Picture' in Kamenka, *Feudalism*).

[174]Hexter, 'The Myth of the Middle Class in Tudor England' reprinted in *Reappraisals*.

[175]E. A. Wrigley, 'A Simple Model of London's Importance in a Changing English Society and Economy, 1650-1750', *P. & P.*, 37, (1967); 'Family Limitation in Pre-Industrial England'. *Ec.H.R.*, 2nd ser., xix, no. 1 (1966); *Population and History* (1969), especially ch. 3.

produce findings that do not fit into it. Yet by and large, as is evidenced, for example, in the way I myself uncritically accepted the framework when trying to explain changes in witchcraft beliefs, the outline of English history seems uncontentious and unarguable. England starts in the century after the Norman invasion as a poor, rural society, thinly inhabited by 'peasants' and lords, similar in many ways to its Continental neighbours. Then, by some strange accident which has never yet been satisfactorily explained, sometime between the later sixteenth century and the mid-eighteenth it took a different course from its neighbours. If this picture is correct, the problem of explaining what is unique about England leads us to the seventeenth and eighteenth centuries. But before we narrow our view, let us examine the evidence more closely.

3

English Economy and Society in the Sixteenth and Seventeenth Centuries

We may now examine the English evidence. When dealing with a country with an average population of over five million over a period of two centuries, moreover a country where there were very great regional contrasts as well as marked differences between the aristocracy, gentry, middling and poor, it is possible only to sample briefly, and to refer to previous studies. It should be stressed that the rich and the inhabitants of large towns may have differed very considerably from the patterns we will discuss and furthermore that there were very considerable changes over time and over space. Nor can we deal adequately here with more than a small number of the criteria of 'peasantry' we have suggested. The weight of proof for the thesis we will be pursuing will have to come from future work. Yet with all these qualifications it does seem possible to provide a firm answer to the question: was England in either the sixteenth or seventeenth century a 'peasant' society, similar to either the 'classical' or 'west European' peasantry?

We may start with the individual and work upwards and outwards. The vicar of Earls Colne in the country of Essex wrote a Diary which has survived and been both published and analysed.[1] Ralph Josselin was not just a vicar, but also a farmer who built up an estate in the village and between 1660 and his death in 1683 drew about half his income from the profits of land, rather than from his ecclesiastical living. The 660 pages of his printed diary give us the most intimate and detailed insight into the mind and activities of a yeoman farmer that we possess. Day by day or week by week between 1644 and 1683 he noted details concerning harvests, prices, weather, land purchases and sales, debts and loans and many other economic matters. He also noted the activities of his wife and children and of other villagers. From all this we can look into the

[1]Alan Macfarlane (ed.), *The Diary of Ralph Josselin 1616-1683* (British Academy, Records of Economic and Social History, n.s.iii, 1976).

life of a man who lived in a small Essex village without any long interruption between 1641 and 1683. We may wonder how nearly Josselin fits the model we have elaborated. The answer is clear. It is difficult to envisage anyone further from the ideal-type 'peasant.' On almost every one of the criteria described above, his thought, life-style and activities were totally contrary to that of the model. Only in the fact that he was engaged in agriculture to a considerable extent and hence subject to the uncertainties of the weather and prices does he fit our image at all. His Diary makes it clear that the basic unit of ownership in his case was not the household or family, but Josselin himself. He describes a situation of complete, absolute and exclusive private ownership. He was not merely the trustee or organizer of a small corporate group who jointly owned the land. The land held in his name in deeds and court rolls was not family land, but his land.

The difference can best be illustrated by taking the two extreme situations which can occur. In traditional Russia the head of a household could be removed from his headship for mismanagement or misbehaviour.[2] In Josselin's case, on the contrary, he threatened on several occasions to disinherit his only surviving son. He was finally driven to such a state that he wrote

John declared for his disobedience no son; I should allow him nothing except he took himself to be a servant, yet if he would depart and live in service orderly I would allow him 10 li yearly: if he so as to become gods son, I should yet own him for mine.[3]

As we have seen, in a peasant society, birth or adoption plus participation in the basic tasks of production give people an inalienable right to belong to the small property-owning corporation. They cannot be 'disinherited' since their right is as strong as anyone else's. In Josselin's case his children's access to property was through his gift. It is a central and crucial difference to which I shall devote the next chapter. I shall also write further on the question of inheritance. We are told that in Russia there was no written will, since it was clear that all males should receive an equal share of what was, in nature, theirs. It was a matter of splitting up temporarily a communal asset, the shares returning to the common pool when the demographic situation had changed. In marked contrast, Josselin's own will and the provision for his children recorded in the Diary and manor court rolls of the parish show that we have in his case a fully developed system of individual

[2]Shanin, *Awkward Class*, p. 221.
[3]Macfarlane (ed.), *Diary of Ralph Josselin*, p. 582.

inheritance, in which each child was given a part at the discretion of the parents.[4]

Ownership was not based on the household; nor was production. The Diary makes it clear that the basic unit of production in Josselin's case was neither the extended family nor even the smaller household of parents and children, for Josselin did not co-operate in production with his own parents, with his siblings or with his own children. His sons did not work the farm but were apprenticed to other masters over fifty miles away. As in most of modern Britain, parents cannot and do not expect their children to invest their labour into a 'family pool,' so it was in Josselin's case. His children all left home as soon as they started to be net producers, the girls at between ten and fourteen, the boys at fifteen.[5] This also meant that the household was not the basic unit of consumption; the children visited home, but belonged to other, non-related, consumption units. There was thus no basic link between the family and the farm, between the social and the economic unit; neither ownership, nor production, nor consumption was based on the family. Among the consequences of this was the lack of attachment to a particular house or landholding. Josselin's grandfather was a wealthy yeoman who farmed in Roxwell in Essex, but Josselin's father sold off the patrimony and went to farm in Bishop's Stortford, where he lost most of his estate. Josselin then settled in Earls Colne and built up a farm there. His children showed the same geographical mobility, most of them settling well away from their father. As for the purpose of Josselin's agricultural activity, it was certainly not mainly for his own use, but for exchange on the market in order to obtain cash with which to buy other commodities. In fact he only worked a small part of the estate himself, letting out the rest to other, non-related, villagers for a money rent. He estimated that in the years 1659-1683 his landholdings brought in a total of approximately £80 *per annum*. Given the cost of foodstuffs at the period, less than one quarter of this sum would have been consumed directly in the form of food.

It would be possible to continue in this fashion through all the major indices of peasantry, noting that Josselin's economic behaviour was highly 'rational' and market-orientated, that his own marriage and marriages of his children were not arranged by kin but were on the basis of individual choice, that his family life was far from the 'patriarchal' stereotype both in relation to his wife and his children. For those who seek proof, it would be instructive to read some of the classic accounts of

[4]Alan Macfarlane, *The Family Life of Ralph Josselin; An Essay in Historical Anthropology* (Cambridge, 1970), pp. 64-7.
[5]Ibid., p. 93.

peasantry cited above, and then to read Josselin's own Diary. Yet even if we accept unequivocally that Josselin was not a 'peasant,' though he farmed, it would be possible to dismiss this as an exceptional case on several grounds. Firstly, he kept a Diary, which suggests that he was an unusual man, Secondly, he was University educated and hence moved in a broader intellectual world than most of his neighbours. Thirdly, he was a devout Puritan and a vicar. He thus belonged to the 'intelligentsia' rather than to any possible peasantry. Some counter-arguments can be brought forward from the Diary. Although his Diary shows strong divisions between the wealthy and the poor, it does not anywhere give an impression nearly as strong as that obtained from writings on India or Russia of a great split between the 'Great' and 'Little' traditions, between the 'intelligentsia' and the 'mere peasants.' Secondly, it is clear that Josselin's horizons and mentality were very different from the ideal-type peasantry long *before* he had been to University or thought of being a minister. One early account of his youthful musings describes a mind that hardly fits the peasant stereotype, although he was at that time merely the son of a failing Essex farmer.

I made it my aim to learn and lent my mind continually to reade histories; and to shew my spirit let me remember with grief that which I yet feel: when I was exceeding young would I project the conquering of kingdoms and write histories of such exploits. I was much delighted with Cosmography taking it from my Father. I would project wayes of receiving vast est(ates) and then lay it out in stately building, castles, libraries colleges and such like.[6]

He wrote this describing the time when he was aged twelve. Yet even with these counter-arguments, the case cannot be proved from the life of a single individual.

Fortunately, there are a considerable number of other sixteenth- and seventeenth-century diaries and account books still surviving. When I undertook a survey of English diary-keeping, I searched most of the more detailed diaries and autobiographies for the period up to about 1720,[7] but no one showed an attitude to land and economics that could be termed 'peasant' in the way we have defined it. From the documents of wealthy people such as Pepys, Mrs. Thornton, Blundell, D'Ewes and Harlakenden, through the middling-level of Heywood, Stout, Eyre, Jackson, Loder and Sarah Fell, down to the level of the apprentice

[6]Macfarlane (ed.), *Diary of Ralph Josselin*, p. 2. Keith Thomas has rightly commented that 'Josselin is just a small agrarian capitalist. I don't think Marx or anyone else would be upset by him' (personal communication). But if it turns out that he is normal, there are certain grounds for wondering when all traces of 'peasantry' had vanished.
[7]For a brief survey see Macfarlane, *Family Life*, ch. 1.

Roger Lowe, there is plenty of evidence of a highly-developed and monetized society.[8] A sophisticated and 'rational' approach is evident and most of the authors keep scrupulously careful accounts. Of course it could be argued that, by definition, peasants do not keep diaries. Yet there is a strong impression in all these works that there was no great gulf between the writers and the town and country dwellers around them; their neighbours and kin enter the pages as equally individualistic, rational and calculating human beings participating just as fully in a market economy and a highly mobile society. The unspoken assumption behind most of these personal documents seems to be that almost every external object has its price and its owner, that everything from land and houses downwards is a commodity which may be exchanged on the market. Such a view would appear to be just as strongly developed in the supposedly more remote north, the world of James Jackson of Holm Cultram in Cumberland, William Stout of Lancaster, or Henry Best of Yorkshire,[9] as it was in Essex or London where Josselin and Pepys wrote. Furthermore, there is no evident contrast in this assumption between the earlier personal documents of the later sixteenth and early seventeenth century and those of a century later.

From the level of the individual we may move up one layer to that of the parish. We may ask to what extent detailed local studies of particular 'communities' fit with the predictions of the sociologist's model of peasantry in the sixteenth and seventeenth centuries. We may look in a little detail at the situation in two very different parishes which I have myself studied for a number of years, Josselin's parish of Earls Colne in Essex, and the parish of Kirkby Lonsdale in Cumbria. It is known that England showed enormous regional variation in agriculture and social structure reflecting its history and settlement as well as physical differences in climate and soil. It is therefore sensible to

[8]*The Diary of Samuel Pepys* (1970 onwards, in progress), eds. Robert Latham and William Matthews; *The Autobiography of Mrs. Alice Thornton of East Newton, Co. York*, (Surtees Soc., lxii, 1873), ed. C. Jackson; *Blundell's Diary: Comprising selections from the diary of Nicholas Blundell Esq. from 1702 to 1728* (Liverpool, 1895), ed. T. E. Gibson; *The Diary and Correspondence of Sir Simons D'Ewes, Bart.* (1845), ed. James O. Halliwell, 2 vols.; *The Account Book of Richard Harlakenden, senior and junior, 1603-1643*, Ms. in E.R.O. Temp. Acc. 897; *Rev. Oliver Heywood's Diary, 1630-1702* (Brighouse, 1882), ed. J. Horsfall Turner, 4 vols.; *The Autobiography of William Stout of Lancaster, 1665-1752* (Manchester, 1967), ed. J. D. Marshall; *Adam Eyre, A Dyurnal* (Surtees Soc. lxv, 1875), ed. H. J. Morehouse; 'James Jackson's Diary, 1650-1683' *T.C.W.A.A.S.*, n.s., 21 (1921), selections by F. Grainger; *Robert Loder's Farm Accounts, 1610-1620* (Camden Soc., 3rd ser, 21, 1936), ed. G. E. Fussell; *Household Account Book of Sarah Fell of Swarthmoor Hall, 1673-8* (Cambridge, 1920), ed. N. Penny; *The Diary of Roger Lowe of Ashton-in-Makerfield, Lancashire, 1663-74* (1938), ed. Williams L. Sachse.

[9]Jackson and Stout are cited above. The farming book and accounts of Henry Best are printed in C. B. Robinson (ed.) *Rural Economy in Yorkshire in 1641* (Surtees Soc., 1857).

pick two areas which were as different as possible. The parish of Earls Colne, with a population of about a thousand persons in the middle of the seventeenth century, was relatively near to the dominating London market in the centre of the economically precocious and religiously radical area of East Anglia. Enclosed before our period begins, it seems to have combined arable corn production, cattle farming, and a considerable production of hops and fruit. In every respect it can be compared with the upland parish of Kirkby Lonsdale on the edge of the Yorkshire moors, far from London and depending mainly on sheep and cattle for its wealth. The parishes were chosen not only for the contrast but because each is described in a particularly full and detailed set of local records.[10] To what extent were these and other English villages inhabited by 'peasants'?

We have seen that peasantry is basically an economic and social order founded on household ownership. This means that the most widespread and most important form of ownership will be family ownership; small peasant farmholdings will constitute the bulk of the landholding units. The position is concisely put by Thorner as follows:

In a peasant economy half or more of all crops grown will be produced by such peasant households, relying mainly on their own family labour. Alongside of the peasant producers there may exist larger units: the landlord's demesne or home farm tilled by labour exacted from the peasants, the *hacienda* or estate on which the peasants may be employed for part of the year, the capitalist farm in which the bulk of the work is done by free hired labourers. But if any of these is the characteristic economic unit dominating the countryside, and accounting for the greater share of the crop output, then we are not dealing with a peasant economy.[11]

If we use this index and look at Earls Colne at any point in the sixteenth or seventeenth centuries we see that it was not a peasant economy. It was dominated by large landlords, in the early period by the Priory and the Earl of Oxford, later by the Harlakendens. In 1598 a detailed map and a survey were made of the parish, showing the ownership of land. From these the area of demesne land farmed and owned directly by the lord of the manor can be estimated. It can be seen that approximately two-thirds of the parish was demesne and thus, at the end of the sixteenth century, was owned by one person. Most of the rest was copyhold land which, in practice, was held by about twenty individuals. In effect this means that about three-quarters of the people

[10]A list of the main sources used in the study of these parishes is contained in the bibliography. The methodology employed and a more detailed description of the documents is given in Macfarlane *Reconstructing*.
[11]In Shanin, *Peasants*, p. 205.

in the parish held nothing beyond a house and garden. By the definition quoted above, this was clearly far from a peasant economy, not composed of self-sufficient, small, farming households. The fact that the large manorial estate was a rational enterprise, run strictly for economic profit, is shown by the detailed account book of the family which survives for the early seventeenth century. A certain number of the landless were employed as casual labour on others' land, but numerous documents show that there was also a very great deal of non-agricultural activity in the town. As well as baking, brewing, butchering, tailoring, there was considerable employment in the East Anglian cloth industry.

The lord's Account Book and Josselin's Diary both show that the bulk of food production, particularly the growing of fruit and hops, was not for local consumption, but for cash sale in nearby markets at Colchester and Braintree, from where it found its way to London and other parts of the country. This is not an area of subsistence agriculture, but cash cropping. Thus what at a preliminary glance looks like a rural village filled with small yeoman families, turns out on closer inspection to be one dominated by a few large landowners, with a multitude of small producers, agricultural and otherwise. The parish was fully involved in a capitalist and cash marketing system and differed almost as much from the traditional peasant society as does modern Kent or Essex.

Another feature which we would expect to find would be the continuity of families through time and a lack of geographical mobility. This was not the case, for in Earls Colne the families present in, for example, 1560, were different from those present in the same parish in 1700. Even in a peasant society with little disruption by war or famine, there is likely to be considerable change in families as they die out in the male line. But the situation is much more dramatic in Earls Colne. For example, of 274 pieces of property listed in a rental for the two Earls Colne manors in 1677, only twenty-three had been held by the same family, even if we include links through females, some two generations earlier in 1598. A massive shift can be seen in even shorter periods. Comparing two sixteenth century rentals for Earls Colne manor we find that of 111 pieces listed in 1549, only thirty-one were owned by the same family some forty years later in a rental of 1589, again including the links through women. The result is that individuals appear, build up a holding, then the family disappears, all in a generation or two. It also seems to have been the case that most people, especially younger sons, and daughters, would end up in a parish other than the one in which they were born. If we take the records for the period 1560-1750, and take a sample of approximately one-twentieth of the individuals mentioned in the parish, namely those starting with the letter 'G,' we may trace the number who were recorded as both baptised and buried in the parish register. The figure is an under-estimate of those who actually *did* remain for their whole life in the parish, since the burial register is missing for twenty years and there is clearly under-registration of burials in the later seventeenth century. Yet even allowing for this, it is of interest that according to the parish register only approximately one-third (41/125) were both baptized and buried in Earls Colne. Most of these were infants and small children. Only seventeen persons stayed beyond their tenth birthday and were buried in the parish. Even some of these may have left for a while, to be buried on their return or on a visit. Another sample are the persons mentioned by Ralph Josselin as residing in Earls Colne. Taking a sample of fifty men and twenty-five women, in only one third of the male cases and one sixth of the female, do we know that the person was both baptised and buried in the parish. The parish in the sixteenth to eighteenth centuries, far from being a bounded community which contained people from birth to death, was a geographical area through which very large numbers of people flowed, staying a few years or a life-time, but not settling with their families for generations.

Another index of peasantry lies in the pattern of social mobility: we have seen that in traditional peasantries a family would move as a whole and there would be a tendency towards what Shanin calls 'cyclical mobility,' an undulating wave-like motion over time. There were certain negative and positive feedback mechanisms which kept a family oscillating about a mean. There is no spiralling accumulation whereby the rich continue to get rich and the poor to get poorer.

The records from Earls Colne and elsewhere suggest that certain individuals rose, and then one of their children likewise did so. Families did not move in a block, but shed some of their younger or less talented children. As a result, after several generations, as for example noted by Margaret Spufford,[12] grandchildren of the same person could be at extreme ends of the hierarchy of wealth. One long-term effect of this pattern is the well-known general phenomenon by which England is characterized between the fifteenth and eighteenth centuries, a growing split between a wealthy minority of landowners and an impoverished labouring force. One of the central themes of much social history since Tawney has been the way in which absolute division grew so that by the eighteenth century it is possible to speak of 'classes' rather than estates. In Earls Colne, comparisons of the distribution of land at the start of the sixteenth and end of the eighteenth century support this idea of

[12]In a talk to King's College, Cambridge Social History Seminar, February 1974.

increasing differentiation. This contrasts with the situation in parts of the world where temporary increases in production are invested in demographic or social expansion, rather than being accumulated and hoarded by one heir.

It seems abundantly plain that we are not dealing with a 'peasant' village in Earls Colne in the sixteenth to eighteenth centuries. Comparison with the records of other Essex villages, particularly the neighbouring parish of Great Tey and those of Hatfield Peverel, Boreham and Little Baddow, suggests that Earls Colne was not exceptional within Essex. Yet it could be argued that Essex as a whole was exceptionally advanced. We may briefly look at some published studies of other parishes in the lowland region of England.

The open-field parish of Wigston Magna in Leicestershire has been described by Hoskins. Although the turnover of family names was not quite so great as that in Earls Colne, of eighty-two family names in 1670, 44% had been present one hundred years before, 20% two hundred years before.[13] In other respects the pattern of social mobility and the land market seem to have been of the same order as in Essex. We are told that there 'always had been, as far back as the records go, a good deal of buying and selling of land between the peasant-farmers of Wigston,' but by the later seventeenth century 'the fines, conveyances, mortgages, leases, and marriage settlements alone for this period, in such an incessantly active land-market as Wigston are bewildering.'[14] It is also clear from the inventories that the farmers were producing for the market. The pattern of social mobility was one which led to the opposite situation to that described for Russia. There was a growing cleavage between rich and poor. Wigston witnessed, as did the whole of the Midlands, the emergence of a group of farmers in the late fifteenth century who were above the average in wealth, as can be seen in the Lay Subsidy of 1524.[15] During the later sixteenth century and the seventeenth century there was a growing problem of poverty, while a few families accumulated almost all the land in the village. By the time of a survey of 1766 the village had become completely polarized between a rich few and numerous landless labourers.[16]

The same splitting apart of the village combined with an active land market is documented for the Cambridgeshire village of Chippenham studied by Margaret Spufford. This parish in the sheep and corn area of Cambridgeshire witnessed a growth of larger-than-average holdings even in the fourteenth and fifteenth centuries.[17] But the author argues

[13]Hoskins, *Midland Peasant*, p. 196.
[14]Ibid., pp. 115, 194-5.
[15]Ibid., pp. 141-3.
[16]Ibid., pp. 217-9.
[17]Spufford, *Communities*, pp. 65ff.

that the crucial period in which the small farmers were pushed out was between 1560-1636. Economic polarization meant that a roughly egalitarian distribution in 1544 was replaced by one where large absentee landowners held almost all the land in the survey of 1712. During the crucial period of growing inequality, over half the transactions in the manor court were sales of property — presumably to non-kin. The author also believed that there was a good deal of emigration, which helped to keep the population from growing during most of the period.[18]

It is clear that geographical and social patterns differed and that mobility may have been less pronounced in some areas, as David Hey has argued for the Shropshire parish of Myddle and Cicely Howell for another Leicestershire parish.[19] Yet in no local or regional study of any area in lowland England in the sixteenth or seventeenth centuries, and many have been undertaken, have I come across any evidence to suggest any of the features which we have seen go with 'peasantry.'[20]

Since I am attempting to investigate the English, and not merely the *lowland* pattern, it is necessary to pursue our search to the upland region of the north and west. Furthermore, if we are to find a pre-industrial peasantry anywhere in the country, it seems likely that it will be in the higher, supposedly more remote and backward upland area. It is generally agreed by those familiar with such regions that kinship and the family were more important in the highland zone. There, if anywhere, we will be dealing with a domestic economy, based on extended kinship and family labour. Groups of kin are the basic unit of production in a peasant society. Associated with low geographical mobility this will lead us to expect a high degree of kin co-residence in an area with 'peasants.' It is therefore relevant that a number of local historians have spoken of the 'kindreds' and 'clans' of these upland areas, in contrast to the dispersed kin of the lowlands. Describing Troutbeck in Cumbria, Scott noted the frequent occurrence of identical surnames and wrote that 'These families — we might rather call them clans — intermarried so frequently that their descendents are inevitably related many times over . . .'[21] H. S. Cowper, describing Hawkshead in north Lancashire wrote of 'what we venture to term, in default of a

---

[18]Ibid., p. 90.
[19]David Hey, *An English Rural Community: Myddle under the Tudors and Stuarts* (Leicester, 1974); C. Howell, 'Stability and Change 1300-1700,' *Jnl. Peasant Studies*, vol. 2, no. 4, June 1975.
[20]W. G Hoskins, *Provincial England* (1964); Peter Clark, *English Provincial Society from the Reformation to the Revolution: Religion Politics and Society in Kent, 1500-1640* (1977), *The Agrarian History of England and Wales* (Cambridge, 1967), vol. iv, (ed.) Joan Thirsk, chs. 1, 7, 8, 9.
[21]S. H. Scott, *A Westmorland Village* (1904), p. 261.

better word, the clan system — the cohabitation of hamlets and areas by many folks owning the same surname and a common origin.'[22] More recently Mervyn James has suggested that 'upland' areas in the Durham region were more familistic and Joan Thirsk noted that while the 'clan' was strong only in Northumbria, in many upland areas 'the family often exerted a stronger authority than the manorial lord.'[23] Speaking of the northern fells, and in particular the areas of partible inheritance, Joan Thirsk writes that 'the family was and is the working unit, all joining in the running of the farm, all acepting without question the fact that the family holding would provide for them all . . . .'[24] Of all the upland areas of England, the area most likely to be inhabited by peasants was southern Cumbria, that is, parts of the Lake District, west Yorkshire and north Lancashire. It is known that a special form of social structure, based on small family estates, existed there. A peculiar form of land tenure had emerged in an area of weak manorial control and difficult communications.[25] As Scott wrote of Troutbeck, 'Under the system of customary tenture there has grown up a race singularly sturdy, independent, and tenacious of their rights . . . Instead of the land being occupied by two or three squires, and a subservient tenantry, this single township has contained some fifty statesman families, which have held the same land from generation to generation with the pride of territorial aristocracy.'[26] The security, the mobility, the equality, all seem to indicate a 'peasant' society.

In this region lies the parish of Kirkby Lonsdale, lying along the Lune valley in a cradle of the hills, its seventeenth century stone walls and substantial farmhouses still visible. The parish produced oats, barley, wool and cattle in an area stretching from the rich riverside meadows in the south up to high fells on the east. The approximately two thousand five hundred inhabitants in the late seventeenth century were distributed in nine townships, including the market town of Kirkby itself. Each township had a different tenurial and social system. Before considering the nature of ownership in this parish, we may look at some of the indications of peasantry which we have already used in the southern area.

[22]H. S. Cowper, *Hawkshead* (1899), p. 199. Also speaking of 'kindreds' in this area is C. M. L. Bouch and G. P. Jones, *A Short Economic and Social History of the Lake Counties 1500-1830* (Manchester, 1961), p. 90.
[23]Mervyn James, *Family, Lineage and Civil Society* (Oxford, 1974), p. 24; *Agrarian History of England*, iv, (ed.) J. Thirsk, pp. 9, 23.
[24]'Industries in the Countryside' in F. J. Fisher (ed.), *Essays in the Economic and Social History of Tudor and Stuart England* (Cambridge, 1961), p. 83.
[25]A recent description of this phenomenon is J. D. Marshall, 'The domestic economy of the Lakeland yeoman, 1660-1749' *T.C.W.A.A.S.* n.s. vol. lxxiii (1973).
[26]Scott, *Westmorland Village*, pp. 20-1.

One such index is geographical immobility; in a traditional peasantry both families and individuals tend to remain for their lives in one village or group of villages. This does not seem to have been the case in Kirkby Lonsdale. To start with the crude index of the survival of family names, we may look to see how many of the twenty-eight surnames of those who held lands in just one of the townships, Lupton, in 1642 according to a tenant list were still present two generations later in a list for 1710. The answer is twelve; thus fewer than half were still present. Of course, we have to allow for change of name at marriage, or the chance that unrelated individuals with identical surnames had come into the parish. Further research will establish how many of the holdings were in the same family throughout this period. What is certain is that the rate of change of ownership increased in the middle of the eighteenth century so that there was hardly a farm owned by the same family throughout the period 1642-1800. It is also clear from preliminary work that even before the introduction of turnpike roads and other pressures which are believed to have destroyed the old patterns, there was very considerable mobility of farm holdings. There is no evidence whatsoever, from the figures, from the wording of wills or from the contents of legal cases that families and farms were closely attached by sentiment. It is symbolic that the farms were hardly ever called after the families, but after natural features: Foulstone, Greenside, Fellhouses. Contemporaries seem to have talked only occasionally of the 'Burrows of Foulstone' to differentiate them from other persons of the same name in the parish.

Even more striking than the movement of whole families is the degree of individual mobility. Although there is some out-migration, and daughters often move to a nearby village at marriage, one of the central features of peasant societies, as we have seen, is their low rate of geographical mobility of individuals. Except in times of crisis, a man born in a village is likely to remain there all his life, working on the jointly held estate and receiving his rightful share when married. Girls would stay to work for the communal labour pool until marriage. It is now known that nothing like this occurred in Kirkby Lonsdale in the seventeenth century. Preliminary figures published some years ago showed that a very considerable proportion of the children left home in their early or middle teens.[27] It is possible to make such calculations because a combination of a parish register and a listing of inhabitants allows us to see whether those baptized in the parish remained there. In Lupton, for example, of twenty males baptized in the period 1660-1669 who were not recorded as buried before 1695, only six were present in the

---

[27]Macfarlane, *Family Life of Ralph Josselin*, pp. 209-210.

listing of that year. Fourteen had disappeared from the township. Women were even more mobile. Of twenty-three girls baptized in the same period whose burial is not recorded, not a single one was present in the listing of 1695. A search for both boys and girls for the decades after this also suggests that very few stayed in Lupton after the first few years of their lives. Far from settling down on a family farm, younger sons and all daughters moved away. Even the eldest son often went away for a number of years before returning to take over a holding. The central feature of the situation seems again to have been the opposite of the 'peasant' situation. Rather than the holding absorbing the children's labour, the parental home shed the children just as they began to be net producers. If extra labour was needed, it was hired in the form of labourers or servants. This was related to a particular and peculiar household structure.

It was earlier argued that it is characteristic of peasant societies that in operation and sometimes in residence as well, the basic unit is the 'extended family.' Married sons and their wives and parents work together and consume together, pooling labour and sharing proceeds. Thus households are often large and contain more than one currently married couple, for example a 'stem' family with a married couple, their married son and wife, and grandchildren. It is clear that in Kirkby Lonsdale such complex and extended households were absent. The listing for Lupton in 1695 does not show a single instance of a married child living with his or her parents, not even with a widowed parent. The Killington listing mentions two cases only among 222 names; a widow living with a married son, and a widower with a married daughter. The idea that two married couples should live or work together is never expressed in any of the documents. Nor are there any cases of anything equivalent to the Indian joint family where brothers and their wives live together or work a communal estate together. Throughout Kirkby Lonsdale, the listings for the nine townships with very few exceptions indeed show only nuclear families, parents and unmarried children. Wills fairly frequently mention that children are married, but in such cases the married child seems to have lived elsewhere.

It is obvious that analysis of residential or household structure, by itself, is not enough to disprove the absence of 'extended' or 'joint' families. Co-residence is only one of the indexes. Although the Kirkby Lonsdale families did not live in complex households and do not seem to have been 'eating from the same pot,' as they would have done for example in pre-revolutionary Russia, they could still have been acting as joint families in terms of ownership, production and consumption. It is well known that the joint residential unit, for instance in India, is often more an ideal than an actuality, and that most people, most of the time, may live in nuclear households even in peasant societies. It might be that operationally there was some form of co-operation. We might find a group consisting of several married couples, parents, brothers and wives and children living in the same village and working a communal holding.

Literary evidence makes us suspect that even joint families defined in terms of operation rather than residence did not exist. It was not just a matter, as Arthur Young put it when attacking the settlement laws, of young people's 'abhoring' the thought of living with their fathers or mothers after marriage.[28] It was a question of discipline, self-government, independence. A description of norms which would astound an 'ideal-type' peasant is given in 1624 by William Whately when counselling young people.[29]

When thou art married, if it may be, live of thy self with thy wife, in a family of thine own, and not with another, in one family, as it were, betwixt you both . . . The mixing of governours in a household, or subordinating or uniting of two Masters, or two Dames under one roof, doth fall out most times, to be a matter of much unquietness to all parties; Youth and age are so far distant in their conditions, and how to make the young folks so wholly resign themselves unto the elder, as not to be discontented with their proceedings; or to make the older so much to deny themselves, as to condescend unto the wills of the younger . . . in the common sort of people (is) altogether impossible. Whereof, as the young Bees do seek unto themselves another Hive, so let the young couple another house . . .

This advocates not merely a physical separation, but a social one also, the setting up of an economically and jurally independent unit. We find that the Kirkby Lonsdale records support this idea of separate units.

Detailed records of the economic structure and landholdings, as well as the listings, make it almost certain that families did not operate as communal units in production and consumption. Despite earlier quoted remarks about the concentration of family names, the listings do not reveal heavy concentrations of people with the same surname, possibly kin, living near to each other. In Killington, for example, the majority of the surnames of heads of households only occur once in the listings. In only nine cases did surnames occur in more than two households. The most common surname in the parish was Barker, fifteen of the 222 persons in the chapelry being called by that name and eleven being called Atkinson. If we concentrate on these two names, we find

[28]Quoted in W. E. Tate, *The Parish Chest* (Cambridge, 1960), p. 214.
[29]W. Whateley, *A Care-cloth or a Treatise of the Cumbers and Troubles of Marriage* (1624), sigs. A6-A6v.

that although each of them was to be found in eight separate house-holds, this was by no means a situation of a group of 'kindred' farming a set of neighbouring estates or one large farm. In the case of the Barkers, there were three households with three Barkers in each, one with two people of that name, the other five households merely contained one person of that name, usually as a servant. The Atkinsons were even more spread out, with one set of three, one of two, and the rest single individuals. Since both these names were common in the region, it is quite likely that a number of the individuals were not related. If we turn to the wills, there is nowhere, in the nearly two thousand for the parish, a suggestion that brothers were farming jointly. The probate inventories show where people's livestock was at the time of their death and to whom they owed debts; in neither case is there any hint of com-munal farming. The unit of production was the husband and wife and hired labour, not children. This helps to explain and is given support by the incidence of servanthood in the area.

It appears from studies of India, Russia and other peasant societies, that farm servants and domestic servants are relatively rare and unimportant in traditional peasantries. Farm labour is family labour. In Kirkby Lonsdale, a search of the listings shows that the absent child labour was replaced by hired labour. In Killington, of an adult male population of approximately eighty, ten were stated to be servants and nine were day labourers; thus approximately one quarter were hired labour. Another quarter were stated to be 'pensioners' in receipt of parish poor relief. Thus one half of the population was supporting or paying for the labour of the other half. There were also thirteen women stated to be servants. It seems to have been the case that move-ment into an unrelated household, either as apprentice, servant or day labourer, was a central feature of the area. In other words, instead of the unit of labour being determined by the demographic expansion and contraction of the family as sons were born and grew and parents died, people regulated the amount of labour by hiring outsiders. As their holding expanded, they could bring in more hands. Half the parish hired the other half. In this situation, economics was not dependent on demography. Furthermore, with a free labour supply, two important consequences followed. Firstly, there was no great incentive to marry young and to have many children; young adults could be hired without the inconvenience of having to feed and clothe them in their young and unproductive years. Secondly, there was an incentive to saving and accumulation since such saving could be used to purchase more land and more labour. Expansion was not limited by the inelasticity of labour. A consequence of this was that the pattern of social mobility in the area was very different from that experienced in peasant societies.

It has been suggested that the typical pattern of peasant societies is one in which families move as a whole, and over time will accumulate, have more children, partition the estate and become poorer again. Thus there are no long-term divisions into permanent 'classes.' The pattern in Kirkby Lonsdale was totally different. Families did not move as a whole; daughters and younger sons often moved downwards while the eldest son would move upwards. We have to trace individual mobility, rather than family mobility, for the pressure of impartibility and private as opposed to family estates was dominant.[30] Furthermore, there are traces of a growing separation between the rich and the poor, which turned into a permanent class barrier, even in this supposedly egalitarian region. In Killington at the time of the 1695 listing, approximately one third were in receipt of poor relief or 'pensioners.' In the main township of Kirkby Lonsdale, in the year of the listing some fifty-two persons were listed in the poor overseer's accounts as receiving alms. If we assume that they had roughly the same number of dependents as the poor in Killington, this would again constitute one third of the population. We are witnessing the formation in this rural area during the seventeenth century of a permanent and large category of landless and largely propertyless labouring families. The townships were already divided into certain individuals who owned the farm and shops, and others who worked for them.

If we combine the various features described above we may present an over-simplified general model which depicts this parish as populated by a set of highly individualistic farmers and craftsmen who are also highly mobile in both the geographical and social sense. This is further confirmed if we look at the extensive web of debts and credit to non-kin revealed in the probate inventories. The model is also both supported and integrated into one ideal-type life portrait in a description of what life was like in one of these northern valleys. The account was written in the nineteenth century, looking back to the eighteenth, but from the accounts we have looked at, it would appear to hold true of the second half of the seventeenth century also. Bearing in mind the stability and 'family property' complex of an Indian or East European peasant, it is worth quoting the description in full.[31]

The farm labourer of the dales, then (and he is more often than not the son of a small farmer or yeoman), is nothing akin to his southern brother . . . he is early sent to school, but at fourteen leaves home to earn his living. He has been well

---

[30]The detailed evidence to support these assertions will have to await a future publication.
[31]*The Annals of a Quiet Valley* by a Country Parson, edited by John Watson (1894), pp. 94-100.

schooled, in a way, and looks forward to "service." At the half-year hiring —
Whitsuntide or Martinmas — after he has attained his "first majority," he goes
to the nearest country town and stands in the market place. He is attired in a
brand new suit, with a capacious necktie of green and red. These articles he has
donned upon the memorable morning, and as a gift from his parents they
constitute his start in life . . . As an outward and visible sign of his intention, the
lad sticks a straw in his mouth and awaits the issue . . . After waiting a greater
part of the morning and seeing many of his fellow men and maid-servants hired,
he is accosted by a stalwart yeoman, who inquires if he wants a "spot" — a
place, a situation. The lad replies that he does: that he is willing to do anything:
and that he will engage for £4 the half-year — "if it pleases . . ." At sixteen or
seventeen he is stalwart enough to hire as a man, and now his wages are
doubled; he asks and obtains £12 for the year, or even £14 if entering upon the
summer half. The farm servants of the dales "live in," and have all found . . . In
proportion, the girls are much better off in the matter of wages than the men.
There is probably less competition among them, owing to the fact that there is a
great temptation for country girls to migrate and enter service in provincial
towns . . . Many of the men, when about thirty years of age, are able to take
small farms of their own. Nearly all the statesmen's sons do this, and probably
without any outside help, for, as a class, these labourers are not only industrious
but thrifty. I knew a man who had saved £120, which sum he had divided and
deposited in three banks . . . From the fact of "living in," as nearly all the valley
servants do, it need hardly be said that early marriages are rare. All the better
men look forward to the time when they can have a farm of their own; and when
they obtain a holding, they then look out for a wife.

Here we see all the features: the absence of tie between sons and their
father's holding; geographical mobility; hired labour; saving and thrift;
late age at marriage; the movement of girls away from the area. In every
respect it is a contrast with a classical 'peasantry.'

Local studies of other northern parishes and towns do not contradict
and often support what has been found for Kirkby Lonsdale. Yet it
would be foolish to over-stress the case and there may have been areas,
for example in northern Cumbria, Redesdale and the Northumberland
border, or the Cornish peninsula, where farm and family were more
closely identified. We still await the discovery of a 'peasant' community
in England in the sixteenth and seventeenth century.

So far we have drawn on two types of evidence, autobiographical and
local studies, in order to support the argument. There are now a very
considerable number of studies which suggest that what we have found
in relation to selected features of the society were more general characteristics of the country. Historians have found evidence of very
considerable geographical mobility and turnover from the sixteenth
century onwards by using taxation records, manorial documents,

repetitive listings, ecclesiastical court depositions and other sources.[32] They have found that the household size was small and it structure simple.[33] They have noted the very great fluidity of the social structure, with rapid upward and downward social mobility.[34] It has been guessed that 'probably between a quarter and a half of the population were servants at one time or another,' and that perhaps a quarter to one third of the families in Stuart England had servants.[35] This picture of mobility and wage labour, of nuclear-family households where the children moved away from home before marriage and often lived in separate villages, does not in any way fit the stereotype of peasantry elaborated in the first chapter. It would be possible to investigate other features associated with the peasant model in order to show that they also did not fit, but sufficient has probably been written to suggest that we are not by the sixteenth century dealing with a peasant society. This poses the further question of why this should have been the case and how long the non-peasant had been established. Put in another way, what was it about the society which meant that, despite its agricultural base combined with towns and highly developed stratification, it was different from those other agrarian societies with which it has been classified?

[32]S. A. Peyton, 'The village population in the Tudor Lay Subsidy Rolls,' *English Hist. Rev.*, xxx (1915); E. E. Rich, 'The population of Elizabethan England,' *Ec.H.R.*, 2nd ser. ii (1949); P. Laslett, 'Clayworth and Cogenhoe' in *Historical Essays Presented to David Ogg*, eds. H. E. Bell and R. L. Ollard (1963); Julian Cornwall, 'Evidence of Population Mobility in the Seventeenth Century,' *Bull. Inst. Hist. Res.* xl (Novemb., 1967).

[33]Philip Styles, 'A Census of a Warwickshire Village in 1698,' *Univ. Birmingham Hist. Jnl.* iii, (1951-2); Laslett, *Household*, ch. 4.

[34]Lawrence Stone, *The Crisis of the Aristocracy, 1558-1641* (Oxford, 1965), and 'Social Mobility in England, 1500-1700' *P. & P.*, 33 (April, 1966); Hexter, 'Myth of the Middle Class' in *Reappraisals*; Alan Everitt, 'Social mobility in early modern England' *P. & P.*, 33 (April, 1966). The whole of the famous 'gentry' controversy is also, of course, relevant; for one summary of the debate see Hexter, 'Storm over the gentry' in *Reappraisals*.

[35]P. Spufford, 'Population Movement in Seventeenth Century England,' *Local Population Studies*, no. 4 (Spring, 1970), p. 49; Laslett, *World we have lost*, p. 13. On servanthood, see also Laslett, 'Clayworth and Cogenhoe,' p. 169.

4

Ownership in England from 1350 to 1750

The central feature of 'peasantry' is the absence of absolute ownership of land, vested in a specific individual. The property-holding unit is a 'corporation' which never dies. Into this an individual is born or adopted, and to it he gives his labour. In such a situation women have no individual and exclusive property rights and individuals cannot sell off their share of the family property. It would be unthinkable for a man to sell off land if he had sons, except in dire necessity and by common consent. There is unlikely to be a highly-developed land market. As we have already seen in the case of Josselin's proposed disinheritance of his only son, the inhabitants of Earls Colne lived in a different world. The transfers in the manor court rolls, the deeds concerning freehold property, the lengthy cases from the village in Chancery, and all other sources bearing on economic life in the parish suggest that by the later sixteenth century ownership was highly individualized. Land was held by women in their own right, men appearing to do suit of court 'in the right of their wife.' Land was bought and sold without consideration for any wider group than husband and wife. It was, in fact, treated as a commodity which belonged to individuals and not to the household. There is no hint, for example, in the statements concerning transfers in the court rolls, that a plot was passed to a family rather than an individual. Examination of the manor court rolls back to the start of the sixteenth century does not suggest that family or household ownership had ever been practised. Since this appears to be the crucial foundation of the difference between a peasant and a non-peasant social and economic structure it is worth digressing briefly to consider whether the situation in Earls Colne was abnormal, in the lowland area of England in the sixteenth and seventeenth centuries.

In discussing the question of family and individual ownership in this period three distinctions need to be made: between 'chattels' and 'real estate,' between freehold tenure and other kinds of tenure, and between the rights of wives and the rights of children. The legal and practical situation concerning goods or chattels was very different from that concerning real estate. By Common Law, the wife had rights to one third of her husband's estate, including goods, but the children had no rights in their parent's goods.[1] By ecclesiastical law, during the sixteenth and seventeenth centuries 'by a Custom observed, not only throughout the Province of York, but in many other Places besides,' including London, if there was only a wife, the husband could dispose of only one half of his goods by will, if there were children, only one third.[2] Thus, assuming that he had not sold his goods and bought land, or given the goods away during his lifetime, within certain parts of England up to the repeal of the custom by an Act of 1692, wives and children had a certain stake in the father's goods or 'chattel' estate. The heart of the matter lies in the question of real estate, principally land, for it is here that we will see whether the family and the land-holding were identified.

A simplified summary of the position of women in relation to real estate shows that contrary to the situation in peasant societies, women could be *true* landholders. In the case of freehold land, a woman could hold and own such property. During her marriage or 'couverture,' the husband 'gains a title to the rents and profits,' but he may not sell or alienate it.[3] If the man holds the title and marries, the wife has an inalienable right to at least one third of his estate for her life by common law. She had a right to this 'dower' even if she remarried or the couple were divorced (*a mensa et thoro*) for adultery, as long as she did not elope and live with her lover.[4] There was no way of excluding a woman from her Common-Law dower, though it might be increased, or the particular share of the estate specified, by a 'jointure' which set up formally a joint estate for husband and wife for life. The situation with regard to non-freehold land, and particularly copyhold land, was very different. Except when an heir was under fourteen years of age, and only until he or she reached that age, a married woman did not automatically obtain any rights over the real estate of her husband.[5] Copyhold estates were not liable to 'freebench' as it was known, unless by the special customs of the manor it was stated to exist.[6] Although it would appear that most manors in England did have such a custom up to the

---

[1]Maitland, *English Law*, ii, pp. 348-355.
[2]H. Swinburne, *A Treatise of Testaments and Last Wills* (5th edn., 1728), pp. 204-5.
[3]Blackstone, *Commentaries*, ii, p. 433.
[4]Ibid., p. 130; Maitland, *English Law*, ii, p. 419.
[5]*The Order of Keeping a Court Leet and Court Baron* (1650; facsimile reprint), p. 36. This text speaks of the 'heir,' without distinguishing males and females. In practice the age varied, depending on local custom.
[6]Blackstone, *Commentaries*, ii, p. 132.

eighteenth century, as E. P. Thompson has pointed out, there were a
minority of cases where no freebench was allowed.[7] Earls Colne was one
of these, for in the court roll of June 1595 it was stated:

At this court the steward of the manor by virtue of his office commanded an
inquisition to be made whether women are indowerable of the third part of the
customary lands of their husbands at any time during the marriage between
them. And now the homage present that they have not known in their memory
nor by the search of the rolls that women ought to have any dowry in the
customary tenement of their husbands but they say that in times past diverse
women have pretended their dowries but have always been denied and therefore
they think there is no such custom.

In such a situation a woman could be made a joint owner with her
husband by a surrender to their joint use in the manor court, or the
estate could be bequeathed by her will. Both these devices were used. In
other areas of England her position was much stronger; by the custom
of 'tenant right' or 'border tenure' which encompassed our other parish
of Kirkby Lonsdale, a widow had the whole estate for her widowhood.[8]
But here, as elsewhere, the right was for less than that in freehold estate,
for the widow usually lost her freebench if she re-married or
'miscarried,' in other words had sexual intercourse. Women could also
hold copyhold property in their own person, either by gift, purchase, or
through inheritance, for example when there were no male heirs. To a
very limited extent, therefore, we can view husband and wife as a small
co-owning group. We may wonder whether we can add any further
members of the family to this corporation.

The situation with regard to freehold property seems abundantly
clear. Maitland stated that 'In the thirteenth century the tenant in fee
simple has a perfect right to disappoint his expectant heirs by
conveying away the whole of his land by act *inter vivos*. Our law is
grasping the maxim *Nemo est heres viventis.*'[9] Although Glanvill
produced some rather vague safeguards for the heir, Bracton in the
thirteenth century omitted these and the King's Courts did not support
a child's claim to any part of his parent's estates. For instance, Plucknett
cites a case of 1225 to this effect.[10] The only major change between the
thirteenth and sixteenth centuries was that by the Statute of Wills in
1540 a parent could totally disinherit his heirs not only by sale or gift
during his lifetime, but also by leaving a will devising the two-thirds of
his freehold estate which did not go to his widow. Swinburne, a leading

[7]In Goody, *Family*, p. 354.
[8]A. Bagot, 'Mr. Gilpin and manorial customs', *T.C.W.A.A.S.*, n.s. lxii (1961), p. 238
[9]Maitland, *English Law*, ii, p. 308.
[10]Plucknett, *Common Law*, p. 529.

authority on testamentary law, nowhere mentions the children's right to any part of the real estate of their parents.[11] This had been formalized in the Statute *Quia Emptores* of 1290, which stated that 'from henceforth it shall be lawful for every freeman to sell at his own pleasure his land and tenements, or part of them . . . ,' with the exception of sales to the church or other perpetual foundations.[12] In this crucial respect, English common law took a totally different direction from Continental law. As Maitland put it,

Free alienation without the heir's consent will come in the wake of primogeniture. These two characteristics which distinguish our English law from her nearest of kin, the French customs, are closely connected . . . Abroad, as a general rule, the right of the expectant heir gradually assumed the shape of the *restrait lignager*. A landowner must not alienate his land without the consent of his expectant heirs unless it be a case of necessity, and even in a case of necessity the heirs must have an opportunity of purchasing.[13]

Thus by English Common Law children had no birth-right and could be left penniless. Strictly speaking it is not even a matter of 'disinheritance'; a living man in the sixteenth century has no heirs, he has complete seisin or property. The only restriction is the right of his widow to one third of the real estate for life. A son in effect has no rights while his father lives and they are not co-owners in any sense. In the case of freehold real estate in the sixteenth century the children had no automatic rights. The custom of primogeniture might give the eldest child greater rights, where the estate was not disposed of, than other children; but ultimately even the eldest son had nothing except at the wish of his father or mother, except where the inheritance had been formally specified by the artificial device of an entail. Even such entails could be broken quite easily in the sixteenth and seventeenth centuries.[14] As a result, as Chamberlayne put it in the seventeenth century, 'Fathers may give all their Estates un-intailed from their own children, and to any one child.'[15]

Children had no stronger rights in the non-freehold property of their parents. About one third of all English land was held by copyhold tenures in the early seventeenth century. Originally most of this land was held 'at the will of the lord,' which meant that, in theory, at a person's death his heirs had no security. But gradually over time in many areas of England copyhold estates became heritable. In practice,

[11]Swinburne, *A Treatise of Testaments*, p. 119.
[12]A. W. B. Simpson, *An Introduction to the History of the Land Law* (Oxford, 1961), p. 51.
[13]Maitland, *English Law*, ii, pp. 309, 313.
[14]Blackstone, *Commentaries*, ii, pp. 116-8, describes some of the devices for doing so.
[15]E. Chamberlayne, *The Present State of England* (19th impression, 1700), p. 337.

as we see in Earls Colne by the late sixteenth century, a copyholder could sell or grant away his land, or he could surrender it to the lord 'to the use of his will.'[16] In this he could specify his heirs. Thus at the start of the sixteenth century a man could alienate his land from his children while alive. After the Statute of Wills in 1540, all socage land tenures, including copyhold, became freely devizable by will, though in practice, wills dealing with socage land had been made for at least a century before the Statute. We have seen that a widow might have a free-bench, but children had *no* inalienable rights. Children had no legal claim against a person to whom their parent's land had been granted or given. In sum, neither in the case of freehold or non-freehold, except where an entail was drawn up, did a child have any rights. Even entails were contrary to the idea of 'family estate,' since they could take the land away from children, as easily as ensuring them a portion.

It might be argued that too much has been made of will-making and the possibility of selling land and too little of intestacy. It could rightly be pointed out that if a landholder died without leaving a valid will his property would go to his rightful heirs. These heirs would first of all be his descendents and then other family members. This 'family-centred' system is one which is still present and seems natural to us. As Maitland observed,

At the end of Henry III's reign (i.e. the 1270's) our common law of inheritance was rapidly assuming its final form. Its main outlines were those which are still familiar to us, and the more elementary of them may be thus stated: — The first class of persons called to the inheritance comprises the dead person's descendants; in other words, if he leaves an "heir of his body," no other person will inherit.[17]

This being the case, the apparent consequence is that we should look to see how common will-making was and how often, in practice, land was alienated from the family when male heirs were available.[18] If it were discovered that a large proportion of land was, in fact, passed on to kin at death by intestate inheritance, and few male heirs were disinherited, then it might be argued that the free alienability of land is not as important as we have maintained.

---

[16]A seventeenth century example, from the court held on 26th December, 1639, is as follows: 'John Brewer who held for himself and his heirs one customary messuage with appurtenances . . . surrendered into the hands of the lord . . . the said messuage with appur-tenances to the use and behoof of his last will . . . .' Surrenders 'to the use of a will' are recorded as early as the 1440's in the court rolls for Earls Colne. Pre-Statute wills concerning copyhold land for another area are printed in F. G. Davenport, *The Economic Development of a Norfolk Manor 1086-1565* (1967), Appdx. xiii.
[17]Maitland, *English Law*, ii, p. 260.
[18]I am grateful to Keith Thomas for pointing out this objection.

From local records and autobiographical material I have received the impression that the disinheritance of male heirs by the use of a will was very infrequent in the sixteenth and seventeenth centuries. Occasionally one comes across interesting examples such as the will of John Hill, a skinner of London who in 1636 tried to protect his wife as follows:

if any surviving friend should be any wise troublesome unto her in the behalf of my two children I do bequeath to each of them, John and Susan, 40s. a piece and the rest to my wife . . . . I doubt not of her care of my children especially of Susan and for John I fear she will find some trouble by him yet I desire her to do her best endeavour for some trade here in London if god please to give him grace to apply himself diligently unto it, but if he will not take good ways here, I desire that he may be sent overseas to some plantation as she shall think meet.[19]

Yet even here the son is not totally disinherited, for when his mother died he would not have been debarred from making a claim. Furthermore, it is clear that even in areas such as Cumbria, where will-making was far more widespread than in the south and east, less than a third of the landholders left wills containing disposition of their landed estate duly proved at court. In other areas the proportion making wills was much lower, the poor left very few wills, and the wills that were made often did not mention real estate at all.[20] This would appear to lessen the importance of alienability.

While these are important arguments and more work will need to be undertaken on the will-making population along the lines initiated by Margaret Spufford, in the end these counter-propositions miss the point of the thesis we have been pursuing. We are concerned to examine the nature of the unit of ownership. It has been suggested above that fully developed, individual, private ownership with complete right of alienation was present by the sixteenth century. In no sense can father and son, or 'the family,' be said to be joint-owners from birth, as they would have been in our model peasant society. To show that when the father dies the land does, in fact, usually go to the sons, or that when there is no will the family have first claim, is irrelevant. This can be seen from family law in England in the later nineteenth century. As Maitland stated, it was in essence similar to the law in the later thirteenth century in that descendants had the first claim if there was no will. But this fact would hardly be taken in that context to be proof that a free market in land and private, absolute and individual ownership was not fully developed, just as no-one would argue in such a way

[19]Will dated 13 August 1636 in the London County Record Office, DC/C/320 bundle 8.
[20]W. G. Hoskins, *Provincial England* (1963), pp. 105, 155 note; Spufford, *Communities*, pp. 144, 197 note.

today. The point is not that peasants do not, on the whole, sell off or bequeath away their land; it is that they cannot do so, for it is not their individual property. For our argument, therefore, it only needs to be shown that the possibility of complete alienation was present and was very occasionally enforced. Although it will, in fact, be shown that there was a very considerable land market and that in certain areas, from at least the late fourteenth century, most land was transmitted by sale rather than by inheritance, this is not the essential proof of the argument. We are not talking about statistical tendencies, but of a legal, *de jure*, system of private ownership, where the devices of gift, sale and last testament were all expressions of the fact that the society and the law recognized that, ultimately, ownership was in the individual and in no larger grouping.

It has been necessary to spend some time on this topic in order to show that what we find in Josselin and in Earls Colne was only a particular instance of a central characteristic of sixteenth century English law and society. The family as the basic resource-owning unit which characterizes peasant societies does not seem, in law at least, to have existed in England. England was here not only very different from the Third World societies, where the introduction of English Common Law in the nineteenth and twentieth centuries caused such dislocation,[21] but also from Europe at that time. If the essence of peasantry is the identification of the family with the ownership of the means of production, it is difficult to see how England can have been a peasant society in the sixteenth century. The consequences of this situation are apparent in the records for Earls Colne.

From 1540-1750 there survive over three hundred written wills for inhabitants in Earls Colne, indicating a fully developed system of individual inheritance. They included land, houses and goods. This is in direct contrast to the situation in a traditional peasant society, as we have seen, where the agricultural assets are not being bequeathed, but partitioned, usually before death, and where, consequently, a will would be a violation of children's rights. Furthermore, if we look at the principal land registration record, the manor court roll, we find a fully developed land market with the sale and mortgaging of land to non-kin. At least half of the transfers of land registered during the sixteenth and seventeenth centuries were between non-kin. For example, during the five-year period 1589-1593 in the manor of Earls Colne, fifty-one parcels of copyhold land were transferred. At least twenty-one of these

---

[21]Many examples could be cited of such dislocation, for example E. Boserup, *The Conditions of Agricultural Growth* (1965), p. 90, or G. Myrdal, *Asian Drama* (1968), ii, pp. 1036-7.

were sales of copyhold land to non-kin for cash, while a number of others were surrenders at the end of mortgages or leases. Just under half the transfers were by 'inheritance' between kin. Detailed examination of this period shows that this cannot be explained by suggesting that the vendors were heirless individuals, or very poor individuals 'falling off' the bottom of the economic ladder. What we are witnessing is a continual process of amalgamation, exchange and accumulation, in which estates were constantly changing shape, ownership and value. They were not tied to specific families.

Although by the middle of the sixteenth century a man could give away, sell or devize any or all of his real estate, excepting the widow's share, either in his life or by will, if he did not do so the estate would by custom or common law descend to a particular child. In Earls Colne, as in most of England, the first-born male would inherit the estate by law. Although no written statement to this effect has been discovered for Earls Colne, detailed study of wills and court rolls shows this to be the case. It also shows that the severity of male primogeniture was modified by the giving of 'portions' to younger sons and to daughters. In general, however, from at least the beginning of the sixteenth century the major share of the landholding went to one child. Maine has pointed out that this 'Feudal Law of land practically disinherited all the children in favour of one.'[22] In essence, primogeniture and a peasant joint ownership unit are diametrically opposed. The family is not attached to the land, and one favoured individual is chosen at the whim of the parent, or by the custom of the manor. It has already been suggested that primogeniture and complete individual property in real estate are intimately interlinked, both apparently firmly established in England by the thirteenth century.[23]

If peasantry and primogeniture are in principle opposed, we would expect the rule to be limited to parts of western Europe. This seems to have been the case. Lowie long ago noted that 'the widespread European dominance of primogeniture' marked it off from Africa and Asia and a recent survey of property rights states that primogeniture among the upper classes 'has been a great rarity in the world.'[24] Yet even within Europe, England seems to have been by far the most extreme in its application of this principle, as contemporary commentators quoted by Joan Thirsk show.[25] Indeed, while primogeniture among the gentry and aristocracy was fairly widespread in Europe, further research may show that England was the only nation where primogeniture was

[22]Sir Henry Maine, *Ancient Law* (13th edn., 1890), p. 225.
[23]Maitland, *English Law*, ii, p. 274.
[24]R. H. Lowie, *Social Organization* (1950), p. 150; Kiernan in Goody, *Family*, p. 376.
[25]Goody, *Family*, p. 185.

widespread among those at the lower levels in society, in other words amongst those who might have constituted a 'peasantry.' Although there were considerable regions where partible inheritance was common, and younger children could be provided with cash or goods, it is clear that a custom such as this would have profound consequences. This is particularly the case where it is combined with the possibility of disinheritance. It is important to realize that *primogeniture* or any form of impartible inheritance *per se* is not diametrically opposed to the restricted form of 'peasantry' characteristic of much of western Europe. It was not just extreme impartible inheritance which distinguished parts of England from peasant societies. It is this combined with the fact that ownership or 'seisin' lay in the individual, plus restricted rights conferred by marriage for his or her spouse, but no larger unit.

The parish of Kirkby Lonsdale presents an interesting comparison in this respect, for it was an area with particularly strong customary property rights. As stated, the tenurial situation varied between each of the nine townships in the parish. According to Machell,[26] who travelled through the parish in 1692 and whose findings are corroborated and expanded by Nicholson and Burn,[27] the landholding structure in the nine sub-townships at the end of the seventeenth century was as follows:

Kirkby Lonsdale: some tenants free (about one third), some customary, some customary at fine arbitrary, some arbitrary (copyhold), some heritable.
Casterton: tenants about half free and half customary, paying a fine certain for three years rent.
Barbon: six or seven freeholds; all tenants are finable and arbitrary (i.e. copyhold), they were sold to freehold in 1716.
Middleton: the tenants purchased their estates to freehold in the time of Elizabeth and James I.
Firbank: all freeholders, having purchased their customary tenures in 1586.
Killington: all freeholders, having purchased their customary tenures in 1585.
Lupton: only about two freehold tenements, all the rest customary.
Hutton Roof: some divided customary estates, but generally bought themselves free.

This illustrates the variability even within a parish.

We may examine in more detail two townships which were adjacent, but which contrast strikingly in their tenurial situation, namely Lupton and Killington. In Lupton there was an absentee lord of the manor, but he owned very little of the township land directly; there was

[26] J. M. Ewbank (ed.). *Antiquary on Horseback* (Kendal, 1963), pp. 18, 26, 29, 36, 39.
[27] J. Nicholson and R. Burn, *The History and Antiquities of the Counties of Westmorland and Cumberland* (1777), i, pp. 243-265. The evidence concerning Killington comes from W. Farrer and J. F. Curwen, *Records relating to the Barony of Kendale* (Kendal, 1924), ii, p. 416.

no 'demesne.' Almost all the land was held by customary tenants with holdings of between fifteen and forty acres apiece and some rights in the common grazing. In Killington the form of tenure had originally been the same as that in Lupton, but in 1585 the customary holdings had been converted to freehold. One consequence was that there were two persons styled 'gentleman' living in Killington according to the listing of inhabitants of 1695, whereas there were none in Lupton. But even these were minor gentry. The largest landholder's holding in Killington before the Civil War consisted of a capital messuage, Killington Hall, forty acres of arable, twenty acres of meadow, one hundred acres of pasture and one hundred acres of moss and furze called 'Killington Demesne,' another messuage with sixteen acres of land and a water mill.[28] This was roughly five times the size of the average holding in Killington, but since there were about forty estates in the township, it constituted only an eighth of the total land area.

As argued earlier, it is clear that English 'freehold' tenure in the seventeenth century, which gave an individual complete and total rights over his land, is diametrically opposed to the form of landholding that is characteristic of peasant societies, where there is a form of joint family ownership. It thus seems very likely that whatever may appear superficially to be the case, Killington after 1585, Firbank after 1586, Barbon after 1716, Middleton since the early seventeenth century, and parts of Kirkby Lonsdale and Hutton Roof, had a form of land tenure system incompatible with peasantry. Yet in the areas with 'customary' tenure, particularly Lupton, where nearly all was held in this way, some form of family estate might have existed, surviving longer there than in the other townships. We therefore need to examine this system, known as 'border tenure' or 'tenant right' in more detail.

The parish of Kirkby Lonsdale lay within the barony of Kendal, and consequently all the manors, except the rectory manor, were held of that barony.[29] 'Customary' tenure was therefore part of that general border tenure which has been particularly well documented since it was a peculiarity of the area and the subject of considerable litigation in the seventeenth century. An excellent contemporary description is given by Gilpin and there have been a number of other descriptions.[30] Supposedly in exchange for armed services on the border, the tenant

---

[28]The details come from an inquisition of 1639, reprinted in Farrer and Curwen, *Records . . . of Kendale*, ii, p. 437.

[29]Farrer and Curwen, *Records . . . of Kendale*, ii, p. 305.

[30]Bagot, 'Mr Gilpin and manorial customs'; C. M. L. Bouch and G. P. Jones, *A Short Economic and Social History of the Lake Counties 1500-1830* (Manchester, 1961), pp. 65 ff; J. R. Ford, 'The Customary Tenant-right of the Manors of Yealand,' *T.C.W.A.A.S.*, n.s. ix (1909), pp. 147-160; W. Butler, 'The Customs and Tenant Right Tenures of the Northern Counties . . .,' *T.C.W.A.A.S.*, n.s., xxvi (1926), pp. 318-336.

held by a form of tenure which lay somewhere between ordinary copyhold as known in the south of England, and freehold. As with copyhold, the tenant paid certain fines and rents to the lord, though these were usually fixed and small, and performed certain services or 'boons.' But unlike copyhold, the land was not held 'at the will of the lord,' but by the custom of the manor. The landholdings were known as 'customary estates of inheritance' and could be transferred from one 'owner' to the next without the permission of the lord, only being registered, and a fine being paid, in the manorial court. The estates were 'descendible from ancestor to heir under certain yearly rents.' Furthermore, 'the copyholder had no property in the timber on the land; the customary tenant owns everything, as if it were freehold, except the minerals beneath the soil.[31] Customary tenants could devize their lands by will, and it descended automatically to their children or other legal heirs, if no will was made. The situation has been described as 'tantamount to freehold' and in regard to security of tenure this was the case, though the fines, rents and services made it akin to copyhold in other respects.[32] The estates could be bought and sold by ordinary deeds of bargain and sale, though they would also be registered as admittances in the court roll.[33] This was a form of transfer exactly similar to freehold.[34] The major restriction on the tenant was that the inherited estate should not be sub-divided. In order to provide a warrior for the border, the customs stated that all of the holding should go to one person, the widow, then a son, and in default of a son to only one daughter. As we shall see, this was a very strict form of impartibility.

One supposed result of such a system was that wealth was evenly distributed between equal 'family farms.' This equality was noted by those who had witnessed the collapse of the old tenurial system in the second half of the eighteenth century. Looking back to the first half of that century, a writer in 1812 described how 'excepting the estates of a few noblemen and baronets, the land was divided into small freeholds and customary tenements, in the occupation of the owners . . . .'[35] Another supposed result was that a certain family would be identified with an estate, and it would pass for many generations down the same family.

Yet if we look a little more closely at the precise nature of ownership, the pattern is not so simple. We have noted that, since farm and family

[31]S. H. Scott, *A Westmorland Village* (1904), p. 16.
[32]Butler, 'Customs and Tenant Right Tenures,' p. 320.
[33]Ibid., p. 319.
[34]Ford, 'Customary Tenant-right,' p. 157.
[35]J. Gough, *Manners and Customs of Westmorland* (Kendal, 1847; first printed in 1812), p. 25.

are merged in peasant societies, it is the family or household as a group which owns the farmholding, the head of the family merely being the *de facto* manager. Individual ownership is alien. This is absolutely the opposite of the case in both Lupton and Killington, where it would be difficult to envisage a more individualistic form of landholding, either by freehold or customary tenure. There is no evidence in any of the multitudinous court records or customs of the area that the property was jointly owned by the family. In fact, all the indications are in the opposite direction. Firstly, it is clear that in both townships, the landed property was transferred to one person, who was not merely the nominal title holder but the owner in an exclusive sense. This owner might as easily be a woman as a man. If anything, the individualism of ownership was even more extreme than in most copyhold tenures in the south, for whereas in Essex, for example, all daughters received shares in the estate as co-parceners if there was no male heir, in Lupton the principle of indivisible property prevented this division. By the custom of that manor, and generally under tenant-right tenure, in the event of no sons surviving, the holding went to one daughter only. As Machell put it, quoting from a Chancery decree of the early seventeenth century, there was a general custom in the barony of Kendal 'that the eldest daughter/sister/cousin inherits without copartnership in tenancy.'[36] This was a direct equivalent to the custom of male primogeniture in the area. The general principle was that the holding belonged to one person, and could only be transferred to one person; it was not owned by a group of brothers, for example, and partitioned between them as in classical peasant societies.

It is not possible to deal here with the considerable areas of partible inheritance in England, particularly in the upland areas. One of the best documented of these was in Dentdale, which lay alongside Kirkby Lonsdale. The contrast between the two parishes is very instructive and has been illuminated in a general way by Joan Thirsk.[37] It would be very useful to obtain an account of the relations between family and economy in such a region, testing out the hypotheses concerning a peasant social structure. It would also be useful to know more concerning women's rights. In peasant societies, land is not owned individually, and therefore when a woman marries out of a village or family, she may not take land with her, though she may own movable objects or livestock. But in both Lupton and Killington, as elsewhere in England, women's property rights were extensive. A number of the

[36]Ewbank, *Antiquary on Horseback*, p. 3.
[37]Joan Thirsk, 'Industries in the Countryside' in F. J. Fisher (ed.), *Essays in the Economic and Social History of Tudor and Stuart England* (Cambridge, 1961).

wills for these two townships mention women holding landed property, and it has already been mentioned that a widow would succeed to her husband's estate, followed by one daughter, when a son had not survived. Men could thus hold land 'in the right of their wife.'

If further proof of individualistic property rights is needed it may be found in the numerous proceedings in cases which come from the parish of Kirkby Lonsdale to be heard in Chancery. The court dealt with numerous disputes where one individual sought to obtain rights over a specific piece of land or other property. Reading through the roughly seventy thousand words of information in sixteenth and seventeenth century cases from this parish has not once given any hint or suspicion that there was a strong link between a family group and a holding in the sense that some group larger than the individual owned the property.[38] The head of the household or registered landowner clearly owned the property in the full sense, and was not merely the organizer of a joint labour group. There is no trace of the family as the basic unit of ownership and production.

It might be objected that the wife and children did, in this area, have inalienable rights in the family property. It could be pointed out that by tenant-right, the widow inherited the whole of her husband's estate during her 'pure' widowhood, that is as long as she did not re-marry or have sexual intercourse. Furthermore, Kirkby Lonsdale was within the Arch-diocese of York where, as we saw earlier, there was a custom until 1692 that a wife and children each had a right to one third of their husband/father's movable goods at his death. If we look more closely at both Common Law as it applied to freehold lands, and to manorial customs, it is clear that this was not a joint estate. The wife had rights only as long as she was a widow, and the children had no inalienable rights in their parent's land or other real estate. Even with movable goods, a man could give them all away in his lifetime, just as he could sell or give away all his land. In Kirkby Lonsdale, as in the rest of England, the principle that 'no-one is the heir of a living man,' that children had no inalienable rights in a family estate, appears to have been present. Thus a father could totally disinherit a son if he so wished; primogeniture merely meant that an eldest male heir would inherit if no will or transfer before death had been made to the contrary. It did not mean that a son would automatically inherit. Thus, for example, in Lupton we find in the will of John Wooddes in 1682 stating that because the eldest son Roland 'would never doe my counsell nor be

[38]The standard description of this source is W. J. Jones, *The Elizabethan Court of Chancery* (Oxford, 1967). Printed extracts for the later sixteenth century appear in C. Monro, *Acta Cancellaria* (1847).

ordered by me neyther is a fyth man to serve the quenes majestie nor the lords for these causes and consideration' the whole estate was given to the younger son, who was merely to pay his elder brother £6-13-4d. In Killington, a man could do what he liked with his real estate, with the exception that a widow had one third as a dower for life. In Lupton, he could do what he liked before his death, or after the death of his wife, on condition that the inherited estate was not divided.

One consequence of the highly developed private property rights in the area was the enormous amount of litigation in the central courts of equity, primarily Chancery. Another result was the making of a very large number of wills dealing with chattels and real estate. It has already been pointed out that wills are either unknown or regarded with great dislike in peasant societies. Since the dying father is not the private owner of the property, he cannot devize it to a specific individual. The sons are co-owners with the father, just as they are co-workers. But in Kirkby Lonsdale numerous wills were made, and they embody the principle of devizability of land, thus extending the father's power after his death. For example, in the township of Lupton, with a total population of about one hundred and fifty persons at the end of the seventeenth century, there were one hundred and fifteen wills during the period 1550-1720. Many of these were concerned with allocating cash portions to younger males and to girls who would not normally benefit directly from the landholding, but they also frequently confirmed the disposition of real estate.

Further evidence for a lack of any strong link between family and land can be found in the very active land market throughout England in the sixteenth and seventeenth centuries. Historians have long been aware of this and have documented the extent of this phenomenon. Tawney devotes a passage to 'The Growth of a Land Market among the Peasants' in which sales, mortgages and leases, which are widespread in sixteenth century records, are put down to the 'play of commercial forces within the ranks of the customary tenants themselves, through the eager purchasing of land which we noticed as one feature of rural life at the close of the Middle Ages, and through the growth of a cash nexus between individuals side by side with the rule of custom.'[39] Numerous examples of what is termed 'Land Hunger' are given for the same period by Mildred Campbell, and local studies of particular villages confirm the picture.[40] Hoskins describes for Wigston Magna in the sixteenth century how the deeds 'record a multitude of such transactions,' for 'There was . . . and always had been, as far back as the records

[39] R. H. Tawney, *The Agrarian Problem of the Sixteenth Century*, (1912; Harper Torchbook edn., 1967), p. 72.
[40] M. Campbell, *The English Yeoman* (New Haven, 1942), pp. 72 ff.

go, a good deal of buying and selling of land between the peasant-farmers of Wigston.'[41] Again, numerous instances are given. If another example is needed, the land market in three Cambridgeshire parishes in the sixteenth and seventeenth centuries has recently been described in detail by Margaret Spufford. There, for example in Chippenham, the sale of many small plots during the period 1560 to 1636 led to the disappearance of many of the middling-sized holdings and the polarization of village society between rich and poor.[42] There is no evidence in any of these discussions of the land market that estates were fluctuating in size in relation to the family cycle or number of children; those who could afford to do so, bought land, whether they had large or small families, whether they were young or middle-aged. The impetus to sales seems to have been economic, rather than demographic. Nor is there any real evidence that people tried to keep particular holdings within the family; both land and houses were exchanged for more convenient and profitable investments with little apparent concern for 'keeping the name' on a particular piece of land. Furthermore, the majority of sales and transactions were between people who were not kin, extra-familial rather than intra-familial transfers.

It is now possible to see not only that England from the start of the sixteenth century exhibited many features which do not fit with the predictions of the peasant model, but also *why* this should have been the case. Already highly individualized ownership had severed the link between a family group and land. The family was not the basic unit of ownership, nor was it in all probability the basic unit of production and consumption. This was not a change that occurred during the sixteenth and seventeenth centuries as England moved *from* a peasant social structure at the start to a market-capitalist, industrialized society towards the end. The legal and ideological framework was already largely developed at the start of the period. This suggests that if we are to find the reasons for the collapse of a different system, we must search earlier. If there was no recognizable peasantry in sixteenth and seventeenth England, when had it disappeared? One recent suggestion is that whereas there was clearly a 'peasant' social structure in the late fourteenth century, as argued by Rodney Hilton, recent evidence suggests that it had collapsed by the middle of the fifteenth century.[43] Since there was no obvious break between 1380 and 1450, this leaves Blanchard and us puzzled. It is clearly time to consider the period between the Black Death and the end of the fifteenth century, particularly in terms of the central feature of the basic unit of ownership.

[41] Hoskins, *Midland Peasant*, p. 115.
[42] Spufford, *Communities*, pp. 65 ff.
[43] The suggestion is made by Ian Blanchard in a review of Hilton's *Peasantry* in *Social History*, 5 (May, 1977), pp. 662-3.

When we turn to recent studies of the post-Black Death period it soon becomes apparent that, with the notable exception of Rodney Hilton and Cicely Howell,[44] there is a general agreement that most of the characteristics of a real peasantry disappeared soon after the Black Death. This could be seen as interlinked to a change in the nature of feudalism at the higher level. We are told that 'late medieval lordship, indeed, has not much in common with feudal *dominium*' in this 'loosely-knit and shamelessly competitive society . . . .'[45] The intertwining of family and land, with the consequent geographical immobility, absence of a land market, retention of the land in particular families, all had rapidly vanished. Andrew Jones in his study of Leighton Buzzard in the later fifteenth century has shown that of 909 transfers of land in the period 1464-1508, 66% went from one family 'group' to another during the lifetime of the owner, while only 15% went to the family in the owner's lifetime and 10% at death.[46] Thus not only was there a very active market for land, but such property was on the whole going to non-kin. Furthermore, the trend goes back before this, for the 'court rolls of the last years of the fourteenth century reveal a clearly flourishing land market.'[47] Speaking of the late fourteenth century Hilton also found for the Midlands that, possibly as a result of the 'very considerable mobility of the peasant population,' or for other reasons, 'between a third and a half of holdings went outside the family after the death of the head of the household.'[48]

Rosamond Faith has also documented the active land market of the fifteenth century and noted that this trend began in the fourteenth century. She states that while the

idea that land 'ought to descend in the blood of the men who had held it of old' is of course common in many peasant societies . . . there does seem to have been a period in English history — roughly that of the fourteenth and fifteenth centuries — when in many rural communities this fundamental idea was in practice abandoned. Family claims to land were disregarded, or seldom pressed, and in place of the strict and elaborate arrangements which had previously governed the descent of land, there came to be no laws but those of supply and demand.[49]

---

[44]Hilton, *Peasantry* ch. 1; C. Howell, 'Peasant Inheritance,' C. Howell, 'Stability and Change 1300-1700,' *Jnl. Peasant Studies*, Vol. 2, no. 4, (July, 1975).
[45]K. B. McFarlance, 'Parliament and "Bastard Feudalism,"' in R. W. Southern (ed.), *Essays in Medieval History* (1968), p. 260.
[46]Andrew Jones, 'Land and People at Leighton Buzzard in the Later Fifteenth Century,' *Ec. Hist. Rev.*, 2nd ser., xxv, No. 1 (Feb., 1972), p. 20.
[47]Jones, 'Leighton Buzzard,' p. 23.
[48]Hilton, *Peasantry*, p. 41.
[49]Rosamund J. Faith, 'Peasant Families and Inheritance Customs in Medieval England,' *Agricultural Hist. Rev.*, vol. xiv, pt. 2 (1966) pp. 86-7.

Faith's evidence is mainly from the south of England, and shows that, for example, at Brightwaltham, family transactions 'dropped from 56 per cent of the total in 1300 to around 35 per cent throughout most of the fourteenth century and fell very sharply to 13 per cent after 1400.'[50] In 1400, '87 per cent of the total recorded land transactions' in the Ramsey manors were 'non-family,' in 1456, 83 per cent.[51] Thus she believes that 'when we turn to the court rolls of the fourteenth and fifteenth centuries,' the 'old patterns of inheritance had been abandoned,'[52] though it is naturally very difficult to be sure about the earlier period since court rolls only commence in the second half of the thirteenth century. Thus we find that on an average manor in the fourteenth century, for example one of those owned by St. Alban's, when a man died 'the land which his son or daughter or widow inherited was no longer likely to be the traditional family holding, but land which had passed through the hands of several different families quite recently.'[53] But Faith is unwilling to let go of the model entirely, even when the data contradicts it, so that she is forced to end up rather lamely that 'the idea of "keeping the name on the land" may still have been important, as an idea — perhaps as an aspiration — but it no longer reflected what was happening in the village.'[54]

The work of those associated with the Pontifical Institute and Father Raftis also supports the picture of a vanished peasantry. De Windt's detailed study of Holywell cum Needleworth near Huntingdon is summarized:

In short, familial retention of property was not obsolete in Holywell in the first half of the fifteenth century. It was, however, overshadowed by non-familial interests. Thus, between 1397 and 1457, although such a source as the Court Book recorded a total of 43 cases of familial retention of property — 24 instances of blood right inheritances and 19 cases of direct conveyances within a family—there were 21 cases of direct conveyance outside a family and, most important, 98 instances of land being taken up from the open market that had fallen vacant and been unclaimed by heirs or relatives of former tenants . . . the conclusion is inescapable that by the fifteenth century in Holywell, the day of total commitment . . . the further identification of the family's interests with the preservation of the tenement — was over.[55]

The author believed that the crucial change occurred in the middle of the fourteenth century with the 'severe shocks' to the economy caused by

[50]Ibid., p. 90.
[51]Ibid., p. 91.
[52]Ibid., p. 89.
[53]Ibid., p. 89.
[54]Ibid., p. 92.
[55]De Windt, *Land*, p. 134.

the Black Death.[56] A similar picture of the fifteenth century is drawn by Raftis; and a recent reviewer has concluded, on the basis of his own work on Somerset and Derbyshire, as well as the studies noted above, that it 'appears that by the 1450s the cohesive family unit had disappeared, shattered, fragmented into atomistic elements.'[57]

A study of the Cambridgeshire parish of Chippenham from before the Conquest up to the eighteenth century enclosures led Margaret Spufford to conclude that 'Enclosure is sometimes thought of as the death knell of the "small peasant" farm. In Chippenham it was no creator of inequality; it set the seal on a process which had begun by the late fourteenth century.'[58] This supports the view that the years from the later fourteenth century to the eighteenth need to be looked at as one period. In a recent study of Westminster Abbey and its estates Barbara Harvey has also documented the active land market and absence of a tie between family and land from the second half of the fourteenth century. She states that, after 1350, 'the family sense of inseparable association with a particular holding, which had been so marked a feature of rural society in the early Middle Ages weakened; indeed, in some places it more or less disappeared.'[59] The author believes that one cause of this change was jointures for married women, which 'helped to bring into existence one notable feature of peasant landholding' in the later medieval period, namely 'the fading importance of inheritance as the mode of transmission of land.'[60] This change was reflected in the very terminology of the transfers, which often spoke of a transfer to a man, his heirs and assigns (*sibi et suis et assignatis suis*). Thus, 'at the very moment when the customary tenant was admitted' the monks 'admitted the likelihood that he would want to sell his interest in the land instead of transmitting it to his heir.'[61]

Another recent study, by Chris Dyer, documents the very active land market and the relatively small proportion of the total transactions which were within the family. Studying some West Midlands villages over the period 1375-1540, he finds high emigration rates: 'about three-quarters of all families disappeared every forty to sixty years in the fifteenth century.'[62] Detailed tables show that the number of trans-

[56]Ibid., p. 192.
[57]Raftis, *Tenure*, pp. 208-9; Blanchard in *Social History*, 5, pp. 662-3.
[58]Spufford, *A Cambridgeshire Community: Chippenham from Settlement to Enclosure* (Leicester, 1965), Dept. of English Local History Occasional Papers, 20, pp. 54-5.
[59]Barbara Harvey, *Westminster Abbey and its Estates in the Middle Ages* (Oxford, 1977), pp. 318-9.
[60]Ibid., p. 299.
[61]Ibid., p. 305.
[62]C. Dyer, 'Peasant Families and Land-Holding in Some West Midland Villages, 1375-1540' in Richard Smith (ed.), *Land, Kinship and Life Cycle* (forthcoming, 1979). I am grateful to Dr Dyer for permission to use his unpublished material.

actions 'within the family' in the later fourteenth and fifteenth
centuries on three manors very seldom rose above a quarter of all the
transactions. In Hanbury they dropped as low as thirteen per cent in the
years 1420-39, having been only twenty-five per cent in 1376-1394; in
Kempsey it was only nine per cent in 1432-9, having been twenty-four
per cent in 1394-1421. What is most notable is that the proportion of
intra-family transactions was generally higher in the sixteenth century
than it had been in the earlier periods. Furthermore, the number of land
transactions was greater in the earlier period than in the later.[63] As the
author states, 'on most manors there was a marked increase in the
number of transfers within the family, both before and after death, in
the early sixteenth century,' for 'in the late fourteenth century and much
of the fifteenth century land holding was very fluid.'[64] The turnover of
holdings was, in the earlier period, 'very rapid, so that as many as 10 per
cent of holdings could change hands in a year, and some holdings went
from tenant to tenant with bewildering rapidity.'[65] Dyer admits that all
this is likely to 'create the impression that the peasant family had disin-
tegrated in the fifteenth century,' but argues that this is a 'great exaggeration.' His counter-evidence, however, is as revealing as is the
preceding information, for he produces only one case, and in this a
holding stayed in the family for three generations, over a period of
about seventy years, before it was sold.[66] A strong impression remains
that the land market was more active, land was treated more fully as a
'commodity,' and intra-familial transfers were less important in the
fifteenth century than even in the supposedly 'capitalistic' later
sixteenth century.

Dyer's findings are supported by figures obtained from the court rolls
for Earls Colne manor from the fifteenth to eighteenth centuries. The
figures are as shown on page 99.

If we look first at the total number of transactions, it will be seen that
the court was as active in 1401-5 as at any later time. The 'land-market'
was, if anything, less in evidence in the early eighteenth-century than at
the end of the fourteenth. This is partly an optical illusion since the
table takes no account of the size of the parcels that came into court. As
a result of consolidation of landholdings, the pieces in the last period
were a good deal larger than those in the earlier five-year periods. Yet
there can be little doubt that land exchanges were as important in 1400
as in 1700. Secondly, we may look at the proportion of land remaining
within the family. In the first period, less than one quarter went to 'kin,'

[63]Dyer, 'Peasant Families and Land Holding.'
[64]Ibid.
[65]Ibid.
[66]Ibid.

Land transfers: Earls Colne manor, copyhold land

period	total number of land transactions	grants from the lord	inter-vivos (non-family)	all transactions within family
1401—5	30	4	19	7
1501—5	28	4	18	6
1603—7	30	0	19	11
1701—5	18	1	5	12

Notes: the format follows that adopted by Chris Dyer, distinguishing trans-actions within the family, whether between living persons (inter-vivos) or inheritance after death, from all others. The period 1603—7 was chosen because the court rolls for the year 1602 are missing. The sources used are described in the list of manuscript sources used for the study, on page 207.

either at death or by transfer within life, and the figure was roughly the same in the next period. But as time passed, the family interest rose rather than declined, so that in the third period over one third went to 'kin' and in the early eighteenth century over two thirds went within the family. Ironically, if we use this as a simple index, it was not until the late seventeenth century that this village began to be inhabited by 'peasants.'

The impression that intra-family transfers were unimportant in the first two periods is strengthened if we look in more detail at the precise nature of the transfers. 'Intra-family' is really too crude a category, for the principal form of transfer which we would expect to find in a peasant society trying to maintain the family holdings is that between parents and children. Yet this is only one of the several types of intra-family transactions that appear within the last column of the table above. We need therefore to break down the information further, as shown on page 100.

The table shows, though the numbers are very small, that transfers from parents to children were fairly rare at the start; thus of the total of thirty transfers, only two were of this kind. Even these two are not quite what they seem if we are interested in the succession of sons to their father's holdings and the continuity of the 'family farm.' One of the two was to a daughter, and the only case of a parent's (in fact a mother's) transferring land to a son was immediately followed by the sale of the property by the son. Thus it is not possible to find a single example of either permanent inheritance or gift of customary land from parents to a son in Earls Colne in the five-year period. Gradually such transfers

Land transactions within the family: Earls Colne manor, copyhold land

period	between husband and wife	from parents to children	other
1401–5	4	2	1
1501–5	3	3	0
1603–7	3	8	0
1701–5	1	10	1

Note: in the 1603–7 period a number of the transfers were from a husband to a wife with remainder to the children, these have been counted as 'from parents to children', as have transfers to grandchildren. The 'other' category consists of one case of transfer between brothers, and the other a case where land was left to an 'heir' unspecified.

began to appear and increase, so that by the end of the period family transfers across the generations were quite important. In the last period, there were seven transfers from parents to sons, one to a daughter, and two to grandchildren. Again, it would seem that the stereotype of peasantry fits better in the supposedly proto-industrial and capitalist early eighteenth century than it does at the start of the fifteenth. Of course the figures are very small and much more work needs to be done, particularly on the size of the holdings, before we can be certain about what happened. Yet the results are enough to cast doubt on any simple theory of the gradual break-down of family inheritance.

As noted, there are still some medievalists who in one breath admit that there was no tie between land and family, and yet use the term 'peasants' when speaking of the later fourteenth or fifteenth centuries. Yet on the basis of the material mentioned above, it does not seem unduly perverse to conclude that if the central feature of peasantry is the strong link between the family group and the land, 'peasants' in this sense had disappeared by or soon after the Black Death. We have therefore pushed them back from the eighteenth to the thirteenth century. Almost all our authorities agree that the peasantry had in practice vanished by the later fourteenth century. They all, however, look back to an earlier period when a peasantry really *did* exist, and therefore spend time puzzling as to why they should have disappeared. Having failed to find any strong evidence of a peasantry back to the Black Death, we may legitimately wonder what the situation was like in what may be termed the heartland or 'golden age' of English peasantry, namely the thirteenth century. Here we will need to proceed very carefully, since many medievalists are opposed to the interpretation which I will suggest. It is now very widely recognized that, *de facto*, there was no peasantry in the later fourteenth and the fifteenth centuries. It was therefore possible to move quickly and superficially, as with the sixteenth and seventeenth centuries. Before the Black Death not only is the evidence much scantier, but we encounter the formidable and widely accepted work of Homans, Kosminsky, Postan and Vinogradoff which rest on the strong assumption that this was a classical 'peasant' society.

5
Ownership in England from 1200 to 1349

At first sight it would seem incontestable that the situation in thirteenth- and early fourteenth-century England was essentially similar to that in peasant societies. In the areas of partible inheritance it was like the 'classical' model; in the areas of impartible inheritance like the 'west European' system. Thus, while the champion, open-field areas with impartible inheritance gave rise to a stem-family organization similar to that, for instance, in southern France, the woodland areas of partible inheritance resembled a Russian joint-family system. As Homans put it, 'A Russian peasant family resembled one of Kent or Norfolk much more than one of the Midlands. It belonged to the class of joint-families: a group of descendents of a common ancestor, the brothers inheriting jointly and living in one community.'[1]

Homans found proof of the existence as part of both systems of the French principle of *retrait lignager*, whereby land could not be sold off without first offering it at a reasonable price to the children. He argues that even if a younger child could not expect much, he at least had a life right to maintenance in areas of primogeniture, as long as he was prepared to work and not to marry. Thus there were birth rights in 'the family land.' The birth rights of eldest sons in areas of primogeniture and of all the sons in areas of partible inheritance were held to be even stronger. Land flowed down through 'the blood'; it could not be alienated from the family.[2] These views are repeated by historians such as Raftis, Howell and Hilton.[3] This question of ownership is central to the notion of peasantry. The crux of the matter is *who* owned the land. It would be easy to assume that it was the family group; but if we look more closely at both the *de jure* and *de facto* situation, as reflected in

[1]Homans *Villagers*, p. 207.
[2]Ibid , pp. 110, 124-5, 137-8, 142-3, 195-7.
[3]Raftis, *Tenure*, pp. 43, 48, 60, 63; Howell, *Peasant Inheritance*, pp. 113-4, Hilton, *Bond Men*, pp. 38-9.

both legal text-books and in the proceedings in the court rolls, it will appear that this is a misinterpretation. Land did *not* belong to the family group, but to an individual. This was the case with both freehold and customary tenures from the thirteenth century onwards. There were no inalienable birth rights, either of the eldest child or any other.

As in the later period it is necessary to make a preliminary distinction between movable and immovable property, or between 'chattel' and 'real' estate. With regard to the former, namely cash, clothing, furniture, Bracton summarized the position in this way: Men and women *sui juris* could make wills, provided that they left their best and second best chattel to lord and church, as appropriate.[4] After that, they could leave their property to their 'kin' or to 'other persons as it pleases . . . .' The other major restraint was that, once debts and funeral expenses had been paid, the chattels were to be divided into three parts if a wife and children survived, then one third should go to each of them and one third could be disposed of. If only a wife remained, half should go to her. But not only was it possible to convert most of the property into real estate, and thus avoid passing it on to the children, but it was the custom in 'cities, boroughs and vills,' including London, that children should have no automatic rights even in the chattels: 'as to the children of such persons . . . they shall rightfully take no more of the deceased's estate, of his movable property . . . than was specifically left them, except by favour of the testator.'[5] The reason given for this extreme freedom is very revealing. Bracton argues that 'a citizen could scarcely be found who would undertake a great enterprise in his lifetime if, at his death, he was compelled against his will to leave his estate to ignorant and extravagant children and undeserving wives. Thus it is very necessary that freedom of action be given him in this respect, for thereby he will curb misconduct, encourage virtue, and put in the way of both wives and children an occasion for good behaviour, which indeed might not come about if they knew without doubt that they would obtain a certain share irrespective of the testators wishes.'[6] The insecurity and individualism of the system are apparent, and particularly revealing when we remember that Bracton is describing mid-thirteenth century England.

Turning to the other aspect, real estate, it now seems clear that there was no rigid division between villeins and non-villeins in their holding of land. The discovery of substantial numbers of 'peasant' land charters shows that 'many of the charters combine in the same transactions the free and the unfree elements of the village: villein and villein land, with

[4]Bracton, *Laws*, p. 178.
[5]Ibid., p. 180.
[6]Ibid., p. 181.

freemen and free land.'[7] Villeins might hold freehold land, and freemen might hold customary land. Furthermore, if we are estimating whether there was a real peasantry, we need to look at the very considerable number of small freeholders who might, with their security of tenure, be reckoned to be the backbone of such a peasantry. In analysing freehold and customary holdings, it is useful to have a rough estimate of the amount of land held by such tenures in the thirteenth century. One set of estimates is provided by Kosminsky on the basis of the Hundred Rolls and court rolls. He estimates that about 40 per cent of arable land was held by customary tenures, all of which 'can be called peasant land.' Another 30 per cent was 'freehold' in a certain sense, but he estimates that about one third of this was held by 'non-peasants,' that is, by large ecclesiastical or lay landowners. 'On the other hand, part of the peasant land is concealed because it appears in the form of tiny manors.'[8] Roughly speaking, we can say that of the land supposedly held by a 'peasantry,' one third was held as some form of 'freehold,' two thirds under customary tenures. We may look first at the position in relation to the third held by freehold, since the evidence is much clearer here. The matter is so central to the argument that we will repeat with elaboration and with application to the thirteenth century, where it also held true, the description of the nature of freehold tenure which we gave for the sixteenth and seventeenth centuries; for there had been no essential change during the years between, apart from the rising power to bequeath freehold land by will as well as during life.

There can be no doubt that with regard to freehold land there was no legal link between *family* and land under Common Law. By the beginning of the thirteenth century ownership lay in the individual, not in any larger group. We may add further proof to the discussion in the previous chapter. As Bracton summarized it, the heir 'acquires nothing by the gift made to his ancestor since he was not enfeoffed with the donee.'[9] A son has no rights while his father lives, unless they have been formally transferred to him in a court of law; they are *not* co-owners in any sense. This is illustrated by the fact that in the thirteenth century, and to a certain extent later, the heir has no automatic seisin in his dead ancestor's property. We are told that:

If a stranger 'abates' or 'intrudes' upon land whose owner has just died seised, he has committed no disseisin. The lawful heir cannot say that he was disseised unless he had in fact been previously seised. In other words, the heir does not inherit his ancestor's seisin. Like everyone else, an heir cannot acquire the

---

[7]Postan, *Essays*, p. 110.
[8]Kosminsky, *Studies*, pp. 203-5.
[9]Bracton, *Laws*, p. 66.

privileges of seisin unless he enters, stays in, and conducts himself like the peaceful holder of a free tenement.[10]

Again there was nothing comparable to the French custom, equivalent to the principle of *le roi est mort: vive le roi*, whereby *le mort saisit le vif*.[11] It is true that the custom of primogeniture gave the eldest male child greater rights, where the estate was not disposed of, than those of the other children. But even the eldest son had nothing except at the wish of his father or mother, except where, on the estates of some land-owners, the line of inheritance had been formally specified by the artificial device of an entail. Even such entails could be broken — and it was theoretically just as possible to entail the land *away* from the family, as to keep it in the family line. The earlier form of the entail, the *modus*, could be used, as Bracton observed, to 'enlarge his gift and make strangers (*alienos*) *quasi*-heirs, though in truth they are not heirs at all . . . .'[12] Such a condition can 'prevent descent to right heirs,' as Bracton shows in the case of a man who died on a crusade.[13] We may thus conclude by stating that on approximately one third of the land held by 'peasants,' there was a complete antithesis to family ownership. A man, or woman, held as an individual, not in trust for his heirs; could sell or otherwise permanently alienate his acquired and inherited estate without consideration for the wishes or needs of his descendants.

The strength of private rights over property is shown in diverse ways throughout Bracton's long discussion of property rights. Parents may give all their property to one daughter, for instance, even though the 'normal' custom would be, when there were no sons, for all to be equal heirs. 'If the father or mother, or both, give their whole inheritance (to one daughter) in maritagium nothing falls into the pot, since nothing remains to be divided among the co-heiresses.'[14] A tenant in fee simple may (unless this is expressly forbidden in the original grant) transfer his 'seisin' to another owner, even if the chief lord objects.[15] The central point is that the parents and children are not *joint-owners* by natural law: a parent has an individual right which he may pass on (by a

[10]Plucknett, *Common Law*, pp. 722-3; for a fuller treatment see Maitland, *English Law*, ii, pp. 29-80. The assize of Mort D'Ancestor was introduced specifically to deal with this problem, but it was not based on a writ of disseisin but abatement. As Maitland remarked, 'were seisin itself a heritable right there could be no place for the mort d'ancestor, since its whole province would be covered by the novel disseisin' (*ibid.*, p. 60).
[11]Plucknett, *Common Law*, p. 723.
[12]Bracton, *Laws*, p. 67. There is a further discussion of the ease with which entails could be broken and their limited use until the later seventeenth century in George C. Brodrick, *English Land and English Landlords* (1881; reprinted, Newton Abbot, 1968), pp. 23-4, 31-2, 43.
[13]Ibid., p. 73.
[14]Ibid., p. 224.
[15]Ibid., pp. 140-3.

positive act, or by failing to transfer the right elsewhere). 'Inheritance' is therefore a form of *succession* to a right, '*hereditas est successio*,'[16] not the *continued* enjoyment of a right which was already present from birth.

So far there can be little argument, and the thesis would probably be conceded by even the most staunch adherents to the idea of peasantry. But with regard to the other two thirds, held by the 'custom of the manor,' the position is thought to be the reverse. The situation is made more difficult since at no date between 1250-1750 could a single book have summarized the customs of the manors in England. As a seventeenth century steward put it, in words which also apply to the thirteenth century, 'Customs . . . of this nation are so various and differing in themselves as that a man might almost say that there are as many several customs as manors or lordships in a country, yea and almost as many as there are townships or hamlets in a manor.'[17] We are often forced to infer the customs from the court rolls or from even more indirect evidence. In order to examine the contention that on customary holdings, in complete contrast to freeholdings, the land was possessed by the 'family' and not the individual, that there were inalienable blood rights which ensured that the family was attached to a particular holding over the generations, we may examine critically the views of three writers who have most forcefully put forward such a view, and supported it with the most evidence. But in concentrating on them, it should be stated that their argument seems to have been accepted by some other medievalists who have worked in tenurial matters.[18] The arguments of G. C. Homans, J. A. Raftis, and C. Howell overlap with each other and may be summarized as follows.[19]

Despite the *de jure* position in Common Law in the thirteenth century that customary land was held 'at the will of the lord' and was not inheritable or alienable by the tenants, the *de facto* position under *customary* law, the customs of specific manors, was that both villeins and freemen could and did pass on land to their heirs or other people, either by gift or sale. As Homans put it, as long as a tenant performed his services, his seisin was secure.[20] He could, through a surrender in the manor court, pass on the land to the person of his or her own choice. While it is true that 'medieval lawyers' may have argued strongly

[16]Ibid., p. 184.

[17]A. Bagot, 'Mr Gilpin and manorial customs' *T.C.W.A.A.S.*, n.s. lxiii (1961), p. 228.

[18]For example, DeWindt, *Land*, p. 124; Postan, *Essays*, pp. 114-136.

[19]The sources for this summary are Homans, *Villagers*; Raftis, *Tenure* and *Warboys*; *Two Hundred Years in the Life of an English Medieval Village* (Toronto, 1974); Howell, *Peasant Inheritance*.

[20]Homans, *Villagers*, p. 109; the developed rights of villeins against their lord is also alluded to, for example, by Rogers, *Six Centuries*, p. 44.

against this principle,[21] it is now clear from the study of court transfers that, as legal historians themselves recognize, while 'it is said that in *strict law* the copyholder remained a tenant at will,' '*by the custom* (he) could have an inheritance just as a freeholder could.'[22] One side of this flexibility will also be extensively illustrated in a later section, where it will be shown that land could be sold by villeins. Establishing the fact, that a thirteenth century villager *could* pass on his land to his heirs clinches no argument concerning the connection between land and the family — it merely places the owner in roughly the same position as a freeholder or a seventeenth century customary tenant, both of whom we know had this right, but also had the right to alienate it from the family. It is merely an extension to the customary tenant of the individual right to alienate property, to 'own' it in a fuller sense. It allows him to sell or give away his land, as well as to pass it on to his heirs. It cannot be assumed, as some do, that because the *father* has a customary right to transmit his real estate to his property, his *children* have a right to inherit that estate from their father. These are separate issues — as many a disappointed heir could testify. In order to prove the case, two further principles must be established.

It is argued that since this was customary land and bound by the 'customs,' and since such customs frequently specified a rule of inheritance, such as male primogeniture, ultimogeniture, or partible inheritance between all sons, family inheritance was secured. As Homans put it,

A villager was not free to bequeath his holding to whom he would. Its descent was fixed by custom and that custom was local custom, varying from place to place. A holding in any manor descended according to the custom of that manor . . . According to the custom of impartible inheritance, a villager's holding . . . went at his death to one of his sons and one only.[23]

At first sight this appears to be an unexceptionable argument, but in view of the extensive land sales which will be documented later, we need to look at it more closely. The over-simplification in it appears if we compare the situation again with freehold and the later history of copyhold. Freehold property in the thirteenth century and later was under exactly the same type of constraint, namely that it should descend by male primogeniture, but in that case it was the custom of the country or common law. In the event that land had not been alienated in a freeholder's lifetime and after his widow's death, it should go to the oldest

[21]Howell, *Peasant Inheritance*, p. 114.
[22]A. W. B. Simpson, *An Introduction to the History of the Land Law* (Oxford, 1961), p. 158. 'Copyholder' is a later term and should not be used of the thirteenth century.
[23]Homans, *Villagers*, p. 110.

son. The situation is identical. Yet we know that freehold land was bought and sold and alienated freely from the family, and no-one has argued that there was a right by blood dominant.[24] Furthermore, the situation in relation to customary land in the sixteenth and seventeenth centuries appears to be almost identical to that in the thirteenth. Each manor had its custom, and, on the basis of this, land would often descend to the 'right heirs,' namely the eldest son or all the sons. Court rolls of the sixteenth century appear to have the same wording, referring to the hereditary right of an heir.[25] Taken by themselves they would give exactly the impression made by thirteenth century courts. Yet the presence of other documents enables historians to see that there was little attachment between family and land. The position was, as with freehold land, that a man could allow the custom to dictate the situation, could die without making a sale or alienation of his land, in which case his eldest son would inherit. But very often he chose to do something else — either selling off part, giving it away, making provision for his younger sons or daughters, or in other ways acting in a way that made the custom merely an unrealized possibility. Again there is the apparently logical, but unwarranted, assumption that because there are rules of inheritance, estates *must* be transmitted according to such rules — a proposition which would clearly be ridiculous with regard to present property transmissions and cannot be assumed to be the case, without proof, in relation to the thirteenth century.

So far it has merely been shown that customary holdings were in many respects, *de facto*, like freeholds — hereditable, governed by rules of inheritance in cases where the estate had not been disposed of. A further argument is that there were restraints on alienation; these were of two kinds, namely that the main property could not be alienated from the heir, and secondly that younger children, even in areas of primogeniture, had certain inviolable 'birth rights,' from which they could not be excluded. This is the crux of the matter. It should be realized that

---

[24]It needs to be stressed that here and throughout the argument I am only considering small landowners, those who could conceivably have constituted a 'peasantry.' The position among larger landowners may well have been very different. As James Campbell kindly reminded me, 'The evidence, which is abundant, for the extent to which the upper classes certainly do assume a natural right of blood to land, notwithstanding the wide powers of alienation *inter vivos* which the Common Law rules for fee simple tenure allowed, shows that free alienation could exist with a strong sense of family or primogenitary rights . . . there is abundant evidence, certainly in the upper classes, about whom we know most, that a sense of connection between blood and land was felt very strongly indeed' (personal communication).

[25]Just one example may be given, from the Earls Colne Manor Court roll for 1595. It is stated that 'Joan Tracer died seised of the premises . . . and that Marion the wife of John Peartree and Edith the wife of Henry Bridge are cousins and next heirs of the said Joan Tracer . . . and have right to the premises . . .'

if either can be shown to be the case, it would set this type of property off from all others and also from the customary tenures after the fourteenth century when we have strong evidence for the absence of family inheritance. What is being argued by Hilton, Homans, Howell and Raftis is that customary land in the thirteenth century was somehow bound to the family in a different way and more fully. What is the evidence for this?

It is argued that 'family land' could not be alienated from the heirs. An extensive search of medievalists' work has brought forward only a few shreds of evidence for this assertion which, as we have seen, goes against all that we know concerning other forms of tenure, and the same form of tenure a hundred years later. One argument is that since it was against the supposed interests of the lord of the manor, alienation from the family would be prevented. Homans argues that 'the lord of the manor may have had good reasons for wishing to restrict the alienation of the lands of his tenants,' since such alienation would have lead to complications in extracting rents and services. But even Homans is not convinced by this argument, since he only weakly continues, 'Perhaps, therefore, the interest of the lords of manors was to prevent alienation.'[26] This matter is further discussed by Paul Hyams, who gives it no great weight, and by Postan, who admits that his evidence is merely theoretical, since there is none to show that lords of the manor actually forbade alienation on these grounds.[27] Even Raftis, one of those most committed to the idea of a permanent family holding, admits that the lord was 'apparently indifferent to the conveyance of customary land out of the hands of the family.'[28] Indeed, a rapid turn-over led to *extra* entry fines and there were thus pressures in the other direction. Richard Smith estimates that approximately three-quarters of the lord's income in the period 1259-1300 on a Suffolk manor came from fines paid on transfers of land.[29]

The second argument is from sentiment. We know, so some authors say, that these were peasants; we know that peasants have a very strong desire to 'keep the name on the land,' therefore alienation was neither common nor regarded with favour. This view underlies a good deal of the writing on the subject. For example, Homans states that 'Men of the Middle Ages would have summed up these facts by saying that no part of an established holding ought to be "alienated." There was a strong

---

[26]Homans, *Villagers*, pp. 200-201.
[27]Paul R. Hyams, 'The Origins of a Peasant Land Market in England', *Ec. H.R.*, 2nd ser., vol. xxiii, no. 1 (April, 1970), pp. 21-3; Postan, *Essays*, p. 113.
[28]Raftis, *Tenure*, p. 65.
[29]Richard Smith, (personal communication); the figure is a rough estimate.

sentiment against what was called "alienation." '[30] We will deal later with the question of sentimental attachment to the land, and, in so far as a vague attitude like this may be disproved, will show that there is little evidence for it. Furthermore, if it existed up to the middle of the fourteenth century, it is most curious that it should suddenly vanish overnight, never to reappear, except among wealthy yeoman and gentry families.[31] Since the argument is also circular, taking for granted what it sets out to prove, we may leave it for the time being.

A third argument is that the owner did not have the *right* to alienate his customary holding by the custom of the manor, that he was forced to leave it to his children or child. At first sight a certain amount of support for this view appears to exist in court transfers cited by Raftis and Homans. But if we examine the texts they cite as evidence, they do not bear the interpretation put upon them. It should be remembered that we are not dealing with sentiment or what is *thought* right, we are not dealing with Homans' view that 'a main principle governing the organization of families in the champion country . . . was that an established holding of land ought to descend intact in the blood of the men who had held it of old.'[32] We are dealing with something deeper, the argument that children had a right, at birth, to the inheritance, a form of joint ownership. Put in Homans' words, this was 'a system of custom, according to which the rights of every member of a family in the means of subsistence possessed by the family were established from birth to death and from generation to generation,'[33] or, in the words of Raftis, 'that various persons in every village had a right by blood to the tenements,' implicitly *before* they formally inherited them.[34] This view has been put particularly strongly recently by Cicely Howell:

The most fundamental of these principles was that family land belonged to the whole family; every member had a claim to support from it, from generation to

---

[30]Homans, *Villagers*, p. 195.
[31]Again it needs to be stressed that we are not speaking about wealthier landholders, who may well have wished to retain family land, but about those with fifty acres or less who would elsewhere have constituted a 'peasantry.'
[32]Homans, *Villagers*, p. 195.
[33]*Ibid.*, p. 214-5.
[34]Raftis, *Tenure*, p. 206. Among the nobility and gentry such a 'right' may well have been strongly felt, and even among small landowners there may often have been such a feeling. But only a realization of the wide gap between this situation and the 'model''peasant societies in the rest of the world where a child did not only have a strong expectation, but was by birth a co-owner with his father, will make it possible to explain the major differences between England and other societies to be documented in the next chapter. It is for this reason that we have stressed this point. Of course, in practice, most heirs may not have been disappointed, just as they may not be to-day, but the fact that the possibility was there, with 'individual' as opposed to 'group' ownership, is, to my mind, of central importance.

generation. Responsibility for its management could lie with a generation-set, or with a single representative, but the position was one of stewardship, not of ownership.[35]

She argues that such a situation 'was strong in England in 1700,' which, as we have seen above, is totally incorrect. Is it correct for the thirteenth century?

When examined closely, Raftis's work, though he appears to accept this argument, gives it no factual support, for he admits that 'the son could lose his right to inheritance by various means.'[36] He argues that 'rights to land through blood' remained for a long period, and that customary rules of inheritance worked well. He concludes that 'the permanent pattern of rights in land was a matter of blood relationship which were recognized but not established by court records.'[37] Yet there is no evidence that the situation on customary estates in the thirteenth century was different from that in the sixteenth century or freeholds in the thirteenth century, namely no evidence that a man, whom it is admitted has individual seisin, and often sells his right to his child, was *forced* to leave his inherited estate to his children or other blood relatives and could not sell it. The two possible cases cited by Raftis, showing some kind of birth rights of children, are also discussed by Homans and may be analysed in discussing his views.[38] The documentation which is put forward by Raftis to support the idea of a blood right on the part of heirs is exactly similar to transfers in court rolls of the sixteenth century or later, and does not establish this fact. Thus, for example, he argues that 'the customary tenant retained a close tie to the land because he had a hereditary title, or to a right by blood, as documents such as the above example from Wistow say, to the tenure of the holding.'[39] The document quoted states that a certain Alice Kabe surrendered her land into the court and 'An inquiry was issued by proclamation whether anyone ought to hold that cotland by blood, and no one appeared.' This is exactly what would happen in a later period; it is as if a tenant had died, in which case, as with freehold land, there are customs as to whom should have the first option. It is possible to cite numerous examples from sixteenth century court rolls using the same method of proclamation.[40] But this is not to say that if Alice had decided to surrender the

[35] Howell, *Peasant Inheritance*, pp. 113-4.
[36] Raftis, *Tenure*, p. 49.
[37] Ibid., p. 62.
[38] Ibid., p. 15; cases from Over and Gravely.
[39] Ibid., p. 33.
[40] One example in the court held in November 1638 in Earls Colne is as follows: 'it is shown by the homage (jury) that John Bounds after the last court and before this court died seised of certain customary tenements held from the lord of this manor and that Sam Bounds is his son and next heir, but because none came therefore proclamation was three times made . . . .' Sam Bounds later came and took the land from the lord.

holding to a neighbour for a certain sum of money, she would not have been allowed to do so. The same can be said of other examples. For instance, at Warboys in 1347, 'The jurors announce the death of Robert Berenger . . . And the court further announces that John his son is nearest heir by blood to that property according to the custom of the manor.'[41] The formula again merely states that *in the absence of prior alienation by the father*, the tenement should pass, according to the custom, to his son. By the late sixteenth century, when exactly the same wording is used, we know that the father could have sold the tenement or devized it to non-kin by a will. It is essential not to confuse the right of a son as against non-kin in the absence of other provision by the father with an absolute right *against* the father and *in* the property on the part of the children.[42]

Homans has attempted to assemble the most evidence to show the inalienability of holdings. His proof is as follows. He first cites a case where a younger brother gives his elder brother his 'right' in an area of Borough English in 1299. Homans draws from this the more general conclusion that 'the consent of the heir was commonly required if a tenement was to be alienated in any way from the customary line of inheritance.'[43] This is not a legitimate inference if it is implied that such consent was needed *before* the death or surrender by the father or owner. Undoubtedly if a property was not alienated and there was a blood heir, he would need to give his consent for a more distant heir to inherit. But this is not, of course, any proof that such an heir had *rights* of an inalienable kind when his father held the property. The next piece of evidence is held to prove that 'Every son had the right, in custom, to expect a portion.'[44] When we look at the passage referred to, however, it is clearly dealing with cash and goods, movables, not with landed estate. The position is stated to be very similar to that obtaining for the Archdiocese of York up to 1692, where children have a right to some kind of 'portion.' But, as has been pointed out above, it was quite possible for a father to give away all his goods before his death and thus deprive his children, or to invest all of his money in real estate which would not necessarily go to them. In any case, we have clearly strayed from the connection between the family and the land.

Although he concedes that younger children might, in practice, be disinherited from the holding, Homans argues that younger sons had a

---

[41]Raftis, *Tenure*, p. 34.
[42]This mistake is easy to make when merely using manor court rolls; it becomes very apparent when the same wording is used, but other documents exist to check the actual transmission of holdings.
[43]Homans, *Villagers*, pp. 124-5.
[44]Ibid., p. 135.

birth right in the family estate. At first Homans implies this by the word *might*, with its ambiguity of whether this was a right or a favour. He thus argues that 'instead of taking his portion and going out into the world, a son who was not to inherit his father's holding might properly choose to stay and live on the holding.'[45] The argument is then apparently strengthened by arguing that the younger son could stay 'so long as' he did not marry, in the sense of 'on condition that.' Homans writes that 'he was not simply unable to take a wife; he was not allowed to take one.' Yet if we look at the document cited, this is based on one ambiguous word. The English translation is given that Walter may have a house and one quarter of wheat 'so long as' he remains without a wife — the latin word for this is *dum*, which is just as likely to mean 'while' or 'during,' as 'on the condition that' he does not. Further examples are cited to show the rights of younger brothers as against the elder. The findings by F. M. Page that on certain Cambridgeshire manors, 'the son who succeeded was not free from obligation to his father's other children,' that by the custom they received an acre each until they moved away or married, is cited. Entries for Gravely and Over, also in Cambridgeshire, are cited to show that younger children seem to have received small portions of the tenement while the eldest received the largest.[46] This again is no proof that the children had birth rights. It merely shows that there was an intermediate form of inheritance custom between strict impartibility and full partibility. It is clearly a restricted custom and does not apply to most of England, and it does not add to the arguments concerning family rights, just as the discovery of widespread areas of full partible inheritance does not do so.

Another argument, put forward by Howell, is as follows.

Bracton is specific in stating that, as late as the thirteenth century, primo-geniture for socage holders did not entitle the eldest son to all the family messuages, but only to the first choice: if there was only one messuage, he should have it, but if there were more than one messuage, the remainder should go to the other children in order of seniority, and those who received no land should receive the equivalent in cash or kind.[47]

If we look at Bracton in the passage cited, it is clear that Howell has misinterpreted the passage in two ways.[48] Firstly it is clear that Bracton is talking here of *specific* cases where a certain holding is divisible — for instance where daughters inherit as co-parceners. Furthermore, he is not talking about *socage* holders. Further down the same page he makes

[45] Ibid., p. 137.
[46] Ibid., pp. 432-3; F. M. Page, 'The Customary Poor Law of Three Cambridgeshire Manors', *Cambridge Hist. Jnl.*, vol. iii, no. 2, (1930), pp. 127-9.
[47] Howell, *Peasant Inheritance*, p. 117.
[48] Bracton, *Laws*, p. 221.

it clear not only that he is not dealing with socage tenure, but also that he is only speaking of specific instances. He writes that 'If a free sokeman dies leaving several heirs who are parceners and the inheritance is partible and has been divisible since ancient times, let the heirs, no matter how many there are, have their equal parts . . . If the inheritance has not been divisible *ab antiquo*, let the whole then remain to the eldest. If it is a villein socage local custom must then be observed.' Thus Bracton's observations are either irrelevant, or give a case opposite to that argued by Howell.

No evidence has yet been encountered to show that parents could not alienate their land from their children. The nearest Homans comes to attempting to do this is in relation to leases. This is contained in a central chapter, where he hopes to establish that alienation was not only morally disapproved of, but impossible.[49] His evidence is as follows. He cites a number of thirteenth century court rolls that show that *leasing* by a customary tenant was circumscribed: he could not lease land beyond his own lifetime, could not make something equivalent to a will whereby the fate of his property beyond his death was specified. The example cited shows this to be true. The jurors in Halton in 1296 state that 'no tenant of the lord can demise his land except for his lifetime . . . .'[50] This is interpreted much more widely by Homans, when he argues on the basis of this one instance that 'clearly this custom would prevent any permanent alienation of land from villagers' holdings.'[51] This is a *non sequitur*, since the permanent alienation, as opposed to leases, would occur by sale or gift, and this case nowhere touches on these matters. The next case cited is also interpreted too broadly. It concerns a woman called Juliana who bought some land, but the jury decided that '*post mortem nulli poterit vendere, legare nec assignare.*'[52] The meaning of this is subtly changed by the translation, for Homans gives the English version as 'she could sell it, bequeath it, or assign it to no one after her death' and takes this to prove that 'she certainly did not acquire the rights which go with a purchase in our modern use of the word,' i.e. the right to alienate it permanently. The interpretation hinges on the phrase 'after death.' It was the case in the thirteenth century, before the power of assigning land by wills, introduced later, that both freehold and customary land could be sold or alienated only during the lifetime of the owner and not *post mortem* by will. It would seem that this case is referring to that power, otherwise it would make nonsense of the numerous land sales in perpetuity which we will

[49]Homans, *Villagers*, ch. 14.
[50]Ibid., p. 196.
[52]*Idem.*
[52]Ibid., pp. 196, 442.

document later and which clearly show that people *did* have the right to
sell land during their lifetimes.

The next instance also is interpreted too simply.[53] It tells of a woman
whose husband had alienated some land which she subsequently
claimed after his death, although 'she could not gainsay in his lifetime'
(*cui in vita sua contradicere non potuit*). Homans states that the woman
'was claiming that her husband might alienate such land only for his
lifetime,' since he held it in the right of his wife, and that it should revert
to her. This is a situation we meet in the case of freehold land and also
with customary land in the sixteenth century. There we can see more
clearly women's property rights. It becomes clear that a man could
lease, rent, or temporarily alienate his wife's real estate during her
'*couverture*,' but could not permanently alienate it. This was the case
with freehold land in the thirteenth century, which we know in other
respects was alienable. Bracton states that 'if the husband makes a gift of
his wife's property it will never be revoked during the life of the
husband, since a wife may not dispute her husband's acts' (*quod viro
suo uxor contradicare non potest*). Yet the property must revert to the
wife after her husband's death and she may sell it then.[54] To find exactly
the same situation with customary land is no proof that land in itself
was inalienable from the family, just as it is not inconsistent for such a
situation in the sixteenth century to co-exist with wide powers of
alienation. At this point Homans declared that 'what has been
established is that on many manors land could be alienated only for the
lifetime of the holder of land, or for the lifetime of those to whom it was
alienated. After their deaths, it reverted to the true heir.'[55] In fact, no
such thing had been proved, and no difference between the treatment of
customary land in the thirteenth century and that in the sixteenth
century has been shown, or between customary land and freeholds in
the early period.

The next illustration is a lengthy and complex one from Newington,
Oxon., in 1293.[56] In this case, a man and his son were alleged to have
come into court and surrendered their rights to others. But the son later
claimed that he surrendered his right only because of the threats of his
father and that he did not really do so, and therefore his father had no
right to surrender his land beyond his father's lifetime and the land
should return to him. Homans interprets this as yet another example of
the rule that 'the holder of land might alienate it only for his lifetime,'
but with an added rule that with the consent of his heirs he might

[53] Ibid., pp. 197, 142.
[54] Bracton, *Laws*, p. 97.
[55] Homans, *Villagers*, p. 197.
[56] Ibid., pp. 197-8.

surrender it for good. There are probably two errors here. The first is to deduce that because in this case an heir's consent was obtained, it was necessary and without it a transfer would be invalid; there are numerous counter examples of sales without the heir's consent, in both this period and later, which could be cited. Secondly, since we do not know the pre-history of the tenurial situation, it is quite impossible to be sure of what is happening. Since the document speaks of the 'right' of the son, and the surrendering of this 'right' with his father, it is quite possible that by an earlier transaction in the court, father and son had been made joint tenants. This could, for example, be affected by a grant from father to son as joint-purchasers, or to the son, who passed it to the 'use' of his father with 'reversion' to himself on his father's death. By customary law, a person had a 'right' only if he had obtained admittance and seisin in the manor court. A son did not obtain this automatically from his father, just as a wife did not obtain it automatically from her husband unless the custom of the manor prescribed a special custom of free-bench. There was thus no normal 'right' to surrender. It is thus possible that the case means something else. It is also possible that in order to avoid just this kind of dispute, fathers liked to obtain their son's permission — but this is a less likely interpretation. One other interpretation is possible. As Homans states, the father was clearly trying to settle the land upon his *daughter* in a marriage settlement. Now there seems to have been particular difficulty in favouring a child other than the heir. We can see this clearly with regard to freehold land. Whereas a man can give away inherited land, according to Glanvill, to whom he will, 'If, however, he has several legitimate sons, it is not at all easy without the consent of the heir to give any part of the inheritance to a younger son, because if this were allowed the disinheritance of elder sons would often occur, on account of the greater affection which fathers most frequently have for their younger sons.'[57] Looked at another way, the principle seems to be that if land is going to follow the rules of inheritance at all, it must follow them strictly, and thus nearer heirs must waive their claims first. This may explain why the son's consent was needed before his sister could obtain the land, and explain why, in general, it could have been easier to have sold land to a stranger than to leave it to a child who was not the first heir. It is certainly not possible to take the case on its face value.

The next case cited by Homans is, as he states, a very compressed one, and it involves a good deal of guesswork on his part.[58] If he is correct in thinking that it concerns a widow's right to alienate her widowright and the claim of what he guesses to be the son of her husband to buy

57 Quoted in Plucknett, *Common Law*, p. 526.
58 Homans, *Villagers*, p. 199.

back the right to the land 'by giving as much as any outsider wishes to give,' there is indeed a curious parallel with the French customs. But to prove that 'the rule at Halton was that if the widow transferred any part of her bench, she might transfer it only to the true heir of the tenement, and not to any outsider' proves nothing concerning the non-alienability of land in general. It was also the custom in the sixteenth century that a widow held her widowright or freebench only for life; often she lost it if she 'married or miscarried,' though in common law she had her 'dower' for life. But in both cases it was not something to be sold off permanently — it was a life right. Yet it would clearly be ridiculous to infer from this that permanent alienation was impossible in sixteenth century customary or freehold tenure. We know that is was indeed possible. The case proves nothing either way.

In the rest of the chapter Homans considers land sales, giving examples of such sales and apparently admitting that they could occur, that permanent alienation without the heir's consent was possible.[59] No further arguments are put forward concerning the restrictions on alienation. The case for an inseparable link between family and land, for 'family ownership' has not been made, though Homans is prepared to conclude that 'the custom . . . was that the holding was not to be divided or alienated.'[60] There is thus, as yet, no evidence of any weight to suggest that land was not alienable and had to flow down through families in the thirteenth century.

We have been warned firmly that

persons with only a passing acquaintance with medieval documents, when searching them for certain items of information and finding such information absent from the documents in question, only too frequently conclude that developments in which they are interested were, therefore, not present at the time or place.[61]

We ought to state, therefore, that the fact that no medievalist has yet produced any worthwhile evidence that the situation in the thirteenth century with customary tenures was substantially different from that in the sixteenth century, namely that there was some kind of blood right, that the children inherited with the father, that the owner was only the steward for the whole family, is not proof that such a situation *did not exist*. If this were all we had to go on, the case would remain open. But there does seem to be fairly strong evidence implicit in the very documents that we have been discussing which proves the opposite case.

[59]For example, *ibid.*, p. 203.
[60]Ibid., p. 214.
[61]Titow, *Rural Society*, p. 24.

One strong set of evidence concerns the frequent land sales which *did* occur, which will later be documented. Even in the thirteenth century, family land was coming onto the market, not just where there were no heirs. Summarizing the evidence for Suffolk manors in the later thirteenth century, Richard Smith, for example, concludes that:

> Patterns exhibited by certain individuals suggest that any notion of the sanctity of the family holding must be viewed with a good deal of scepticism. Although these parents had children to provide for, they engaged in heavy land selling in the years immediately before their death . . . .[62]

Such sales were not merely to outsiders, but even to the supposed joint owners or heirs themselves. Thus 'Reginald sold what would appear to have been a quarter of his holding to his sons in 1276, fifteen years before his death . . . .'[63] This raises an even more fundamental point. In the 'classical' peasant family, all the members of the family are joint-owners; in the west European type, one child is a joint-holder with his father. It cannot, in fact, be said that the father is the owner; the children or child are co-owners when they are born. But in England 'ownership' or 'seisin' lay in the individual. The only person who might share this automatically with a man or a woman (since either could hold the right), was the spouse. This fact was recognized in the custom wide-spread on most manors, of requiring a widow who had held jointly with her husband, at his death to pay a heriot, but not an entry fine. The land was not surrendered to the lord and taken up by a 'new' tenant — the wife had held it jointly, and *vice versa*. But when a son succeeded his father, the form of the transfer in the court roll, where it had to be registered, was in form *exactly* like the transfer to a stranger, and an entry fine was paid. The rights being transferred can be illustrated in this way:

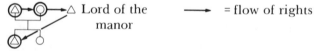

The son came into court and asked to be admitted to a *new* right. That he was not already joint owner with his father, as he would have been in a classical peasantry, is shown by the purchase of such a right from a father during his lifetime. This is an inconceivable situation in traditional India or Russia, where such 'rights' were not for sale. It is also shown in the very frequent instances where a father and son came into court during the father's lifetime and took up a 'joint tenancy,' with reversion to the son after the father's death. Instances of such a procedure are cited by Homans, and he comments that they look rather

[62]Smith, *Life-cycles*, p. 131.
[63]Ibid., p. 130.

'silly' at first sight.[64] In the case he cites, a father surrenders his land to the use of his son John, who is given seisin. The son then grants the land back to his father for life. But Homans points out that it is not so 'absurd,' since 'by a settlement of this sort, the permanent rights in the land were transferred to the son . . . After his father died, the tenement would revert to him and to his heirs.' Homans does not explain why this should be necessary if, as he has argued, such land was inalienable and went to the son and his heirs in any case. Nevertheless, this and many other cases show that with customary land, as with freehold in the period, the heir 'acquires nothing by the gift made to his ancestors since he was not enfeoffed with the donee.'[65] Carried to its extreme conclusion, the child has no automatic right or seisin in his parents' property — it has to be formally transferred to him. He may be able to uphold his right against his peers, but since he has no automatic seisin, he cannot prevent his father from alienating the holding. It could as well be said of customary land in this period, as it could of freehold, that 'All those safeguards of the family which occur on the continent — the community, the inalienable family reserve, the *restrait lignager* and similar institutions, are conspicuously absent,' a view shared by Maitland.[66]

The most likely exception to the idea of individual ownership or seisin would appear to be the case of areas of partible inheritance, where several sons seem to work the holding together. Hallam has shown that in part of thirteenth century East Anglia there are groups of persons called '*heredes*,' '*socii*,' '*parcenarii*' who seem to hold land in common; thus in 1287, almost fourteen per cent of tenants held land in common; in all, nearly a quarter of the five- to 30-acre holdings described in the Spalding documents were held in common.[67] It would be a mistake to infer that even here we have an abeyance of the principle of individual rights; the holdings were jointly held like this until it was desired that there should be a separation, but there were clearly highly individualized rights even when there was commonality. The situation appears to have been equivalent to the sixteenth century custom, for example in some Essex manors, whereby daughters were co-heirs or co-parceners. For a while they would hold as a group, but later the holding would be divided between them. This may have been a life-cycle phase; for a few years after the death of the father the holding was not broken up between co-heirs. But is was clearly possible to do so. There was no necessary and permanent joint ownership, and, although they might be

[64]Homans, *Villagers*, p. 129.
[65]Bracton, *Laws*, p. 66.
[66]Plucknett, *Common Law*, p. 744; Maitland, *English Law*, ii, pp. 308-9.
[67]H. E. Hallam, 'Some Thirteenth-Century Censuses,' *Ec.H.R.*, 2nd ser., x, no. 3 (April, 1958), p. 345.

masked for a while, the individual rights of the heir could be invoked at any time. This possibility is well illustrated in the Suffolk manors studied by Richard Smith; he shows in a number of detailed case studies that 'there was a marked tendency for one of the brothers to emerge as the dominant member of the group because of the others selling all or part of their inheritance to him . . . .'[68] In addition, Barbara Dodwell shows in her study of inheritance in East Anglia that land *might* be held conjointly as *unus heres*, but 'it would be wrong to assume that physical partition was rare.'[69] She further points out that although land *appeared* to be held jointly by brothers, 'It is curious . . . that we so often hear of sons inheriting their father's tenement as though his were a separate holding.' The separate pieces were bought and sold; there was no indissoluble joint estate which could not be alienated to outsiders and had to remain within the family.

The real problem is that court rolls are extremely deceptive and what may appear to be joint is in fact individual tenure. Another example of this occurs in the early fifteenth century manor court rolls of Earls Colne, where there are frequent cases of several named individuals being admitted to a tenement jointly. Thus in 1409 we find the following:

To this court came Richard Meller and surrenders into the ladies hands one cottage with appurtenances sometime Richard Mason's and since Firmyn Shrophams to the use of William Mersale, Robert Kyrton and Thomas Kelet to whom the lady granted thereof seisin to hold to the same William Robert and Thomas and their heirs of the lady to the will of the lady by all ancient services and they give for fine 5s. for such estate thereof to be had and made fealty.

At first sight this looks like some larger, joint, holding. But detailed examination of the court rolls allows one to see from the subsequent history of the particular holding that when the first-mentioned person dies, the other surviving persons come to the court and surrender it to the heirs of the first-mentioned. They are acting as administrators and are later termed 'feoffees' in the court rolls. Later the phrasing is also altered so that the transfer is to A, B and C, 'to the use of A.' Thus this is clearly an individual holding after all.

The fact that 'parceners' or co-parceners had highly individual and separable rights is stated by Bracton. He envisaged two situations where something like a 'joint' estate would exist for a time. Such an estate was formed when daughters all inherited equally and together and when the item, for example a fish pond, could not easily be split between the

[68] Smith, *Life-cycle*, p. 148.
[69] B. Dodwell, 'Holdings and Inheritance in Medieval East Anglia.' *Ec. Hist. Rev.*, 2nd ser., xx, no. 1 (April, 1967), p. 60.

heirs. In the former case, which was equivalent to partible inheritance in customary tenures, he recognized that there was no permanent community of property. In cases where 'there may be several to whom the right descends as to a single heir, because of the unitary nature of the right, as the several daughters of the father or mother . . .' then 'the inheritance, in everything that admits of division, must be divided in equal portions.'[70] This should be done as soon as possible: 'let a division (or) partition of the inheritance be made among them immediately after homage has been taken.'[71] He laid out rules as to how such a division should take place, and how to deal with pieces of property which were not easily divisible.

This lengthy excursus on the relations between the family and the land is necessarily tentative. None of the evidence I have seen, however, gives me an impression that the *de jure* or *de facto* situation with customary land was markedly different from the two areas where we have much more evidence — namely customary land after the Black Death, and particularly in the sixteenth and seventeenth centuries, and freehold land from the thirteenth century onwards. A similar conclusion, but in different words and trying to make a contrary point, namely that parents could provide for their younger children, is made by Joan Thirsk. Her view supports the idea of the freedom of parents, for she writes that 'there were few manors in the Middle Ages, whatever the official manorial custom of inheritance, which did not allow customary tenants to create trusts on their death beds and so dispose of their land in any way they pleased, and at all times freeholders were entitled to dispose of their lands freely.'[72] The case needs further investigation, but it appears that historians of the period have been over-influenced by analogies with other 'peasant' societies and have imposed inappropriate models onto the evidence. If we are looking for a model which economically fits the shreds of evidence we have, it appears that one which would make England entirely different from the stereotype 'peasant' society even in the thirteenth century, is more attractive than that which is presented or accepted, with a few notable exceptions, by medieval historians.

It would therefore be argued that a crucial difference which was plain in eighteenth and nineteenth century Europe was already present in the thirteenth. Engels pointed out that English law alone allows complete freedom of disposal of property:

In those countries where a legitimate portion of parental wealth is assured to

[70]Bracton, *Laws*, p. 194.
[71]Ibid., p. 208.
[72]Joan Thirsk, 'The Common Fields,' reprinted in R. H. Hilton (ed.), *Peasants, Knights and Heretics; Studies in Medieval English Social History* (Cambridge, 1976), p. 19.

children and where they cannot be disinherited — in Germany, in countries with French law, etc. . . . In countries with English law . . . the parents have full liberty to bequeath their wealth to anyone and may disinherit their children at will . . .[73]

More recently, surveying European family systems, H. J. Habakkuk noted that concerning impartible inheritance, 'The best example . . . is provided by England, where the owner has complete freedom to will his property as he pleased . . . ,' but he stresses that the

English case was exceptional; nowhere else in western Europe did the owner enjoy such freedom of testamentary disposition, and nowhere else were the younger children, in cases of intestacy, void of any claim on the family property; in other countries, the portion that a landowner could freely dispose of — the *quotité disponible* — was limited by law, and the children all had a claim to some share in the property.[74]

It is tempting to believe that this was a difference which emerged in the sixteenth and seventeenth centuries. The evidence that we have surveyed suggests that this view would be incorrect.

While it may be conceded that technically we are right so far, that there was no jural link between the family and land, it is likely to be assumed that there will still be a sentimental link. It is argued that, since in an agricultural society land is the basis of wealth and status, it is necessarily regarded as more than a mere commodity. Furthermore, since it is assumed that families did, in practice, stay on the same plot, it is assumed that familiarity bred affection and attachment. It is thought that thirteenth century villagers saw a certain landholding as belonging to a certain family, as the west coast Irish might put it, that it was 'so and so's *place*,' and as a corollary that it was strongly felt that the 'name should be kept on the land.'[75] This view is repeated by some medievalists. For example, Postan writes:

The high preference for land was, of course, part and parcel of the mode of life and of the scale of values characteristic of peasants of most ages and most countries . . . To him land was not only a 'factor of production' . . . but also a 'good' worth possessing for its own sake and enjoyed as a measure of social

[73]F. Engels, *The Origins of the Family, Private Property and the State* (Chicago, 1902), trans. E. Untermann, p. 88.
[74]H. J. Habakkuk, 'Family Structure and Economic Change in Nineteenth Century Europe' reprinted in Norman W. Bell and Ezra F. Vogel (eds.), *A Modern Introduction to the Family* (New York, 1960), pp. 140-1.
[75]I am grateful to Tom Gabriel of Reading University for the information concerning Ireland, taken from his thesis on County Mayo.

status, a foundation of family fortunes and a fulfilment and extension of the owner's personality.[76]

Or, even more recently, Howell writes of 'the strong feeling that land should remain within the village community,' combined 'with the even stronger feeling that land should not be alienated from the family.'[77] Likewise, Hilton has written of the 'deep sense of hereditary family right,' and assumed this sentiment of attachment.[78] The argument appears compelling. The first premise is that land is the basis of wealth: 'I take it as axiomatic that for the peasantry of medieval England land was the main basis of wealth.'[79] What is important economically must also be important emotionally.

Yet the situation is more complex than this. In the first place, although land may ultimately be the source of wealth, as in other agricultural societies, it would appear that there was a high degree of occupational specialization. The proliferation of cottage industries and by-employments, a developed bureaucracy, religious hierarchy and the State, as well as the fact that probably over half the adult male inhabitants of England in the thirteenth century, as we shall see, owned no land, but were servants or labourers, meant that there was already a thick screen of legal, political and social institutions between the land and the people.[80] DeWindt puts this mildly when he states, 'It is clear that susbsistence in Holywell prior to the Black Death did not depend exclusively, therefore, on land, nor for that matter did prosperity. . . .'[81] It is arguable that the presence of cash, towns and markets, trade and the other factors mentioned above already separated England in the thirteenth century from other rural societies. England may have been rural and ultimately dependent on agriculture, but strangely it was almost certainly not a subsistence society where land and its ownership was the only means of wealth. Since 'sentiment' is so difficult to prove or disprove, we have to approach the problem indirectly. One method is through the actual pattern of land ownership. When there is a close

---

[76]Postan, *Medieval*, p. 151. It should, in fairness, be pointed out that Postan is not primarily referring to a sentiment of attachment to a specific ancestral holding, but to 'land' in general. There are, however, very few real peasant societies, if any, where this exists alone, without being accompanied by strong attachments to particular holdings held by a family. The one implies the other and if the latter feature is absent it already suggests that England was different from other peasantries. An abstract love of 'land' in general, for its social as well as its economic benefits, is not of course restricted to 'peasant' societies being present, for example, in nineteenth century English gentry families.
[77]Howell, *Peasant Inheritance*, p. 137; see also p. 139.
[78]Hilton, *Bond Men*, p. 39.
[79]Titow, *Rural Society*, p. 91.
[80]It is widely recognized, for example, that England had at this time the most centralized and bureaucratically organized government of any nation in Europe.
[81]DeWindt, *Land*. p. 202.

emotional bond, families will sell land only in the direst of circumstances and with the general consent of the family. We have seen that the latter permission was unnecessary. If the former had been the case, a land market should be absent, except in extraordinary instances. The same piece of land should be attached to one family for generations, and descend from father to sons or son. We may look at the evidence so far brought forward by the medievalists who have worked on the thirteenth century. Do they show a picture diametrically opposed to the busy land market and alienation of holdings from a family already discovered in the later fourteenth century?

Evidence for a considerable mobility of land was produced as early as 1923 in some articles by Hudson, on the basis of evidence from a Norfolk manor in the late thirteenth and early fourteenth centuries. He was surprised at the very large number of transfers on this manor, on average forty-seven a year, and noted that of the total, only seventy-four were transferred by 'death and inheritance,' while 443 were for 'private convenience.'[82] He concluded that 'more than half the whole number of surrenders were apparently the result of private convenience, and illustrate the entire freedom of the tenants, villein or other, to exchange their lands as they wished. The lord could not stop them, provided they fulfilled the dues laid on that particular land.' Some years later, Homans also noted the extensive land market. For instance, in Hertfordshire the records showed that 'sales and other alienations of small amounts of land were already being made in large numbers in the first half of the thirteenth century.'[83] He argued, however, that the traffic in land was probably more developed in south-eastern England than in the Midlands, a view that had been repeated by a recent writer.[84] Kosminsky noted that the alienation of freeholdings, which we will remember constituted about one third of 'peasant land,' was both frequent and easy.[85]

The discussion took on a new depth with the accidental discovery of a volume of 'peasant land charters' which illustrated a busy land market in the East Midlands in the later twelfth and thirteenth centuries. Postan was naturally surprised to find such an active land market, since it conflicted with the predictions of the peasant model: 'an active market in peasant property . . . belies more than one assumption commonly made about the English village in the twelfth and thirteenth

[82]Rev. W. Hudson, 'Manorial Life; Manorial Courts,' *The History Teachers Miscellany*, i, no. 12 (October, 1923), pp. 181-2.
[83]Homans, *Villagers*, p. 204.
[84]Ibid., p. 204; Hyams, 'Origins of Peasant Land Market,' p. 25.
[85]Kosminsky, *Studies*, pp. 224-5. Recently, Barbara Harvey has written that 'by the end of the thirteenth century, freeholders were practised buyers and sellers of land . . . .' *Westminster Abbey and its Estates in the Middle Ages* (Oxford, 1977), pp. 300-1.

centuries.'[86] Although court roll evidence, which only survives in any
quantity from the middle of the thirteenth century,[87] had prevented us
from going back before then, Postan argues that we can now speculate
further, as follows. 'At the end of the twelfth and in the early thirteenth
centuries land was frequently bought, sold, and leased by villeins
without any recorded licence from the lord,[88] and therefore we have
little record of the size of the market. Yet

What with the deductions from backward-looking entries in thirteenth-century
judicial records and the evidence of under-tenants and that of subdivision of
customary lands and the free appendages to villein holdings, the presumption
of an active village land market in the twelfth and thirteenth centuries is well
supported.[89]

He therefore warns us against the tendency to assume that there was too
great a contrast between the thirteenth century and the fifteenth century
in terms of a land market.[90] Postan's discussion has been complemented
and further refined by subsequent research.

   On the supporting side, there is growing evidence of the frequency of
sales and transfers and also of the equally important fact that many of
these took the land away from the family line. On the basis of thirteenth
century evidence from Taunton manors, Titow concludes that 'the
practical result (of frequent re-marriage) was that family holdings had a
way of wandering about, and the notion of a family holding passing
down from father to son, from generation to generation, belongs to the
same brand of fiction as that of the typical manor.'[91] Barbara Dodwell,
on the basis of a study of inheritance in East Anglia in the thirteenth
century, concluded that as long as villeins 'obeyed the rules,' namely
came to court and paid a fine, they were 'perfectly able to dispose of all
or a portion of their tenements.' Consequently, in the second half of the
thirteenth century, 'there were innumerable licenses to alienate.'[92]
Raftis gives cases of sub-letting, short-term leases and frequent sales in
the thirteenth and fourteenth centuries, and a considerable land market
in freehold properties.[93] In a more recent study, of Warboys in Hunting-

---

[86]Postan, *Essays*, p. 110.
[87]Manor court rolls and other manorial documents suddenly begin to survive in relative
abundance from the last ten years of Henry III (1266). Before 1250 there is very little direct
evidence on this question.
[88]Postan, *Essays*, p. 123.
[89]Ibid., p. 122.
[90]Ibid., p. 132.
[91]J. Z. Titow, 'Some Differences Between Manors and their Effects on the Condition of the
Peasant in the Thirteenth Century', reprinted in W. E. Minchinton (ed.), *Essays in
Agrarian History* (British Agricultural History Society, Newton Abbot, 1968), i, p. 39.
[92]Dodwell, 'Holdings and Inheritance', p. 63.
[93]Raftis, *Tenure*, pp. 74-83.

donshire, he shows that of thirty-one conveyances between 1288-1366, only eleven were known to be from parent to child, six were of unknown type, while fourteen were to non-kin.[94] There is a graphic picture of a very busy land market on Battle Abbey land in the thirteenth century,[95] and Rodney Hilton has concluded on the basis of work by Kosminsky, as follows:[96]

E. A. Kosminsky emphasized the undoubted fact that in the thirteenth century when the market for land — stimulated by the market for agricultural produce — was very brisk, holdings tended to be broken up. One would find the messuage place of a holding, that is the site of the central homestead, being sold separately from the arable land, just as the crofts and curtilages normally attached to the messuage would be detached and sold off. And many were the cases of dealings in acres, half-acres, even quarter acres, in the common fields. In such circumstances, continuous possession of a holding by the same family over many generations would be exceptional in practice . . . .

Further evidence is given in a detailed study of Holywell-cum-Needleworth. While conceding that the parcels of land were often small, DeWindt states that the pieces turned over so quickly that it 'raises the suspicion that the land market may have been utilized less for creating permanent additions to total acreage than to meet immediate and temporary needs or for quick gain.'[97] Faith also cites figures which indicate a similar situation. In the thirteenth century on a St Alban's manor there is a 'brisk land market in odd acres and single messuages.' At Brightwaltham in Berkshire, only fifty-six per cent of the total number of transactions between 1280 and 1300 were within the family, while at Chilbolton, a Winchester manor, in the period 1267 to 1371, only twenty-nine out of seventy land fines were paid by tenants taking up family land, though it is true that the majority of the family transactions occurred in the earlier period.[98] Dyer cites figures from a thesis on the manors of Worcester Cathedral Priory that show that only thirty-two per cent of the land transfers in the early fourteenth century 'took place between relatives,' thus two thirds were between non-kin.[99] John Beckerman cites an inquest of 1291 at Horningtoft, Norfolk, which stated that all the customary tenants had been accustomed to sell their

[94]Raftis, *Warboys*, pp. 157-8.
[95]Searle, *Lordship*, pp. 109, 185.
[96]Hilton, *Bond Men*, p. 39.
[97]DeWindt, *Land*, p. 54.
[98]Faith, *Peasant Families*, p. 88.
[99]Dyer, 'Peasant Families' citing a University of Birmingham M.A. thesis, 1964, by J. West.

lands and tenements, with the lord's leave, 'for time out of mind.'[100] A recent detailed study of an east Norfolk manor by Bruce Campbell gives further strong evidence of a busy land market. In the period 1275-1405 there were one thousand five hundred land transactions, which 'allowing for the incompleteness of the record, indicates a total turnover on this one small manor of perhaps 2,250 transactions and 1,150 acres of land ....'[101] Before the Black Death the market was crowded, large numbers of different individuals were selling land. The author stresses that 'one of the most remarkable features' of this period was the fact that 'peasants were remarkably ready to part with (land) and evinced remarkably little difficulty in buying it.'[102]

Richard Smith has made a detailed study of the land market in some Suffolk manors. At Rickinghill, 1259-1293, there were the amazing number of 519 exchanges of land by purchase. Although these were mainly small plots, the author calculates that about one third of the total land entered the market.[103] At Redgrave, of the 731 market transactions between 1259 and 1292, only 207, or less than one third, were of an intra-familial kind. As Richard Smith pointed out, the fact that there were so many sales *within* the family, particularly between brothers, is further evidence of the highly individualized and monetized system.[104] He concludes that 'the exceptionally active character of the land exchange system cannot be disputed.'[105] Furthermore, he gives detailed case studies to show how estates were built up. For example, taking the sons of one moderately wealthy villager, he found that 'Augustus had apparently acquired 90% of his holdings in the land market, and Nicholas 75% of his land by purchase outside the family ....'[106]

---

[100] J. S. Beckerman, 'Customary Law in English Manorial Courts in the Thirteenth and Fourteenth Centuries' (Univ. of London Ph.D. thesis, 1972), p. 141. I am grateful to Dr. Beckerman for permission to cite his work, and to Richard Smith for his notes on the thesis.

[101] Bruce M. S. Campbell, 'Population Pressure, Inheritance and the Land Market in a Fourteenth Century Peasant Community' in Smith, *Land, Kinship and Life Cycle*, ch. 1. I am grateful to Bruce Campbell for permission to quote from his as yet unpublished article.

[102] Campbell, 'Population Pressure'. In the later thirteenth century on the Glastonbury estates 'more than a third of the sitting tenants had acquired their holdings by various means of open and disguished purchase and sometimes over the heads of the legal heirs whose claims they usually bought out (Postan, *England*, p. 564).

[103] Smith, *Life-cycles*, pp. 59-60.

[104] In a personal communication. I am grateful to Dr Smith for putting a great deal of his unpublished material, as well as his knowledge of thirteenth century manorial economy and society, at my disposal. Some of his own ideas on the subject will appear in the introduction to the volume he is editing entitled *Land, Kinship and Life Cycle*, due out in 1978.

[105] Smith, *Life-cycles*, p. 64.

[106] Ibid., p. 130.

These life-histories of individual landowners are especially valuable in providing an insight into the cash and market economy of pre-Black Death villages. One from a very different area, the West Midlands, shows that there too the situation appears remarkably similar to what we find in the sixteenth century. Z. Razi describes what he calls a 'typical wealthy Halesowen peasant,' John Thedrich, as follows:

He inherited from his father a yardland holding or more yet in fourteen land transactions he purchased and leased at least another yardland. He leased for life a holding of half a yardland or more and another smaller holding for a year. He also leased three meadows for his livestock. In 1314 he acquired from the lord a plot of wasteland to enlarge his barn and in 1320 he bought a parcel of land from his neighbour to extend his courtyard. In 1320 and 1321 he exchanged land with four villagers in order to consolidate his lands in one block. He had sub-tenants and at least two living-in-servants. During the peak periods he used to employ several extra labourers. He and Agnes his wife were amerced forty-three times for selling ale against the assize . . . He sued seven villagers for various debts . . . He was amerced eight times for assault and shedding blood. John Thedrich had between 1294 and 1337 at least 196 court appearances and the fines and amercements which he paid during this time amounted to £2-10.3.[107]

This description has been quoted fully since it not only shows the frequent buying, selling, leasing, sub-letting and exchanging of land, which seems to indicate that it was treated as a commodity, but also because it illustrates the penetration of cash, production for the market and the use of hired labour which will be discussed in the next chapter. Razi's work, and the published court rolls of Halesowen do not suggest that this man was in any way exceptional.[108]

None of this conforms in the slightest to our expectations in relation to a peasant society. Some attempts have therefore been made to minimize or argue away the evidence. Faced with mounting proof of mobility and land sales, Rodney Hilton argues that the demographic situation of both the later thirteenth and later fourteenth centuries made them 'peculiar.'[109]

Another argument is that nearly all the evidence we have for an active land market comes from the south-east of England, and particularly from East Anglia. Paul Hyams argues that there is still no strong proof of a *general* English land market,[110] and that it is likely that

[107] Z. Razi, 'The Peasants of Halesowen 1270-1400: A Social Economic and Demographic Study' (Univ. of Birmingham Ph.D., 1976), p. 110. I am most grateful to Dr. Razi for permission to quote from his thesis.
[108] *Court Rolls of the Manor of Hales 1270-1307*, ed. John Amphlett (Worcestershire Hist. Soc., 1912), 2 vols.
[109] Hilton, *Bond Men*, p. 39.
[110] Hyams, 'Origins of a Peasant Land Market' p. 19 and *passim*.

In the early thirteenth century, central and western England probably lagged behind the eastern counties and Kent in the scale of peasant dealings in land. During the first quarter of the century, it is probably an exaggeration to talk of a peasant land market even there. In the second quarter the regional disparity may have decreased but was still noticeable.[111]

Postan has argued that this may prove to be more a function of the different character of the sources in the areas concerned, rather than a true reflection of the land market.[112] Only further research will answer the question of dating, though if it were to be conceded that a widespread land-market was present throughout most of England by the second quarter of the thirteenth century, even though there were 'noticeable' differences between the areas of partible and impartible inheritance, this would be sufficient for the case I am trying to make.

A final attempt to avoid the full implications is the argument put forward by Postan that this was not a 'true' land market, in that the main motivation was not economic, but demographic. Since the argument illustrates well the way an *a priori* model of peasantry and analogies from other societies are applied, we may cite the text rather fully. Postan writes that

On general grounds, i.e. those of mere common sense and of comparable experience in other peasant cultures, we must assume that in societies in which the family is the unit of ownership and exploitation, the needs and resources of individual families are too unequal and too unstable to allow family holdings to remain uniform or unaltered in use and size. Ideally the size of a family holding in peasant society is one which is large enough to fill the family's mouths and small enough to be worked with the family's hands. This ideal many families could approach; few could realize in full. In all peasant societies (certainly in Europe) there always have been holdings inadequate to the needs of large families or to the resources of rich ones, as well as holdings too large for the unaided labour of small, poor or aged holders.[113]

While conceding that the labour market could iron out some of the differences caused by demographic inequalities, Postan goes on to argue that the purchase and sale of lands was 'an equally obvious remedy.' He claims that the existence of these 'natural' sellers and buyers 'has not escaped the notice of historians' and proceeds to try to prove that most land sales were the result of such transactions.[114] Though partially committed to the notion of 'peasantry,' it appears that other medievalists are not prepared to accept this interpretation.

[111] Ibid., p. 25.
[112] Postan, *Essays*, pp. 134, 145.
[113] Ibid., pp. 114-5.
[114] Ibid., pp. 115-7.

The logical fallacies are exposed by Paul Hyams, who points out that such an argument should mean that a land market exists to a similar extent in all agricultural societies — which it clearly does not.[115] Hyams also refers to the fact that even Homans, an investigator committed to sociological explanations, preferred an economic interpretation.[116]

Other arguments are deployed, some of them drawing on the work of Kosminsky, who also eschewed a demographic explanation. The most detailed analysis is again undertaken by Richard Smith, who, after considering the two explanations, finds that his evidence fits much better with the economic interpretation of Kosminsky and Hyams than that of Postan.[117] It does not appear that there was an 'equilibrium' where family size and landholding were kept balanced through sales and purchases. Another recent detailed analysis of medieval court rolls has also challenged Postan's views.[118] Razi shows that at least one of only two examples which Postan gives for his view that there was 'equilibrium' through the 'poor' buying land, is a misinterpretation: detailed work on the background of the case shows that the people who bought Edith Blanche's land, three out of five of whom were identifiable, were not members of the 'labouring classes' but 'members of solid peasant families.'[119]

In sum, the motives for, and the frequency of, the transfer of land do not resemble the situation in Eastern Europe, traditional India or China, or even parts of the Continent in the fourteenth century, where a land market was virtually absent. The movement of families through space and time, and the purchase and sale of land give little hint of the results of any sentimental attachment to land at this period.

The nature of the unit of ownership is central to the argument. If we are right in the alternative hypothesis suggested here, we should find that individual ownership was associated with many other features which do not fit the predictions of a 'peasant' model. On the other hand, if there really was a peasantry, we should expect to find evidence for it in numerous other areas, for instance the patterns of geographical and social mobility, the absence of hired labour and the presence of complex households. We may now turn to these other features in the thirteenth to fifteenth centuries in order to test the arguments we have been pursuing.

[115]Hyams, 'Origins of a Peasant Land Market,' pp. 19-20.
[116]Ibid., p. 19, note 1.
[117]Smith, *Life-cycles*, p. 69.
[118]Razi, 'Peasants of Halesowen,' pp. 122ff.
[119]Postan, *Essays*, p. 117; Razi, 'Peasants of Halesowen,' p. 122.

6
English Economy and Society in the Thirteenth to Fifteenth Centuries

The previous chapter has traced arguments claiming that to identify the unit of ownership in a peasant society, we must look to the family group, not the individual. Yet it appears on the surface often as if the 'owner' is the eldest male, since he usually takes the lead in decision-making, and if land has to be registered, it is registered in his name. Furthermore, ownership of land normally remains with the community of males; women when they marry out may take a dowry of moveables, but land normally stays with the men. A girl who marries in, is absorbed into a landholding corporation. The idea of a woman's separate property in real estate thus comes up against a double objection — against individual property rights as such, and against the inferior position of women. The idea that she can make a will or sell such property, that after her husband's death the property passes into her private hands, that she can enter into contracts on her own account, all these are unthinkable in a peasant society. Characteristically the *de jure* position of women is low in a peasant society; she is the appendage of the men of the group; her life and honour depend upon them. We would expect to find a similar situation in medieval England if it had been a peasant society.

The property rights and status of women, single, married and widowed, is a complex but central issue which I hope to take up at length elsewhere. All that I can do here is to state that both seem to have been very extensively developed even by the start of the thirteenth century. At first sight the general consensus of historical work would appear to go against this assertion. If we restrict ourselves to the case of unmarried women we know that in most peasant societies they remain under the authority of their parents until marriage, and then pass into the control of their husbands and later, as widows, into that of their own sons. They have no separate rights as distinct from the group. It is therefore no surprise when Eileen Power writes of the upper class that 'in feudal society there was no place for a woman who did not marry and marry young.'[1]

G. G. Coulton invokes the strong authority of Maitland to support his view that the 'old maid' was 'as unusual a phenomenon in the Middle Ages as in modern upper-class French society, quoting Maitland's words as follows:

It is hardly too much to say that the early Medieval law never seems to have contemplated the existence of an unmarried woman of full age . . . Her position is never the subject of statute law, as is that of widows; hence it seems probable that among the higher classes, the independent 'femme sole' was, outside the convent, a negligible quantity.[2]

This quotation clearly implied that an unmarried woman of full age had little, if any, legal freedom and little independent status. Such a view from a historian of Maitland's stature is indeed a powerful support to one of the correlated institutions of peasantry. But when we turn to the page Coulton cites as the origin of the quotation from Maitland we are in for a shock. Not only is the whole quotation missing from this page and nowhere to be found in the rest of Maitland's *History of English Law*, but the page to which we are referred contains a passage which is totally contrary to the supposed passage. What Maitland in fact wrote was

After the Norman Conquest the woman of full age who has no husband is in England a fully competent person for all the purposes of private law; she sues and is sued, makes feoffments, seals bonds, and all without any guardian . . .

In fact, Maitland's whole passage on the legal position of unmarried women fits very badly indeed with the predictions of the peasant model. While public law 'gives a woman no right and exacts from her no duties' (that is to say, she can hold no public office), as regards private rights) 'private law with few exceptions puts women on a par with men.'[3] The legal position of women in general is excellently summarized by Maitland:

in Bracton's day . . . Women are now 'in' all private law, and are the equals of men. The law of inheritance, it is true, shows a preference for males over females; but not a very strong preference, for a daughter will exclude a brother of the dead man, and the law of wardship and marriage, though it makes some difference between the male and the female ward, is almost equally severe for

[1]Eileen Power, 'The Position of Women' in G. C. Crump and E. F. Jacobs (eds.), *The Legacy of the Middle Ages* (Oxford, 1926), p. 413.
[2]G. G. Coulton, *Medieval Panorama* (1938; Fontana edn., 1961), ii, p. 281.
[3]Maitland, *English Law*, i, p. 482.

both. But the woman can hold land, even by military tenure, can own chattels, make a will, make a contract, can sue and be sued. She sues and is sued in person without the interposition of a guardian; she can plead with her own voice if she pleases; indeed — and this is a strong case — a married woman will sometimes appear as her husband's attorney. A widow will often be the guardian of her own children; a lady will often be the guardian of the children of her tenants.[4]

Maitland is therefore able to conclude that 'As regards private rights, women are on the same level as men, though postponed in the canons of inheritance.'[5] There is no talk in his discussion of parental domination, of *patria potestas*, of inferior status, of women's position being dependent on marriage, of lack of property or power. The unmarried woman is equal to a man, owning property in her own name, inheriting estates. Thus a woman who is *sui juris*, is of age and neither single nor widowed, 'can make a will, just as any other person may and dispose of her property';[6] 'Land may be given, before marriage or after . . . to the wife alone and her heirs . . . .'[7]

Detailed studies support this picture of legal independence. We are told that manorial records show 'a substantial number of women tenants of full customary holdings.'[8] Eileen Power remarks that 'A glance at any manorial "extent" will show women villeins and cotters living upon their little holdings and rendering the same service as men; some of these are widows but many of them are obviously unmarried.'[9] Women harvest workers were at times paid at the same rate as men in the fifteenth century according to Thorold Rogers,[10] while 'female reapers and binders at Minchinghampton, Gloucestershire, in 1380 certainly got the same rates, 4d. a day, as the men.'[11] Manorial litigation 'occasionally reveals them as village money-lenders' and we are told that a

considerable body of pleadings in the manorial courts on such matters as debt and trespass seems to have been conducted by women in their own names and only rarely through attorneys. Payments for the relaxation of suit to the manorial court were made by women as well as by male tenants, which suggests, of course, that they were liable as suitors.[12]

---

[4]*Idem*; an example of women excluding men is given by Bracton, *Laws*, p. 190.
[5]Maitland, *English Law*, i, p. 485.
[6]Bracton, *Laws*, p. 178.
[7]Ibid., p. 79.
[8]Hilton, *Peasantry*, p. 98.
[9]Power, 'Position of women,' p. 411.
[10]Rogers, *Six Centuries*, p. 77.
[11]Hilton, *Peasantry*, pp. 102-3.
[12]Ibid., pp. 103, 105.

Hilton concludes that the 'structure of peasant society in England at the turn of the fourteenth century seems to have been such that women as tenants, labourers and entrepreneurs had recognised rights within their communities.'[13] If we turn to another recent study, we find that in the town and manor of Battle in Sussex, the position of women, as described by Eleanor Searle, was as follows:

nothing is more striking in the town's records than the independence and activity of its women. During the C13 and C14, partible inheritance rather than Borough English applied to females. Women could inherit as freely if they were distant blood-heirs as if they were daughters of a deceased burgess. When a woman inherited, she herself took the oath of fidelity to the abbot (if unmarried) . . . in thirteenth century Battle women could, and did, remain unmarried land-holders, buying and selling lands and rent charges as freely and often with no less rigour than men. In the rental of 1240 thirty-six women are listed as burgesses.[14]

Furthermore, in the thirteenth century, women came into the court with their complaints, 'articulate and alone.'[15] The general position is fully supported by further documentation concerning ordinary women collected by Eileen Power in chapter three of her recently published *Medieval Woman*.[16]

　This picture does not fit the idea of peasantry at all well, and this is recognized by medievalists, who are either puzzled or again try to argue it away. Raftis is clearly dismayed when he finds that a large number of widows left with estates did not remarry.[17] Since he assumes that the household was the basic unit of production, and since the husband is dead, he is unable to see how they could work their holding without family labour. When we come to discuss hired labour, we will see that this was perfectly easy since servants and day labourers could be hired when needed. Rodney Hilton provides very considerable document-tation for the high status and economic independence of women in the later fourteenth and early fifteenth centuries. Yet, since this does not fit the general model, he tries once again to limit the period of the phenomenon and then to argue it away as probably 'peculiar.' 'The situation I have described can be taken as true for peasant women only at a particular period in the history of English rural society. It would be

[13]Ibid., p. 106.
[14]Searle, *Lordship*, p. 118.
[15]Ibid., p. 395.
[16]Eileen Power, *Medieval Women* (Cambridge, 1975), edited posthumously by M. M. Postan.
[17]Raftis, *Tenure*, p. 40.

dangerous to extend it beyond the century after the Black Death . . . .'[18] While considering the possibility that the greater freedom of women was a relic from Anglo-Saxon England, he seems to favour an explanation which states 'that women benefited in the post-1350 period from the same demographic and economic conditions which permitted a temporary improvement in the conditions of all peasant tenants and all labouring men.'[19] From Maitland's remarks and other evidence this appears very unlikely; if the century after the Black Death was 'peculiar,' so probably was the century before. But there is no 'peculiarity' if we realize that this was not, in fact, a peasant society at all.

When discussing women's status we have continued to concentrate on the question of ownership. We may now turn to the other side of the question, the unit of production and consumption. In the model peasant society, this unit is again the household. This houshold is characteristically composed of more than the 'nuclear' or 'elementary' family of parents and children, but with a minimal group of those who are co-owners. Wherever there are peasant societies, there is always an ideal of an 'extended' household, and usually a phase in the life-cycle when more than one married couple live together in the same house and 'share the same pot.' Such complex and multiple households tend to break up as brothers decide to separate into their own dwellings, though the unit continues to produce together and share the results of its labour.

Thus we find in India or Russia that the ideal, and for many people at one stage of life, the actuality, of brothers, their wives and children, and their ageing parents living together. In the intermediate form of peasantry of the Irish/French type, parents and one married son will live together as one household for a while. Given this feature, those who argue for a medieval peasantry naturally expect to find complex multigenerational households in thirteenth century England, acting as the basic unit of production and consumption. In areas with impartible inheritance they would approximate to the southern European 'stem' family, and where all sons inherited, one would expect to find laterally extended joint households, with several married brothers and their parents living together. If multi-generational households could be found, this would be strong evidence for the existence of 'peasantry.' If

---

[18]Hilton, *Peasantry*, p. 108.
[19]Ibid., p. 109. Richard Smith informs me that his detailed work on Suffolk court rolls in the second half of the thirteenth century shows women just as active and important as they are in the description of the later fourteenth century by Hilton.

they were absent, it is still possible that while residentially separate, members of the family worked together and consumed together. But in this case England would already be clearly different from all other peasant societies we know.

The two leading proponents of the view that medieval households contained more than one married couple are Homans and Hilton, whose views have been accepted by others, for example Krause.[20] Hilton has repeated his view on several occasions. He writes that 'By the thirteenth century . . . we often find grandparents, the married eldest son and heir, with his wife and children, together with the unmarried members of the second generation.'[21] A few years later, it is again stated that by the twelfth and thirteenth centuries '. . . when documentation becomes abundant, each household at the most seems to have contained grandparents, one married pair of the next generation, their children, perhaps an unmarried uncle and/or aunt and sometimes a living-in servant or two depending on the wealth of the group. This would be the composition of the household at the period of its fullest extension.'[22] This view was repeated elsewhere where, despite the use of the word 'could,' it is clearly implied that the household followed the multi-generational 'stem' model in many cases.[23] The most curious feature of this argument is that hardly any evidence is produced in support of it. Two maintenance agreements are quoted, but that is all.[24] It is notoriously difficult to be certain about household size and structure before the sixteenth century, but it is possible that it was felt unnecessary to document the case more fully since it appeared to have been made so effectively by the sociologist Homans. We may therefore turn to his work.

Homans' central thesis is well-known. Basing himself on the models of the French sociologist LePlay, he concluded that, in general, in the champion area of central England, primogeniture would be strong,

[20]J. Krause, 'The Medieval Household: Large or Small?' *Ec. H.R.* ix, no. 3 (1957), p. 421. Although questioning a good deal of Homans' thesis, one of the latest discussions of the question still accepts that extended households were fairly common in the fourteenth century, Edward Britton, 'The Peasant Family in Fourteenth-Century England', *Peasant Studies*, v, no. 2 (April, 1976) p. 5.
[21]Hilton, *Bond Men*, p. 27.
[22]Rodney Hilton, 'Medieval Peasants: Any Lessons?' *Jnl. of Peasant Studies*, i, no. 2 (Jan., 1974), p. 209.
[23]Hilton, *Peasantry*, pp. 28-9.
[24]Even these two agreements are ambiguous. Neither relates to an unequivocal parent-child arrangement. In one the kinship relationship is not stated. In the other a man surrendered the holding to his heir, who then surrendered it to a man with a different name who guaranteed a room and certain provisions to the original holder. (*Peasantry*, p. 30).

only one son would remain to marry on the family holding, and we would therefore find a 'stem' family structure, of the type found in early twentieth century western Ireland, with parents living with one married son. In the woodland area, with early enclosures and partible inheritance, all the sons would remain and marry. One would find some kind of joint-family, more closely approximating the Russian or Indian experience, with parents and several married sons all living for a while together. They might later agree to live apart, though they would still continue to farm a communal holding.[25] Homans himself concentrates on the champion areas, and does not try to prove the case in relation to the joint household of the partible areas. Since he did not have access to censuses or listings of inhabitants, he was forced to deduce household structure indirectly.

His proof, when examined closely, is very slender, and consists of two arguments. The first is by analogy. Since we know these were peasants and therefore like other peasants, we may assume that their household structure was like that of other peasant societies. Thus he draws on analogies with rural Ireland to show how retirement was organized.[26] Such circular reasoning proves nothing. The second argument derives from manorial records, particularly the transfer of holdings to married children and maintenance agreements for the old. The former proves, says Homans, that sons did marry before their parents' death. But since, he argues, they could not marry before the tenement had been handed over to them, they were naturally encumbered with their aged parents, whom, it is reasonable to assume, lived with them. That they actually did live with the previous generation after marrying appears to be proved by some maintenance contracts, as well as legal cases concerning maintenance.[27] These set out in minute detail which parts of the house the old are to have. They seem to be produced by a 'stem family' system. Since there is no indication as to whether they were ever put into effect, it is really impossible to prove or disprove the thesis directly from such documents. Fortunately, however, the practice of making maintenance contracts, and of sons marrying before their parents' death, did not end in the thirteenth century. We find the same situation occurring in the sixteenth and seventeenth centuries. Those who have used wills and manorial documents have therefore come to the same conclusion that

---

[25]Homans, *Villagers*, book 2 *passim* and especially p. 119.
[26]Ibid., p. 157.
[27]Ibid., pp. 145-7, 152-3. Richard Smith has kindly reminded me that the demographic conditions of the time would considerably lessen the likelihood of co-residence, even if it had been desired.

Homans did, and have argued that there must have been multi-generational stem households in the later period.[28] Yet for this later period there exist a large number of listings, which have conclusively shown that the mean size of the household was very small, about 4.75, and that multi-generational households, for example of the stem-type, were very infrequent. Less than six per cent of the households in the sample one hundred English listings 1574-1821 contained more than two generations. Nor has a single example of co-resident married siblings been found.[29] This is not merely a distortion, as Berkner suggests, caused by the nature of the listings.[30] It really does seem to have been very unusual for a married child or children to have lived with their parents. There seems to be a flat contradiction between two sources.

I have discussed this in the context of a particular case where one has both maintenance agreements, wills and a listing, and it appears clear that the wills and manorial documents cannot be interpreted at their face value.[31] One explanation is that though a son may be specified as inheriting part of the land and marrying, he may still live separately until his parents die. Secondly, it seems that the maintenance contracts laid down a *possible* settlement, but that very frequently it was not put into effect. This interpretation seems to receive support from Richard Smith's recent finding, from analysis of the largest collection of medieval maintenance contracts ever assembled, that three-quarters of them contained clauses which suggest separate residence and quasi-independent economic behaviour of the two generations.[32] Others state that if the two married couples (or a surviving single grandparent) could not live amicably together then they should live apart. Other agreements imply separate residence from the start, without one individual's troubling the other. It is possible that in the second category it was the contingency clause, rather than the main agreement, which was usually followed. Whatever the reasons, it now seems impossible to argue with any confidence that there were anything but nuclear households from the thirteenth century onwards.

The case will only be proven finally, one way or the other, on the basis

---

[28]For example, Spufford, *Communities*, pp. 114-5; Howell, *Peasant Inheritance*, p. 145.
[29]Laslett, *Household*, pp. 126, 150, 153 and ch. 4 *passim*.
[30]L. Berkner, 'The stem family and the developmental cycle of the peasant household: an eighteenth-century Austrian example,' *American Hist. Rev.*, lxxvii (1972).
[31]Macfarlane, *Reconstructing*, pp. 174-5.
[32]I am again grateful to Richard Smith for this information: as he has pointed out to me, such contracts are biased towards the upper echelons of the village landholders. What happened lower down we do not know.

of different evidence. Taxation documents, though coming from the later fourteenth century, form one type of evidence. It is interesting that a recent detailed examination of certain Poll Tax lists should lead Richard Smith to conclude that 'there seems to be good reason to suppose that the general shape and membership of the familial group differed very little from that of early modern England . . . .'[33] It is also to be hoped that some early listings of inhabitants will be found. Unfortunately, the only known listing, for Spalding in Lincolnshire in the twelfth century, is unusable for our purposes, since it is too full of ambiguities.[34]

Even if it could be shown that the residential unit was nuclear, it could still be argued that kinship was far more important in production and consumption than in a later period. The brothers might live at opposite ends of the street, but work as one productive and consuming unit — as is often the case in an Indian village. Again this question can only be approached indirectly. One index is the actual residential pattern of kin, and the number of interactions between them shown in manorial records. In our model peasant society, there is little geographical mobility and families are rooted in one place. After a period, villages are therefore filled with groups of people who are connected by kinship and marriage, sets of people with the same surname or linked through women. It was once believed that this was the case with medieval villages. But more detailed work on specific villages does not bear out this first supposition. Homans realized this, and he dwelt at some length on the fact that the system of primogeniture meant that younger brothers and daughters would move away from the village. Consequently no large clans or kindreds would form. As he remarks 'upon the whole there is little evidence that the inhabitants of an English village in the thirteenth century thought of themselves as a body of kinsmen.[35]

DeWindt's study of a manor near Huntingdon confirms this view. He remarks that 'there is very little indication of clans having formed in the village. Even among the most prolific families, the survival of more

---

[33]Richard Smith, 'The Poll Taxes of 1377 and 1381 and proportions married: A progress report on some current research' (unpublished paper presented to the S.S.R.C. Cambridge Group Conference on European Family Systems, 1976), p. 15. I am most grateful for permission to quote from this paper.

[34]H. E. Hallam, 'Some Thirteenth-Century Censuses,' *Ec.H.R.* 2nd ser., x. no. 3 (April, 1958), pp. 340-361. It is not certain why the lists were compiled and consequently we do not know who was included. It is not even certain that all those listed were alive at the time of compilation. Again I must thank Richard Smith for his advice on this matter.

[35]Homans, *Villagers*, p. 216.

than two continuous lines was seldom encountered . . . whatever the reason, the clan phenomenon was not characteristic of Holywell . . . .'[36] He also states that 'there is an emphasis in the society on the nuclear family — husband, wife and children — and an apparent de-emphasis on the broader kinship group — or extended family — in the absence of distinct clan activities and orientations,' which he finds surprising, since 'the stress on the nuclear family is not normally associated with the medieval experience.'[37] One example he gives of this absence of family co-operation is in the important pledging relationship, where one person would act as a surety for another. This could be a kinsman, but 'the bulk of Holywell's record pledgings from 1288 to 1339 was not confined within family lines but was rather between members of different families.'[38]

Again the most detailed examination of the matter is that by Richard Smith. In his Suffolk manors he found rather more intra-familistic contacts than were reported by DeWindt.[39] The frequency of contacts leads him to argue that on Redgrave manor 'the bulk of the rural population . . . had a social structure that was for the most part familistically organized.'[40] But this is qualified in various respects. Firstly, the intra-family contacts were much stronger in the middling families who constituted a minority of the population: 'both upper and lower quartile families were much less family-oriented than were middle quartile families.'[41] Secondly, the contacts were not between groups of kin, but between individuals; there is no evidence of any kind of clan or kindred. Indeed, the author is led to suggest that the ethics of the villagers in their family life appears to be very similar to that of mid-nineteenth century Preston as documented by Michael Anderson.[42] Finally a comparison of the situation in Suffolk with manors in Yorkshire, Worcestershire, Bedfordshire and Essex shows that intra-familial contacts, and hence the assumed concentration of kin, is up to

[36]DeWindt, *Land*, p. 246 note.
[37]Ibid., pp. 280-1.
[38]Ibid., p. 246.
[39]Richard Smith points out that DeWindt's very low level of intra-family contact can partly be explained by that author's inability to fully reconstitute families from incomplete manor court rolls (personal communication).
[40]Smith, *Life-cycles*, p. 217.
[41]Ibid., p. 386.
[42]Ibid., p. 397 note; Michael Anderson, *Family Structure in Nineteenth Century Lancashire* (Cambridge 1971). Anderson, of course, stresses the continued importance of kin ties, but they were based on what Anderson calls 'normative calculative instrumentalism' and it is to this feature that Smith draws an analogy.

four times as high in the partible, Suffolk, area as in impartible areas.[43]
Thus, while there was some concentration of kin in certain areas of
England, it was, on the whole, very far removed from the situation in
other 'peasant' societies.

There are other features of medieval society which suggest that the
family system was basically different from both the classical and
modified types of peasantry outlined above. We have already mentioned
the question of maintenance and provision for the old. The head of a
household in a peasant society is the organizer and leader of a co-
operative work group based on real or fictive kinship; though land may
be registered in his name, he does not own it exclusively, and just as a
child has rights in productive resources from birth, so an old person has
rights in it until his death. When strength and leadership fail,
effectively leadership is passed on to a child, but the old person can
expect automatically to have access to shelter and food and clothing for
his lifetime. There is sometimes an institutionalized area, such as the
famous 'west room' of Ireland, where the old go, but clearly it is theirs as
of right; it is not something for which they need to make a contract, a
legally binding condition, without which they can be turned out to
wander. We would therefore expect that if England were 'peasant' in the
thirteenth century that the old would gracefully retire, to be looked after
without question, as their children when young had to be looked after
out of a common fund. They had invested their lives' labour, and could
now draw their pensions automatically. This was one of the blessings of
having children, and one of the reasons so often given for encouraging
high fertility in peasant societies. And of course the old person sitting in
the inglenook is one of the central features of the old stereotype of the
medieval peasant.

It has already been suggested that, in practice, the old people did not
live with the young, that at marriage the families normally separated,
and that the 'west room' complex was probably very infrequent. What is
more extraordinary, and complements this, is the fact that it was felt
necessary to draw up a lengthy written contract or maintenance agreement if co-existence was contemplated. In return for surrendering their
individual and personal property rights to a child, the parents asked for
very specific rights in return. It is clear that without legal protection in a
written document they could have been ejected from a property which
was no longer their own. These maintenance agreements were then

[43]Smith, *Life-cycles*, p. 413. Richard Smith has further qualified his statement concerning
'familistic' organization by stating that this means 'only in the sense that the nuclear
family was the basic co-resident domestic group' (personal communication).

registered in the court roll. It is as if parent and child were strangers bargaining; Raftis comments that 'maintenance agreements could just as readily be made with in-laws or strangers' and the form was identical.[44] These documents abound, and Homans quotes several of them which show that the conditions were very exactly specified. In return for surrendering the property a couple in Bedfordshire in 1294 were promised, in return, food and drink and a dwelling in the main messuage, but if the two couples started to quarrel, then the old couple were to have another house and 'six quarters of hard corn at Michaelmas, namely three quarters of wheat, a quarter and a half of barley, a quarter and a half of beans and peas, and a quarter of oats' and all the goods and chattels, movable and immovable, of the said house.[45] In another agreement, a man who surrendered his right in Hertfordshire in 1332 was guaranteed by contract yearly so long as he lived, 'one new garment with a hood, worth 3s. 4d., two pairs of linen sheets, three pairs of new shoes, one pair of new hose, worth 12d., and victuals in food and drink decently as is proper.'[46] In this case the agreement was probably between unrelated persons, but it was no different in general form from a parent-child contract, except in later specifiying that the surrenderer would work for the new owner.[47]

Contemporaries seem to have been well aware that without legal guarantees, parents had no rights whatsoever. Homans quotes and summarizes the medieval poem *Handlyng Synne* by Robert Mannyng of Brunne, written in about 1303. A man gave all his house and land and animals to his son 'that he should keep him well in his old age.' The father did not, foolishly, obtain a witnessed and written contract. The young man married and had a son and 'began to think that his father was too heavy a burden' as Homans continues the story.[48] The son began to mistreat his father.

At last, when his father was shivering with cold, he bade his young son cover him with nothing more than a sack. The boy cut the sack in two, covered his grandfather with half of it, and showed his father the other half, to signify that just as his father had mistreated his grandfather, so the boy when his turn came

[44]Raftis, *Tenure*, p. 71.
[45]Homans, *Villagers*, pp. 144-5.
[46]Ibid., p. 146.
[47]Other examples of maintenance contracts are printed in Raftis, *Tenure*, pp. 44-5; Bennett, *Manor*, p. 254. References to a number of sixteenth and seventeenth-century agreements are listed in Keith Thomas, *Age and Authority in Early Modern England* (British Academy, 1976), p. 34, note 5.
[48]Homans, *Villagers*, p. 155. The story was repeated in the seventeenth century, see Thomas, *Age and Authority*, p. 36, where other instances are also given. The story of King Lear is, of course based on this motif.

would mistreat his father in his old age and cover him when he was cold with only half a sack.

The father could have taken the warning and obtained a written protection at law and indeed it is Mannyng's point in telling the story to warn people not to leave themselves defenceless and at the mercy of their children. A similar story was given as a sermon *exemplum* and is summarized by Rodney Hilton:[49]

a son and his wife take over the family holding. At first the grandfather is fully maintained at his son's board. After a time his rations and clothing are reduced; then he is made to eat with the children. Finally he us put into a "little house at the utmost gate." The old man is not defeated. He pretends to have a coffer full of coin and, playing on his son's hope to inherit, is restored to the house and to full board.

Both stories illustrate not only the extreme individualization of property rights but also the fact that parents had no customary *rights* to the wealth of their children, once the legal title had been passed over. This is again flatly contradictory to the idea of *family* ownership and to the whole model of peasantry. Both Homans and Hilton evade the implications of the agreements and the stories by remarking that 'Rough treatment of this sort cannot have been the common fate of fathers at the beginning of the fourteenth century . . . .'[50] or that 'arrangements in the manor court to safeguard their position illustrate what were their customary expectations, normally (one presumes) respected without a court order being necessary.'[51] The real point is that there were *no* enforceable customary expectations and just as a man would be a fool to hand over his house deeds to a stranger today and then expect to be supported for the rest of his life in lieu of rent, so thirteenth-century mothers and fathers could not depend on their children's good will. To find the essence of 'contract' in this central crucial parent-child relationship, rather than a relationship based on 'status,' is very extraordinary and in no way fits with any conceivable model of peasant society. It is also illustrated in the fact that when aged parents *did* live with their children they were often treated as, and termed, 'lodgers.' Examples of children charging their aged parents for bed and board in the fifteenth century occur in the Plumpton correspondence and parents as 'lodgers' in the seventeenth century are mentioned by Laslett

---

[49]Homans, *Peasantry*, p. 29.
[50]Homans, *Villagers*, p. 155.
[51]Hilton, *Peasantry*, p. 29.

and others.[52] The many law suits between parents and children in early records would make a further study possible.[53]

Thus, what we know about the treatment of the old suggests that there was already a highly developed and individualistic family system. Such a system would both be reflected in, and partly caused by, the method of tracing descent or blood relationships in such a society. When a classical or even attenuated peasant society exists, a neighbourhood tends to become filled with kin by blood and marriage. The multitude of relatives are related to the individual in specific ways and the concepts of descent and methods of tracing relationships provide a fit between the past and the present by explaining how the distribution of people and land came about. The links between people are mapped out and boundaries between different groups are suggested by the method of reckoning descent. It is characteristic of peasant societies that descent is traced from a common ancestor; all the descendants of a certain man are relatives. Such systems are known as 'ancestor-focused' descent systems.[54] That is to say, people project their minds to a relative some generations back and then work down to the present, in order to see who are their relatives. This is most easily achieved by tracing descent through only one sex, usually male, as in the 'agnatic' or 'patrilineal' systems which dominate classical peasant nations such as India or China. It is then possible to form people into discrete groups, known to anthropologists as 'unlineal descent groups' or lineages. But it is also possible to maintain an ancestor-focus and combine this with tracing descent from a common ancestor down through *both sexes*, as in a 'cognatic' system. This system has, for example, been documented for parts of traditional west-coast Ireland, as well as for much of Polynesia.[55] Both systems make it possible for an individual both to relate himself to, and dissociate himself from, his neighbours on the basis of kinship and to recruit help along these lines. It is this system which we would have expected to find if England had been a peasant society in the medieval period.

Expecting to find such a system, it is not surprising that the few medieval and other scholars who have speculated on the subject should

---

[52]*Plumpton Correspondence* (Camden Soc., 1839), ed. Thomas Stapleton, pp. xxvii, cxxiv; Laslett, *Household*, p. 35 note; Margaret Spufford in Goody, *Family* p. 174, mentions a case of 1649 when a man was living as a 'sojourner' with one of his sons.
[53]Cases occur in early court rolls and Chancery proceedings.
[54]There are clear general descriptions of such system in Robin Fox, *Kinship and Marriage* (1967), ch. 6 and M. Sahlins, *Tribesmen* (New Jersey, 1968), pp. 24-5, 54-5.
[55]Robin Fox, *Encounter with Anthropology* (1973), ch. 8; an example of a Polynesian case is described in Raymond Firth, *We, the Tikopia: A Sociological Study of Kinship in Primitive Polynesia* (1936).

have emphasized in one way or another the importance of descent and the importance of ancestors. Du Boulay, for instance, writing about fifteenth century England, argues that the 'notion of the conjugal family' was 'only just beginning, and that men thought dynastically of the line that stretched backward and forwards across the generations.[56] We have seen that Homans thought of landholdings in Kent or Norfolk as belonging to 'the class of joint-families: a group of descendants of a common ancestor.[57] This gives the impression of ancestor-focus, as does Homans' remark that 'in reckoning closeness of blood relationship, men reckoned by degrees of descent from an original mated couple, a man and a woman.[58] But if we look at the medieval situation a little more closely it emerges that the system of descent was not one of 'ancestor-focus,' but rather, as in the modern British and North American kinship system, of 'ego-focus.' In other words, when working out relationships, a person moves outwards from himself, he does not fix his mind on a previous generation and drop downwards.

The evidence concerning medieval notions of tracing the line is largely to be found in Bracton's treatise on methods of reckoning descent of the mid-thirteenth century, which is identical to modern twentieth century methods of doing so.[59] This was realized by Maitland and other legal historians. For instance, in Maitland's account of the system,[60] it is shown that the method that is outlined in the middle of the thirteenth century is in all essentials exactly the same as that elaborated by Matthew Hale in the middle of the seventeenth century, which is the same as that described in considerable detail by Blackstone at the end of the eighteenth century, which in turn is the same as that described by anthropologists for contemporary England.[61] The pivot is the individual, who traces his blood relations without distinction of sex

[56]F. R. H. Du Boulay, *The Age of Ambition*, (1970), p. 125; see also p. 116. The author is mainly writing about the higher ranks in society which may correspond a little more to this picture.

[57]Homans, *Villagers*, p. 207.

[58]Ibid., p. 216. Homans wrote before the basic distinction between two very different types of cognatic system was understood; it was only in the 1950s and 1960s that such systems were thoroughly investigated. For a lucid account of the difficulties of studying English kinship even in 1965, see Robin Fox, 'Prolegomena to the Study of British Kinship' in *Penguin Survey of the Social Sciences* (1965), ed. J. Gould.

[59]Bracton, *Laws*, pp. 188-200.

[60]Maitland, *English Law*, ii, pp. 269ff, esp. pp. 296-7. Maitland points out that Bracton's account of a 'parentelic' system, which was radically different from that used in Roman Law, is clouded by the attempt to use the pictorial representations of the *arbor consanguinitatis* from Roman law books.

[61]Sir Matthew Hale, *The History of the Common Law of England* reprinted Cambridge, 1971), ch. xi; Blackstone, *Commentaries*, ii, ch. xiv; Fox, *Kinship and Marriage*, ch. 6.

upwards, sideways and downwards. It is a system which is highly effective in a mobile, industrial society, but it is a curious system to find in a settled 'peasant' society.

The way a person describes his kin is closely connected to the way he thinks about them. This is true for both what he calls them when referring to them ('my father') or addressing them ('dad'). It is usually the case that where property is held by a group larger than the nuclear or elementary family, as in a peasant society, terms of reference and address do not distinguish between the nuclear family and outsiders, or between the direct line and collateral relatives. For instance, a father and father's brother may both be termed 'father'; such 'classificatory' systems, as they are known, are characteristic of many classical peasantries, for instance India and China. Such a system makes it possible to deal with very large numbers of near relatives. An alternative system, which is tied to the ancestor-focused cognatic system we have previously described, is also used in a situation where every relative's relationship is important. This solution is to make use of a completely developed 'descriptive' system whereby the *exact* relationship to each individual has to be specified. As Morgan describes the traditional Celtic system, for example, it is not possible to talk vaguely of one's 'cousin' or 'uncle'; one has to speak of one's 'father's brother's son,' or one's 'mother's brother.'[62] In order to operate such a system, each speaker must carry in his head an accurate map of the genealogical links in his neighbourhood. If England had been a 'peasant' society in the thirteenth century we would have expected to find that it had one of these systems of terminology, or at least something very different from its present 'Eskimo' system (named after the Copper Eskimos who have the same type). The present system is half way between a classificatory and descriptive system, separating the central line of father, grandfather, son, grandson, for example, from collaterals, but lumping together 'uncles' and 'cousins' in an almost 'classificatory' way.

The present 'Eskimo' system is, as is often observed, particularly well adapted to an industrial and individualistic system, since, to use Fox's metaphor, the individual is at the centre of a series of concentric circles like an onion with various skins. At the centre is the nuclear family, which is isolated: father, mother, son, daughter. The next layer are grand-relatives, parents and children. Then there are uncles and aunts,

---

[62]Lewis Morgan, *Systems of Consanguinity and Affinity in the Human Family* (Washington, 1870), pp. 44-6. For a general introductory description of classificatory and descriptive kinship terminologies and the English system, see Fox, *Kinship and Marriage*, ch. 9.

nephews and nieces. Outside that are the cousins. Some have thought that such an ego-centred and complex system is a product of industrial and urban society. But is is now clear that almost exactly the same terminology was in use from at least the thirteenth century onwards. This was recognized in general by Homans when he wrote that 'the terms for distant kinsmen were made merely by adding prefixes to the terms for persons closer to the small family. There were then, as there are now, great-grandfathers, and grandfathers, great-uncles, grandsons, and cousins of different degrees.'[63] He goes into the question in no greater detail, but on the basis of contemporary court rolls we can confirm that Morgan's description of the English kinship terminology in the middle of the nineteenth century also applies to the thirteenth century. This is what Morgan himself believed to be the case, writing that

Beside the adoption of the Roman as our legal form, the only changes in the English system within the last five centuries, so far as the writer is aware, is the restriction of the term *nephew* and *niece* to the children of the brother and sister of *Ego*, and the substitution of *grandson* and *grandaughter* in their places in the lineal line.[64]

He is suggesting that the earlier system had merged ring two and three of the onion — grand-parents and nephew/neice, but that in basic structure the system of terminology had not changed. Again this sets England apart from other 'peasant' societies very early, and such a system is fully compatible with the intensely individualistic pattern of ownership documented above.

We may now turn more specifically to the basic unit of production. In the model peasant society, farm labour is family labour. The co-working group consists of parents, married children and their spouses, grandchildren, plus extra labour of adopted children and more distant kin as required. The negative consequence is that wage labour, in the form of daily labourers and farm or domestic servants, is absent. The mobility of labour is low, and the institution of servanthood is not present, for example, in traditional China or India. It is therefore clear that the presence of a very large number of landless or semi-landless labourers and servants is incompatible with the essence of peasantry. Hilton writes that the 'altogether landless wage labourers . . . were

[63]Homans, *Villagers*, p. 216.
[64]Morgan, *Systems of Consanguinity and Affinity*, pp. 44-5; see p. 32-7, for a general description of the 'Teutonic' system which England shared.

always a minority. Had they been a majority, this fact would have implied the end of the peasantry, since the essence of peasant society is that the basic form of productive labour within it is that of the peasant family living on its own holding.'[65] The model predicts very few, if any, labourers and servants.[66]

Court rolls often only mention servants and labourers by chance. For a long time, therefore, it was possible to go on fitting medieval society to the model's predictions. During the last twenty years, however, evidence has been accumulating to support Kosminsky's early findings that servants and labourers were already very important in the thirteenth century.[67] On the basis of the 1380-1 Poll Tax Hilton states that 'it can be shown, for instance, that between 50 per cent and 70 per cent of males in East Anglican villages were employees designated as servants or labourers.'[68] By the criteria previously quoted from the same author's work, this was no longer a peasantry.

Nor was this confined to East Anglia. Figures from the same tax for Gloucestershire, once under-registrations had been eliminated, showed very large numbers of servants; at Kempsford, 69 out of a listed population of 157 were servants.[69] Postan's work on demesne servants or 'famuli' has shown the importance of such hired labour.[70] The same author frequently talks of labourers: 'the smallholder could — and we know he did — hire himself out to the lord or to the more substantial villagers; the latter hired labour to supplement the labour resources of their households.'[71] In fact, 'taken as a whole, the smallholding population of thirteenth century villages,' that is to say those unable to live entirely off their own property and thus forced to enter the labour market, 'was very numerous, frequently more numerous than the

---

[5]Hilton, *Bond Men*, p. 37.
[66]Though Lofgren has tried to reconcile the presence of servants with 'peasantry' by suggesting that, in parts of Scandinavia, 'the system of farm servants must then be seen as a flexible way of circulating manpower in the peasant community,' suggesting that they fluctuated with the life cycle (Lofgren, *Family and Household*, pp. 25, 23).
[67]Kosminsky, *Studies*, ch. 6.
[68]Hilton, *Peasantry*, p. 31. Further evidence of widespread servanthood and wage-labour from another area is cited by the same author in *A Medieval Society: The West Midlands at the End of the Thirteenth Century* (1966), pp. 165, 114-5.
[69]Ibid., p. 32.
[70]M. M. Postan, 'The Famulus: the Estate Labourer in the Twelfth and the Thirteenth Centuries', *Ec.H.R.*, Supplements, no. 2.
[71]Postan, *Essays*, p. 115. Elsewhere Postan writes that in the thirteenth century 'perhaps as much as a third of the total rural population was available for whole or part-time employment as wage labour ....' He estimates such wage labour involved one to two million persons (Postan, *England*, p. 568).

middling group, and sometimes more numerous than the rest of the village taken together.'[72]

It is therefore not surprising that 'substantial villagers also employed hired labour. Our sources leave little doubt that in almost every village, some villagers worked for others.'[73] Ritchie showed that wages were high in the late fourteenth century and that many people became labourers.[74] The frequency and importance of servants and labourers on Ramsey manors has been shown by Raftis and DeWindt.[75] The latter cites an extremely interesting chance reference to the fact that in 1308 at Holywell-cum-Needingworth, as well as the ordinary 'famuli' or manorial servants, another 112 labourers appeared at the lord's autumn work, many of whom were probably permanently settled villagers.[76] Searle has also given evidence for the very great importance of hired labour in the thirteenth century, arguing that the total amount of cash spent on their hire was sometimes greater than that on the permanent staff of manorial servants.[77]

Thus, despite the fact that even when there were considerable numbers of servants, they seldom appear in court rolls, as an instance cited by Hilton shows, it is now clear that servants and labourers were common and central.[78] All the evidence indicates that, as in the sixteenth century, it was not children or other kin, but hired labour, who supplemented the labour of man and wife. In a detailed re-analysis of poll tax listings for the later fourteenth century, Richard Smith has found the presence of servants 'on a scale which, if it becomes possible to estimate it firmly, might well be similar to that which characterized England two or three hundred years later.'[79] In other words, in relation to servanthood, England was within the 'unique' pattern of late marriage age and large proportions never married, which was first established by John Hajnal and originally thought to be a *post-medieval* phenomenon. It now looks as if children were put out as servants in other people's households, and labour hired when needed.[80] In every respect, the fluid labour market appears to be diametrically

[72]Postan, *Medieval*, p. 147.
[73]Ibid., p. 148.
[74]Nora Ritchie, 'Labour Conditions in Essex in the reign of Richard II,' reprinted in E. M. Carus-Wilson (ed.), *Essays in Economic History* (1962), ii, p. 93.
[75]Raftis, *Tenure*, p. 209; DeWindt, *Land*, p. 93.
[76]DeWindt, *Land*, p. 93.
[77]Searle, *Lordship*, p. 309.
[78]Hilton, *Peasantry*, p. 35.
[79]Smith, cited in Laslett, *Family Life and Illicit Love*, p. 47.
[80]Hilton, *Peasantry*, p. 51.

opposed to what we would have predicted — fluid despite the attempt of the Statute of Labourers to make it less so.[81]

If further evidence is needed on this point, it is indirectly provided by research into the institutions of adoption and fostering. In a peasant society, the absence of wage labour and servanthood means that alternative methods are needed to iron out the chance unevenness in labour supplies caused by demographic differences between families. Rather than, as Postan conjectures, selling off surplus land, a family with no male heirs would adopt sons.[82] Thus, adoption was a common and important institution in traditional India, China and Russia, and even in pre-seventeenth century Scotland and Ireland. We would therefore expect to find both institutions widespread in thirteenth century England. Fostering appears to have been rare; as Homans commented, 'rarely in medieval England, as often in other peasant societies, a man would give his son to another man to foster.'[83] Full adoption was legally impossible. Bracton spends a few lines discussing the legitimization of a child of one of the partners 'by a sort of adoption.'[84] But as Maitland writes, this is 'really no more than the result of a very strong presumption' of paternity. From 'the time when it (the court) rejects the claims of the "mantle-children" onwards to our own day, we have no adoption in England.'[85] Accepting a servant into the home, or the uncommon practice of bringing up the child of a poor neighbour or kinsman, appears to have been the nearest the English came to fostering or adopting children. Whereas one fourth of the children in some parts of the world are adopted,[86] in England they became wage-earners in another household.

---

[81]In fact the Statute of Labourers is itself evidence of very considerable labour mobility. A great deal of other evidence could also be cited, for instance the fact that threshing corn seems to have been done by paid labour rather than customary labour (Rogers, *Six Centuries of Work*, p. 171), or that treatises on farm management and accounting of the thirteenth-century assumed the widespread use of servants and paid employees (Dorothea Oschinsky, *Walter of Henley and other Treatises on Estate Management and Accounting* (Oxford, 1971) pp. 280ff. 317, 445). An encyclopedia written in *c.* 1260 by an English Franciscan explained how household servants should be treated, pointing out for instance that in law they were equivalent to children (*On the Properties of Things: John Trevisa's translation of Bartholomaeus Anglicus De Proprietatibus Rerum* (Oxford, 1975), i, pp. 305ff).

[82]For a recent discussion of the functions and causes of adoption see Jack Goody, *Production and Reproduction* (Cambridge, 1976) chs. 6, 7. The 'rights of an adopted member were equal to those of descendants' in traditional Russia, we are told (Shanin, *Awkward Class*, pp. 223, 221).

[83]*Villagers*, p. 198.

[84]Bracton, *Laws*, ii, p. 186.

[85]Maitland, *English Law*, ii, p. 399.

[86]For example in the traditional situation in parts of Melanesia: Reo Fortune, *Manus Religion* (Bison books edn., no date), p. 91; Margaret Mead, *Growing up in New Guinea* (1930; Penguin edn. 1942), p. 62.

The absence of wage labour and servanthood in peasant societies is also related to the absence of monetary relationships within the local community. Some surpluses may be sold, but production is mainly for use by the family, without the intervening market. A peasant economy is, internally, a subsistence one, where money, either in the form of cash or its substitutes, is scarce and unimportant. It was once thought that medieval villagers lived in such a 'natural,' non-monetized economy, in which transfers of wealth took the form of labour services or payments in kind, a complex 'barter' economy. This would fit with the model, but there has been a growing weight of evidence that the situation was different.

The work of Kosminsky and Postan has shown that cash was far more important than had hitherto been suspected. As Postan put it, summarizing his earlier work,

> Historians are now agreed that commutation of labour services was by no means a new phenomenon in the late fourteenth century. There was widespread, and on some estates, wholesale, commutation of labour services in the middle of the twelfth century . . . Professor Kosminsky has recently reminded us that by 1279 — the date of the Hundred Rolls — labour dues no longer were the main source of the lord's income from his peasant tenants.[87]

There is a wide variety of evidence, as well as the active land market, to show 'contractual relationships — expecially involving debts — indications of liquid capital resources and the practice of crafts, trades and services . . . .'[88] Peasant cash indebtedness, the contractual hiring to do specific jobs, the sales for cash of small items from the holding, all have been illustrated by Hilton for the later fourteenth century.[89] Searle has shown a very active cash economy, with buying, selling, mortgaging and lending at fourteen per cent interest rates in thirteenth century Battle.[90] A highly monetized economy is documented for Essex for the later fourteenth century on the basis of offences against the Statute of Labourers.[91] More generally, Hexter has cited early

---

[87]Postan, *Essays*, p. 132. A good deal earlier Rogers had stated that 'in the many thousands of bailiffs' and manor rolls which I have read' he had not discovered 'any labour-rent for which an equivalent money-payment could not be substituted' (Rogers, *Six Centuries*, p. 34). For further evidence see M. M. Postan, 'The Rise of a Money Economy' reprinted in Carus-Wilson (ed.), *Essays in Economic History* vol. i, and the same, 'Chronology of Labour Services' reprinted in Minchinton (ed.) *Essays in Agrarian History*, vol. i.
[88]DeWindt, *Land*, p. 282.
[89]Hilton, *Peasantry*, pp. 43-9.
[90]Searle, *Lordship*, p. 127.
[91]Ritchie, 'Labour Conditions in Essex', p. 107. Another description of medieval accounting, which stresses its rational, 'capitalist' features, is given by Hallam in Kamenka, *Feudalism*, pp. 35ff.

fourteenth century account books to show that there was exactly the same 'rational' organized economic attitudes in the early fourteenth century as in the sixteenth century.[92] Further extensive evidence of a cash economy is contained in thirteenth century treaties on estate management and accounting.[93] It would seem that already this was a society interpenetrated at the very lowest levels by the market and cash, by contractual relationships of a kind familiar from later history. Most 'objects' from labour to rights in all types of property, were marketable and had a price. It was not difficult to convert one commodity into another. Production was often for exchange, not for use. If this is true of the thirteenth century in England, it is again at the polar extreme from most other rural societies.

Peasants should be geographically immobile, according to the model, except in times of 'crisis,' being born and dying in the same village — or moving at marriage to a nearby one. As co-owners of resources with their parents, they are, so to speak, glued to the land. Again England does not fit the predictions. There is growing evidence that the geographical immobility which earlier writers took for granted is a myth, both at the individual and family level. Homans was divided on the question, arguing at one point that talk of the 'blood of the village' is evidence that 'the same families must in fact have lived for centuries in the same villages, or such sentiments would have had no chance to become established.'[94] Yet throughout most of his book,[95] he argues that the result of impartible inheritance was that younger sons and daughters left home to seek their fortune elsewhere. Homans did not undertake a detailed local study. Those who have done so have all noted the very considerable geographical mobility. Hallam, writing of Weston in Lincolnshire, showed that even when we omit the possibly most mobile elements, children between ten and eighteen, there was still very great mobility; nearly forty per cent of the adult males and fifty-three per cent of the 'young women' left the manor.[96] It seems likely that

---

[92]Hexter, *Reappraisals*, pp. 86ff.

[93]The rationality, sophisticated accounting, emphasis on profit, and universal translatability of every item into an exact cash equivalent would have surprised Weber; he was unfortunate not to have available the excellent recent edition of *Walter of Henley* and other treatises by Dorothea Oschinsky. That from the middle of the thirteenth century, at least, detailed accounting, auditing, and farming for profit alone, was widely spread was realized by Rogers. This was not confined to large estates and upper-class stewards. As Rogers observed, 'Nothing can be more carefully and more exhaustively drawn than the bailiff's account ... The English bailiff, generally a small farmer, often a serf, must have been at least bi-lingual.' (J. T. Rogers, *The Economic Interpretation of History* (1888), p. 54).

[94]*Villagers*, pp. 122-3.

[95]For example, *Villagers*, p. 119.

[96]Hallam, 'Thirteenth-century censuses', p. 356.

the total emigration was comparable to that for the sixteenth century. DeWindt is forced to argue defensively that 'not all Holywell families in the latter thirteenth century and earlier fourteenth centuries were short-term residents,'[97] but 'the fact that 51 of Holywell's known 140 families from the mid-thirteenth to the mid-fifteenth century failed to maintain residence for longer than a generation appears sobering.'[98] Raftis has found that from the earliest court rolls of a Ramsey manor, emigration of serfs from the domain of the lord was a 'regular feature,' and there seems no great pressure by the lord for them to remain.[99] He states that 'peasants moved widely in the thirteenth century . . . .'[100] Searle found that 'few of the surnames of the 1367 rental' for Battle Abbey 'are found in that of 1443,' yet 'the same is as true of earlier rentals.'[101] Given the features already discussed, this is not surprising. Yet again it sets England apart very early.

In a peasant society, where family and farm are inextricably linked and land is owned by the group rather than the individual, there is a particular pattern of social mobility. Two major features have been noted. Firstly, the family moves up and down the social hierarchy as a group; if one brother grows wealthy, all brothers do so. Secondly, where wealth is partitioned between all the heirs at each generation, there is a tendency for a pattern of 'cyclical' mobility to occur, in which long-term and permanent differences in wealth are avoided. A family that succeeds in one generation and becomes rich has more children so that the resources have to be partitioned between a large number of sons: it becomes 'poor' again. The poorer families coalesce, limit their family size and gradually accumulate wealth. There is an absence of permanent 'class' barriers, and the absence of a permanent group of landless families. We should expect, if England conformed to the model, to find no progressive differentiation, little difference between brothers, and the absence of a landless labouring strata. None of the predictions come true.

---

[97]DeWindt, *Land*, p. 99.
[98]Ibid., p. 175.
[99]Raftis, *Tenure*, pp. 139, 141.
[100]*Ibid.*, p. 167; see also p. 210.
[101]Searle, *Lordship*, p. 362. Rodney Hilton, *The Decline of Serfdom in Medieval England* (Economic History Society, 1969), p. 34, cites this and other evidence to show the very considerable geographical mobility from the later fourteenth century onwards. One difficulty is that court rolls, particularly if landholders are taken as the universe for study, may give a considerable underestimate of total mobility. This can clearly be seen for the sixteenth century when they can be compared to other records. The fact that they do show high mobility, nonetheless, is therefore doubly impressive. Another example comes from the West Midlands, where Razi, 'Peasants of Halesowen,' p. 49, speaks of the 'constant migration from and to the parish' in the early thirteenth century.

Impartible inheritance in many areas of the country meant that we usually witness individual, rather than group, mobility. Different branches of the same family rise and fall simultaneously. Even in areas of partible inheritance it was frequently the case that several brothers would sell off their shares to one of their number.[102] Thus, it does not appear that families moved as a block. There is also evidence of progressive differentiation. Kosminsky long ago argued for growing economic differentiation in the thirteenth century and the rise of peasants with large holdings or 'kulaks'; 'the increased negotiability of land led to an intensification of differentiation between peasant economies, not to its moderation.'[103] This movement threw up a body of permanently landless or almost landless labourers: 'the near-landless peasantry develops under conditions of feudal, manorial production.'[104]

We have already seen that the Poll Taxes suggest that well over half the adult male population in later fourteenth century East Anglia were servants and labourers, and the pattern is reported by most scholars. Titow paints a 'picture of the thirteenth-century English peasantry, as consisting largely of smallholders leading a wretched existence on an inadequate number of acres . . . ,' supplementing their incomes by crafts and wage labour.[105] DeWindt produces evidence for the fourteenth century of a very considerable number of landless and almost landless people in the village: 'there were clearly many persons — and even entire families — not holding adequate parcels of customary land, or any land.'[106] Postan, as we have seen, argued that the land-market was used primarily to even out the distribution of land. But Richard Smith's work on Suffolk supports the view of Kosminsky and Paul Hyams that land sales were used to increase the permanent and cumulative differentiation between rich and poor.[107] He concluded that 'an analysis of the components of the market would appear to suggest that certain forces causing land to become concentrated into fewer hands were definitely operating in this area of Suffolk in the latter part of the thirteenth century.'[108] The rich grew richer and the poor grew poorer,

---

[102]Smith, *Life-cycles*, p. 148.
[103]Kosminsky, *Studies*, p. 212.
[104]Ibid., p. 227.
[105]Titow, *Rural Society*, p. 93.
[106]DeWindt, *Land*, p. 94.
[107]Smith, *Life-cycles*, p. 69.
[108]Ibid., p. 77; but a contrary view is taken by Bruce Campbell with reference to N. E. Norfolk, 'Population Pressure Inheritance and the Land Market in a Fourteenth Century Peasant Community' in Smith (ed.), *Land, Kinship and Life Cycle*.

even in this area of partible inheritance, everyone did not become poorer together as population rose.

I have elsewhere set out a list of the factors which lead to growing inequality.[109] All the more important ones, namely the existence of a land market and of private ownership, a market for surplus agricultural products and cash, appear to be present in thirteenth century England. It would therefore not be surprising to find it diverging from the situation in virtually marketless peasant societies. If we are correct, the situation in the thirteenth century was very similar to that which we witness as population built up again in the late sixteenth century, and land, not labour, again became the scarce factor in production.

The use of a predictive model is both most important and most dangerous when the evidence is insufficient for any firm conclusion yet to be reached. This can be illustrated best with the next two features of medieval social structure, namely the age at marriage and the proportion ever married. Since the fortunes of the family are dependent on the number of labouring hands, and consequently production and consumption in the end flow from reproduction, it is characteristic of classical peasantries that girls marry very young, usually as soon as they can start to contribute to the labour force by breeding. Hence the young age at first marriage found in traditional India, China, Russia. Believing England to have been a basically 'peasant' society of this type until the industrial revolution, social historians naturally found literary and other evidence that country women normally married young — soon after puberty. This was alleged to be the case for the sixteenth and seventeenth centuries, for instance on the basis of young marriages in Shakespeare's plays, and was also thought to be the situation in medieval England.

In the case of the sixteenth century, the keeping of parish registers from 1538 onwards makes it possible to test the assumption. It is now abundantly clear that the prediction is wrong; men and women married in their middle or late twenties, on average.[110] Parish registers will never be found for the thirteenth century; we are therefore left with unreliable and indirect evidence. There are basically three major interpretations which can be made of such evidence. Here we will confine ourselves to the mean average age of women below the level of the gentry at first marriage; the gentry and nobility are better documented, but it is

---

[109]Alan Macfarlane, *Resources and Population: A Study of the Gurungs of Nepal* (Cambridge, 1976), pp. 197-200.
[110]Peter Laslett, *World we have lost*, (1965; 2nd edn. 1971), pp. 84ff; Wrigley, *Population and History*, pp. 86, 106.

generally agreed that their age at marriage may follow a very different pattern from that of the bulk of the population.[111]

One view is that propounded by Homans and J. C. Russell, which is based on the idea that England consisted of two types of peasant social structure. In the impartible areas the marriage age for the inheriting male would be late, since he would have to wait for his father to retire. This would also, by a chain reaction, affect some women. Homans assumes that marriage was late, by implication, for both sexes: 'Marriage is late in Ireland today; it is said to have been late in England in the sixteenth century, when the social order had not greatly changed from what it had been in the thirteenth century.'[112] He gives no evidence for this contention, beyond pointing out that child marriages were condemned in contemporary poetry and suggesting that many landless sons and daughters in impartible areas would have to leave their villages.[113] The general principle is summed up in the rule 'No land, no marriage.' The argument is repeated by J. C. Russell, who states that 'there is some evidence to show that young men were not expected to marry before they had adequate means of support. This normally would postpone marriage for men, and thus for at least a certain part of the women.'[114] He adds some statistical proof from work on the Inquisitions *Post Mortem* and Poll Taxes which seem to show that 'marriage was not very early.'[115] Though he does not write directly on the matter, presumably Homans would argue that where all the sons inherited in the woodland areas, they would *all* have to wait to marry.

It is not difficult to show both logical fallacies and statistical misinterpretations in the Homans/Russell argument, and this has been effectively done by the proponents of the second major thesis. Assuming that England before the sixteenth century fitted better the model of a 'classical' peasantry than the 'west European' model, a number of scholars, chief among them John Hajnal, have suggested that the pattern up to about the fifteenth century was a 'non-European' one of very early marriage for women, at, or soon after, puberty. Hajnal believes that 'the scanty statistical evidence' suggests 'a fundamental change in marriage habits over much of Europe between 1400 and 1650.'[116] Hajnal implies that this transition occurred fairly late, for 'if it were indeed to prove the case that in the Middle Ages the marriage

---

[111]Hajnal, *European Marriage*, p. 116.
[112]Homans, *Villagers*, p. 158.
[113]Ibid., pp. 163, 135-7.
[114]Josiah C. Russell, *British Medieval Population* (Albuquerque, 1948), p. 156.
[115]Ibid., p. 158.
[116]Hajnal, *European Marriage*, p. 122.

pattern of Europe was entirely "non-European," traces of the transition should be visible in some of the early parish register materials.'[117]

We now know that it is not so visible, but he could still argue that the transition had occurred a little earlier. We may look first at the evidence put forward by Hajnal, and then at that of his supporters who believe that a 'non-European pattern,' particularly marriage soon after puberty for village girls, prevailed. Leaving on one side evidence from the Continent and data for the British peerage, Hajnal's arguments are of two kinds. Negatively, he attacks Homans' and Russell's arguments, effectively showing that Russell's figures from the Poll Tax and Inquisitions are fairly meaningless; the sample is too small, the error rates in the Poll Tax too large.[118] He argues that since mortality rates were very high, Homans' deductions from the rule that a son could not marry until he inherited land may not have held back marriage. He could also have pointed out that in 'non-European' societies such as India it is possible to combine very early female marriage with land-holding, and this could also have been achieved in the medieval period. Furthermore, he points out that analogies with post-famine Ireland are misleading. The evidence he brings forward in support of very young female age at marriage is, however, no stronger than Homans'. There is the case of the Wife of Bath in the Canterbury Tales, who married young — but readers of Chaucer will know that other women married at a later age. It is suggested that the age of puberty rose in the sixteenth century, based on legal literature.[119] But from the study of the variability of age at menarche through human societies, even if this could be proved, it is very unlikely that it could have pushed the age at marriage up by more than a year or two — and brought it directly into line with many Asian societies which have a fairly late age at first menstruation.[120] The suggestion that the controversy over the nature of marriage at the Reformation is connected to this problem, though intriguing, is never carried through and I have found no support for it;[121] the only evidence of any weight at all concerns the indirect material from a brief re-analysis of the proportions of unmarried persons aged fourteen or more in the English Poll Tax Returns of 1377.[122] This is a technical matter

---

[117]Ibid., p. 135.
[118]Ibid., pp. 118-120.
[119]Ibid., p. 123.
[120]For the fact that mean average age at menarche almost always falls within the range 13 to 16 years in non-industrial societies, see M. Nag, *Factors Affecting Fertility in Nonindustrial Societies* (New Haven, 1962), p. 105. For a recent discussion of the historical evidence, see Peter Laslett, *Family Life and Illicit Love in Earlier Generations* (Cambridge, 1977), ch. 6.
[121]Nor does a recent survey of the literature support Hajnal's view, Keith Thomas, *Age and Authority*, p. 23 note 63.
[122]Ibid., pp. 118-9.

which cannot be decided here. But it is significant that Richard Smith, whose special period this is, has re-worked both the published and unpublished Poll Tax figures in far greater detail and has concluded that Hajnal was probably wrong. The tendency to undercount the number of women in general, and particularly unmarried women, has distorted the figures, and, to say the least, the Poll Tax cannot be used as evidence of a 'non-European' pattern. But neither can it be used to prove the existence, directly, of late age at marriage. On the other hand, other features suggested by the Poll Taxes fit far better with a late age at marriage pattern than they do with Hajnal's non-European pattern. Thus Richard Smith concluded that the size of the family group and proportion of servants is 'of a level that places it clearly within the "west European" cultural sphere.'[123]

There are other medievalists who believe that evidence from manor court rolls can be used to estimate the age at marriage in medieval England. Furthermore, they conclude that such evidence suggests a relatively young age at first marriage for women, the mean average being about twenty years. There are serious technical weaknesses in the method employed in such estimates, however, since a number of unproven assumptions have to be made concerning the economy and society. An attempt to use a similar method on sixteenth century material, where an independent check could be made by using parish registers alongside the court rolls, suggested that the technique can lead to entirely misleading and inaccurate results.[124]

There is no convincing evidence to show the age at which medieval women married. Since so many of the other economic and social features of the thirteenth century look like those in the sixteenth and fit with a late age at marriage, I would be very surprised if we do not, finally, find that this was the case. It appears that Richard Smith, who has worked very considerably on the subject, both with court rolls and taxation data, is moving towards this view. His thesis on Suffolk concluded that there was 'likely to have been a high marriage age and significant incidence of celibacy,'[125] and more recently he has suggested that the serf lists for Spalding, used by Hallam, indicate an age-structure 'not incompatible with a female age at marriage of 25-6.'[126] Age at first marriage for women from 1540 to 1740 usually fluctuated

[123]Smith, 'The Poll Taxes of 1377 and 1381,' p. 15.
[124]An early brief attempt is Sylvia L. Thrupp, 'The Problem of Replacement-Rates in Late Medieval English Population,' *Ec.H.R.* 2nd ser., 18 (1965), p. 112. A much more thorough attempt is in Razi, 'The Peasants of Halesowen,' pp. 87-91, 229-231.
[125]Smith, *Life-cycles*, p. 384: Dr Smith is here speaking of males.
[126]In a spoken contribution to the conference on European Family Systems, Cambridge, 1976.

around a mean average of 25 years; my guess is that such an average, sometimes rising or falling by up to five years for a short period in certain places, could be traced back to at least the thirteenth century in England if we had the records. This throws no light on the situation on the rest of the Continent, which may well conform to Hajnal's argument.

Intimately linked to age at marriage is the question of the proportion who marry. This is also related to the question of peasantry. Classical peasantries are not only characterized by very early female marriages, but what we may term 'universal' marriage; almost all men and women who are not mentally or physically incapacitated get married. This was true of traditional India and of eastern Europe. In the modified form of peasantry, however, only one son and perhaps one daughter would marry on the farm; the rest would 'travel,' possibly marrying elsewhere. As with the question of age at marriage, those who have looked at the medieval evidence tend to follow one of these two models. Homans puts forward the argument that a large proportion of younger children in areas of impartible inheritance did not marry; 'a man could keep himself alive by taking work as a farm labourer but he could not keep a wife or found a family unless he held land. No land, no marriage.' Consequently both sons and daughters who did not inherit, he argues, moved away from the village and became the single people for whom there were medieval terms *anilepiman* and *anilepiwymen*.[127] His view of considerable numbers of unmarried persons is supported by the findings of some other medievalists, for example Eileen Power.[128] J. C. Russell believes that taxation records indicate, along with age at marriage, considerable numbers of never married persons.[129]

This view is challenged by those who consider medieval England to have been more like a classical peasantry. We have already seen that Coulton appears to have invented a quotation from Maitland to support such a view; and Coulton's pupil, H. S. Bennett, writing of the fifteenth century, states that

It is evident from a brief survey of contemporary documents, that no woman was expected to remain long unmarried, and both legislation and local customs assumed marriage as the natural state for everyone of mature age . . . popular opinion recognized marriage as inevitable, women very easily come to look on matrimony as part of the scheme of things. Probably the idea that a woman had a right to remain single, unless she entered a cloister and became a bride of Christ . . . was unthinkable at that time.[130]

[127]Homans, *Villagers*, pp. 137, 136.
[128]The view of Eileen Power that medieval extents show considerable numbers of unmarried women landholders has already been quoted near the start of this chapter.
[129]Russell, *Medieval British Population*, pp. 154ff.
[130]H. S. Bennett, *The Pastons and their England* (1922; paperback edn., 1968), p. 51.

Such a view is diametrically opposed to the much weightier assessment of the *real* Maitland, but it appears to be supported once again by Hajnal's work. He argues that the fifteenth and sixteenth centuries witnessed a transition from a 'non-European' pattern of universalist marriage to one of selective marriage, with up to twelve or fifteen per cent of women never marrying, by the seventeenth century. Leaving on one side the peerage data, what is the evidence and argument? Firstly, he seeks to discredit the Homans/Russell/Power thesis. In fact, he nowhere directly challenges Homans on this point, but rightly points out that the *inquisitions post mortem* figures are again too small to support Russell's view that half the population were still unmarried at the age of twenty-four.[131] His treatment of Power's view is not a refutation, but an evasion, for he merely states that 'she does not present her material in detail; she seems to expect the reader to feel that a high proportion of spinsters is not an unlikely state of affairs.'[132] It is clear that what is at issue here is the implicit model behind the findings: Hajnal's theory of a 'non-European' or classical peasantry system like India's led him to expect universal marriage, and he consequently quotes with the following emphasis Power's remark that it 'must not be imagined that marriage was the lot of every woman and that the Middle Ages were not as *familiar as our own day* with the independent spinster.'[133] But it is Eileen Power's view, and not Hajnal's, which is supported by recent detailed work on women's property rights and activities already elaborated at the start of this chapter. The balance of local records and legal documents are on her side.

Apart from the negative attacks on the proponents of the view that large numbers of people of both sexes remained unmarried, Hajnal brings forward only one piece of positive evidence. This is again the proportion of women over the age of fifteen who were married according to the Poll Tax of 1377. He argues that the percentage of seventy per cent married is 'of quite the wrong order of magnitude for a population of European pattern.'[134] He admits that there may have been under-registration of unmarried adult women, but he believes that even if we include nuns and others, such omissions only account for about two and a half per cent of the women, which cannot alter the general finding. On the European pattern, 'the percentage of women over fifteen who were married in a country as a whole was below 55 and

---

[131]Hajnal, *European Marriage*, p. 120.
[132]Ibid., p. 125.
[133]Ibid., p. 124. This remark totally contradicts that quoted at the start of the chapter. In the former case Power was speaking about the *de jure* and upper class position, here she is writing about the *de facto*, middling and lower ranks.
[134]Hajnal, *European Marriage*, p. 119.

usually below 50 in the nineteenth century.' He concludes on the basis
of this that the 'marriage pattern of at least some parts of medieval
England in the fourteenth century was not at all like that of eighteenth
century Europe, but much more like that of non-European
civilizations.' He does cautiously add that 'further work on the poll tax
records is needed before much confidence could be placed in such an
interpretation.'[135]

Such work is now in progress, particularly by Richard Smith in the
unpublished work already cited.[136] Again his conclusions do not
support Hajnal. He argues that evasion was probably far higher than
envisaged by Russell or Hajnal, of the order of twenty-five per cent
rather than five per cent, and it was particularly high among unmarried
apprentices and women. As a result it is almost impossible to obtain
meaningful figures. A re-working of the Poll Tax for Rutland suggests,
even if the evasions are not set as high as the level suggested by
medievalists such as Postan and Titow, that 'it is relatively easy to detect
the strong probability of marriage proportions of some 50-55 per cent
within the male population over 14 in late fourteenth century
Rutland.'[137] This is exactly comparable to the figures obtained for post-
1599 English listings of inhabitants at a period when we know that
large numbers of persons were not marrying. Richard Smith's detailed
findings cannot be given here, and we eagerly await their publication.
What is clear is that Hajnal's hypothesis can not be held to have been
proven. In fact, as with the age at marriage, it seems very likely, if we
consider all the features of the economic and social pattern, that Eileen
Power was right. This was probably not a 'universal marriage' society
which later transformed into a selective marriage one. This is not
necessarily to endorse Homans' view that the crucial division was
between heirs who married and non-heirs who did not. Such a simple
argument implies a view of the connection between family and land, a
'quasi-peasantry,' which we have been at pains to challenge at every
level. Yet his general view that unmarried persons were widespread is
likely to be correct, and is again corroborated by other features of the
pattern already described — the large number of servants and
apprentices and casual wage labourers, for example.

The sum total of features which we have outlined in this and

---

[135]*Idem.*

[136]Since it is unusual in a published work to depend so heavily on another's unpublished
findings, I ought to state that I have done so for three reasons. Firstly, the topic is crucial.
Secondly, Hajnal's article is frequently quoted as authoritative and final, whereas I hope
to show there is reasonable doubt. Thirdly, the outstanding quality of Richard Smith's
work makes it unusually reliable.

[137]Smith, 'The Poll Taxes of 1377 and 1381,' p. 6.

preceding chapters leads to a particular type of society radically different from either classical or modified peasantries. Simplifying considerably, a classical peasant society, say in India, was made up of numerous local units or 'villages,' each one fairly similar, self-contained, with its own dialect, gods, and folklore. As the anthropologist Srinivas commented: 'nobody can fail to be impressed by the isolation and stability of these (Indian) village communities.'[138] The whole society was an agglomeration of separate and largely autonomous units. The absence of geographical mobility and permanent economic differentiation, the continuance of families in one area and attachment to the land, is related to a strong sentiment within the local community. The boundaries *between* communities are strong. Outsiders are often treated badly, and a strong contrast is drawn between 'our' place and 'the world'; the nation is made up of many more or less identically constituted units of roughly the same size. Since it was believed that England was also a peasant society, it was believed that this was likewise the case. When Macaulay wrote, he argued that this was so even in 1685, and we have quoted his picture of isolated, backward, rural villages. The fact that certain types of historical record endorse such a view is shown by the statements of the historians of medieval and early modern England who worked between about 1900 and 1950 and whose views are quoted in chapter two above.

It was only the systematic use of a wide range of other documents which begin to survive from the early sixteenth century which shook historians out of this totally mistaken view. Medievalists do not, on the whole, possess such documents. It is therefore not surprising that they should still largely be trapped in a view which we saw clearly expressed by Power and Coulton. Thus recent surveys of medieval society still speak of 'the tightly knit village community' and argue that the late fourteenth century village was 'still an interlocked community.'[139] Hilton frequently speaks of the 'peasant community' in his works, stating, for instance, that 'the solidarity of peasant communities is a well-known fact of medieval social history.'[140] Even those whose work shows that such a tightly-knit community did not exist hark back to a slightly earlier period when it *must* have done so and then 'broken down.' Thus DeWindt writes concerning one Ramsey manor:

if the student . . . approaches the local community as a self-contained and self-sufficient economic and social unit, he again is soon faced with contradictory

[138]M. N. Srinivas (ed.) *India's Villages* (New York, 1960), p. 23.
[139]Paul R. Hyams, 'The Origins of a Peasant Land Market in England' *Ec.H.R.* 2nd ser. xxiii, no. 1 (April, 1970), p. 26; Hilton, *Peasantry*, p. 54.
[140]Hilton, *Bond Men*, pp. 32, 29.

evidence of frequent outside interests and contacts and regular mobility among the peasants under investigation . . .' The great change came in the Black Death, according to this author, however, for then there was a 'fading away of the old, manor-related village organization 'which' brought forth an equally different type of society, where behaviour was strikingly particularistic, independent and even impersonal'.[141]

As Titow correctly writes, the myth 'dies incredibly hard' and all the evidence in fact shows that 'medieval agrarian economy was not self-sufficient, self-contained, or "natural".'[142] What now seems clear is that England back to the thirteenth century was not based on either 'Community' or 'communities.' It appears to have been an open, mobile, market-oriented and highly centralized nation, different not merely in degree but in kind from the peasantries of Eastern Europe and Asia, though only further research will prove whether this was the case.

Other features of the society could be examined in order to show that the characteristics of peasantry appear to be absent; the demographic patterns of relatively slow population growth,[143] the very developed towns and markets, the considerable division of labour and occupational specialization even at the village level, are among the features which it would be worth exploring. But enough has been said, it is hoped, to suggest that there is at least a *prima facie* case for re-examining traditional stereotypes. Only future detailed work will show whether this rejection of the idea of either a classical or modified 'peasantry' or 'domestic mode of production' is correct. It does seem worthwhile, in order to open out the debate, to start with a hypothesis which is opposed to that put forward by many authorities, with the notable exception of the greatest of them, F. W. Maitland, who anticipated much of what has been argued above.

The hypothesis, which we shall develop a little in the next chapter, is that the majority of ordinary people in England from at least the thirteenth century were rampant individualists, highly mobile both geographically and socially, economically 'rational,' market-oriented and acquisitive, ego-centred in kinship and social life. Perhaps this is no surprise, for it would make them very like their descendants whom we are beginning to find out were like this three centuries later.

---

[141]DeWindt, *Land*, pp. 278, 275; see also p. 263.
[142]Titow, *Rural Society*, p. 16.
[143]Possible figures which suggest a trebling or quadrupling of the population in the 250 years after about 1100 are discussed in Postan, *Medieval*, pp. 30-41. This suggests a doubling in 125 years or more. In contemporary Third World societies, and even in many traditional peasantries, a doubling of population every 35 years is not uncommon. If this had happened in England from a base of two million persons in 1100 there would have been a population of over 250 million persons by 1350.

Sixteenth century Englishmen lived in the same country, with much the same legal and political system, geography, language, and roughly the same population. It would perhaps not be surprising to find there was no great difference. It could, indeed, be argued that the *onus* is not on the historian who wishes to show that the social system and economy were very similar in the two periods to prove this, but on those who believe that there was some fundamental transformation between the thirteenth and eighteenth centuries, to produce convincing evidence that this was indeed the case.

7
England in Perspective

If the argument in the preceding chapters is correct, England has been inhabited since at least the thirteenth century by a people whose social, economic and legal system was in essence different not only from that of peoples in Asia and Eastern Europe, but also in all probability from the Celtic and Continental countries of the same period. Even if the causes of this difference were invisible to contemporaries, we would expect that some of the effects should have been apparent to those who moved between England and other parts of Europe. Those foreigners who visited or read about England, and Englishmen who travelled and lived abroad, could not have escaped noticing that they were moving not merely from one geographical, linguistic, climatic zone to another, but to and from a society in which almost every aspect of the culture was diammetrically opposed to that of the surrounding nations.

To survey the whole very considerable philosophical and travel literature of Europe bearing on this problem from the thirteenth to the eighteenth century is beyond the scope of this work. We will therefore single out a few notable accounts or statements, firstly by foreigners who wrote about England, and secondly by Englishmen who were comparing their own society with those around them. Although they made comments on many differences of customs and manners, we will concentrate on half a dozen of the central features that were probably connected directly to the pattern we have elaborated. The highly developed and individualistic market society was one which would lead to unusual affluence, distributed widely over the population. It was a situation of very considerable social mobility, based on wealth rather than blood, and with few strong and permanent barriers between occupational groups, town and country, and social strata. The strong sense of individualism was likely to be found embedded in the laws in the concept of individual rights and independence and liberty of thought and religion. In conjunction, these characteristics would be likely to lead foreigners to think of the English as an arrogant and self-sufficient nation. Thus we should expect foreign observers to notice that England was economically, socially and ideologically very different from the rest of the continent, and for Englishmen comparing their own nation to others to feel the same. If it can be shown that this is not merely an eighteenth-century difference, but can be traced back to the fifteenth century, before the supposed dramatic changes caused by Protestantism and the rise of a new capitalist economy suggested in the chronology of Marx and Weber, it will support the argument that England well before the sixteenth century had already taken a different path from that of the major part of Europe. Only a much more detailed survey of the literature, particularly the reactions of travellers when visiting other countries, will prove the case either way.

One of those who thought most deeply on the differences between England and the Continent, particularly France, during the eighteenth century was De Tocqueville in his work on *L'Ancien Regime*. There could be little doubt that England by then was by far the wealthiest nation, per head, in Europe, and the private property law the most developed. De Tocqueville asked rhetorically 'is there any single country in Europe, in which the national wealth is greater, private property is more extensive, more secure, more varied in character, society more settled and more wealthy?'[1] and asserted that English agriculture was 'the richest and most perfect in the world.'[2] He believed that this was the result of its legal and social system, 'from the spirit which animates the complete body of English legislation.'[3] He was confident that he had not only isolated the 'peculiarities of its laws, its spirit, and its history,'[4] which set England apart from the rest of Europe, but could explain when and why there had developed this fundamental difference. It arose, he thought, from the absence of social barriers, the free mobility, of this highly individualistic society:

Wherever the feudal system established itself on the continent of Europe it ended in caste; in England alone it returned to aristocracy. I have always been astonished that a fact, which distinguished England from all modern nations and which can alone explain the peculiarities of its laws, its spirit, and its history, has not attracted still more than it has done the attention of philosophers and statesmen, and that habit has finally made it as it were invisible to the English themselves .... It was far less its Parliament, its liberty, its publicity, its jury, which in fact rendered the England of that date so unlike the rest of Europe than a feature still more exclusive and more powerful. England

---

[1] Tocqueville, *Ancien*, p. 184.
[2] Ibid., p. 34.
[3] Ibid., pp. 184-5.
[4] Ibid., p. 88.

was the only country in which the system of caste had not been changed but effectively destroyed. The nobles and the middle classes in England followed together the same courses of business, entered the same professions, and what is much more significant, inter-married . . . .[5]

De Tocqueville was less sure of where this momentous difference had sprung from, for he admitted that 'this singular revolution is lost in the darkness of past ages,' though through the etymology of the English word 'gentleman' he could trace it back for 'several centuries.'[6] It seems likely that he thought the turning-point was in the late fifteenth or sixteenth century. He believed that the political and legal systems of the 'Middle Ages' in France, England and in Germany had a 'prodigious similarity' and that likewise 'the condition of the peasants was little different . . . From the confines of Poland to the Irish Sea,' concluding that 'in the fourteenth century the social, political, administrative, judicial, economic, and literary institutions of Europe' had a close resemblance.[7] But by the seventeenth century England was 'already a quite modern nation,' which 'has merely preserved in its heart, and as it were embalmed, some relics of the Middle Ages.'[8] What he meant by this newness is made clear in the same passage. Behind the 'old names and forms,' 'you will find from the seventeenth century the old feudal system substantially abolished, classes which overlap, nobility of birth set on one side, aristocracy thrown open, wealth as the source of power, equality before the law, office open to all, liberty of the press, publicity of debate.' He believed that these were 'all new principles, of which the society of the Middle Ages knew nothing.' We have, of course, argued that wherever we care to look, it is clear that they are *not* new principles and that the change did not occur in the way De Tocqueville imagined. But his characterization of the way in which seventeenth and eighteenth century England already had a different social structure from France is very revealing. Furthermore, De Tocqueville realized that an individualism which had sprung up in England was absent in France. He argued that 'our ancestors had not got the word *Individualism* — a word which we have coined for our own use, because in fact in their time there was no individual who did not belong to a group, no one who could look on himself as absolutely alone.'[9] He warned against a situa-

---

[5]Ibid., pp. 88-9. In his earlier work on America De Tocqueville had also stressed the differences between England and the United States on the one hand, and the Continental countries on the other. The former pair, he believed, already had a much more mobile and egalitarian system by the middle of the seventeenth century (*Democracy in America* (1835; Mentor edn., 1956), ed. Richard Heffner, pp. 47, 248).
[6]Ibid., pp. 89-90.
[7]Ibid., p. 18.
[8]Ibid., p. 21.
[9]Ibid., p. 102.

tion where 'Men being no longer attached to one another by any tie of caste, of class, of corporation, of family, are only too much inclined to be preoccupied only with their private interests . . . to retire into a narrow individualism.'[10] This was the tendency which had emerged in England, and then been transferred to America, for De Tocqueville realized that the open and mobile situation of England in the seventeenth century 'passes finally to America . . . its history is that of democracy itself . . . .'[11] He thus helps to establish that England and then America were considered to have a totally different social structure from that of Continental Europe by the seventeenth century. Furthermore, his description of rural society in eighteenth-century France — the 'peasants' cut off from the towns, from education, from the nobility — indicates a picture which is in sharp contrast not only to England in the seventeenth to eighteenth centuries, but long before. It is unlikely, for example, that any English village from the thirteenth century onwards bore any resemblance to his view of an eighteenth-century village as 'a community of which all the members were poor, ignorant and gross.'[12]

Writing a century before De Tocqueville was another Frenchman, Montesquieu. He visited England in 1729 and plunged into a study of its political and social institutions which he clearly found very alien, writing that 'I am here in a country which hardly resembles the rest of Europe.'[13] In his work on *The Spirit of the Laws* he noted that the social, economic and religious situation, connected to law and politics, was different in England. The English were wealthy, enjoying a 'solid luxury';[14] England was a trading nation as a result of its freedom from restrictive laws and 'pernicious prejudices.'[15] Anticipating De Tocqueville to a certain extent, he pointed out that in France, 'it is contrary to the spirit of monarchy to admit the nobility into commerce. The custom of suffering the nobility of England to trade is one of those things which have there mostly contributed to weaken the monarchical government.'[16] But above all it was the liberty, the independence and the individualism of the English which Montesquieu noticed. They were a 'free people.'[17] As opposed to other nations, he wrote, 'this nation

[10]Ibid., p. xv.
[11]Ibid., p. 90.
[12]Ibid., p. 132. To what extent his description is true even of eighteenth-century French villages is, of course, debatable. But behind the possible exaggerated language there does appear to be the perception of a basic difference.
[13]Quoted in *ibid.*, p. 89.
[14]Montesquieu, *Spirit*, i, p. 314.
[15]Ibid., i, p. 310.
[16]Ibid., i, p. 327.
[17]Ibid., i, p. 307.

is passionately fond of liberty';[18] 'every individual is independent';[19] 'with regard to religion, as in this state every subject has a free will, and must consequently be . . . conducted by the light of his own mind . . . the number of sects is increased . . . .'[20] Montesquieu speculated on why this should be the case, noting that, in general, liberty and individualism were more potent in the north of Europe than the south, 'the people of the north have, and will forever have, a spirit of liberty and independence,'[21] and that, particularly, 'the inhabitants of islands have a higher relish for liberty than those of the continent.'[22] It might, he thought, also have something to do with climate, which 'may have produced a great part of the laws, manners, and customs of this nation.'[23] But he was certain that whatever the roots, the legal system and customs in England were peculiarly favourable to individual liberty; 'their laws not being made for one individual more than another, each considers himself a monarch; and indeed, the men of this nation are rather confederates than fellow-subjects.'[24] In other words, they had formed an association of equal, independent individuals, rather than forming a basically hierarchical and subservient nation of the ruled. This individualism, Montesquieu suggested, was not merely peculiar to England, but was somehow connected to both the economic and the religious system; Protestantism was fitted to northern Europe because independent individuals disliked the idea of a visible head, while Catholicism was appropriate for the south.[25] Furthermore, wealth and trade were related to the difference of laws. The connections were later to be noted by Weber when he quoted Montesquieu as suggesting that England has 'progressed the farthest of all peoples of the world in three important things: in piety, in commerce and in freedom.'[26]

Montesquieu's description of the difference between England and the 'rest of the continent' agrees generally with De Tocqueville's. He differs, however, in explaining the origins and causes of this system. Whereas De Tocqueville, writing in the mid-nineteenth century, had lost its roots in the 'darkness' of the late middle ages, Montesquieu seems to have been aware that the origins were much earlier. He was probably helped in this view by his belief that the northern climate was partly responsible. If this was the case, then as presumably the climate

[18]Ibid., i, p. 309.
[19]Ibid., i, p. 308.
[20]Ibid., i, p. 312.
[21]Ibid., ii, p. 31.
[22]Ibid., i, p. 273.
[23]Ibid., i, p. 307.
[24]Ibid., i, p. 314.
[25]Ibid., ii, p. 31.
[26]Weber, *Protestant*, p. 45.

which caused the laws and customs was centuries old, the difference also must be very ancient. He does not place it in the breakdown of a uniform European pattern in the fifteenth and sixteenth centuries, but suggests that the English system had been different from time immemorial. After spending ten pages describing English law and the English constitution, largely on the basis of Locke's treatises on the same subject, Montesquieu concludes that 'In perusing the admirable treatise of Tacitus *On the Manners of the Germans* we find it is from that nation the English have borrowed their idea of political government. This beautiful system was invented first in the woods.'[27] Nor was it merely the political system that was 'borrowed,' but also, he suggested, the land-law and inheritance system. Crucial here was the fact that, as Montesquieu observed, the Germanic system as described by Tacitus was one of absolute individual property; there was no 'group' which owned the land, and hence no idea that the family and the resources were inextricably linked. In his description of the Salic law he stresses that it 'had not in view a preference of one sex to the other, much less had it regard to the perpetuity of a family, a name, or the transmission of land. These things did not enter into the heads of the Germans . . . .'[28] Montesquieu was clearly not in a position to show how the English could have come to take over this or other aspects of this 'beautiful system.' It is sufficient for our purposes here that this enormously wide-ranging mind should have realized that England was different from every Continental country in the seventeenth and eighteenth centuries, and to have believed this difference probably had very old roots.

We may now move back two centuries to look at the accounts of various foreigners who visited England during the sixteenth century. They were mainly from Flanders and Germany, and their observations concentrate on the physical differences, rather than the social and legal ones. Yet they do tend to confirm that by at least the middle of the sixteenth century evidence of both the wealth and the independent spirit of the English. In an account of the 'bathing excursion' of Frederick, Duke of Wirtemberg, in 1592, to England, the author noted the great wealth of London, a 'mighty city of business' and the fact that people dressed opulently, 'for they go dressed out in exceedingly fine clothes . . . to such a degree indeed, that, as I am informed, many a one does not hesitate to wear velvet in the streets.'[29] The author also noted the agricultural wealth of the country and its profusion of crops, presenting a quaint

---

[27]*Spirit*, i, p. 161.
[28]Ibid., i, p. 283.
[29]Reprinted in W. B. Rye, *England as seen by foreigners in the reign of Elizabeth and James the First* (1865), pp. 7-8.

picture of the countryside as seen through a German's eyes; 'the peasants dwell in small huts, and pile up their produce out of doors in heaps, and so high that you cannot see their houses.'[30] He also stressed English arrogance and lack of subservience: 'the inhabitants ... are extremely proud and overbearing ... they care little for foreigners, but scoff and laugh at them.'[31] During the same decade another German, from Brandenburg, also visited England and later published his journal. This was Paul Hentzner, a jurist and counsellor. He was also struck by the wealth of the English: 'the soil is fruitful and abounds with cattle,' and upon the hills 'wander numerous flocks' of sheep. This is the 'true Golden Fleece, in which consist the chief riches of the inhabitants, great sums of money being brought into the island by merchants.'[32] The inhabitants consumed less bread and more meat than the French, and 'put a great deal of sugar in their drink'; 'their beds are covered with tapestry, even those of farmers ... their houses are commonly of two stories .... Glass-houses (i.e. with glass windows) are in plenty here.' In addition to the material affluence, Hentzner noticed independence of spirit: 'They are powerful in the field, successful against their enemies, impatient of anything like slavery.'[33]

In many ways, the area most like England in Elizabeth's reign was the Low Countries. Yet two accounts by natives of this region also highlight the differences. Emmanuel van Meteren was an Antwerp merchant who lived in London throughout the reign of Elizabeth and travelled through the whole of England and Ireland. He was therefore especially well-qualified to describe English society. He noted the high standards of living, as exhibited in both food and clothing: the English 'feed well and delicately, and eat a great deal of meat .... The English dress in elegant, light and costly garments, but they are very inconstant and desirous of novelties, changing their fashions every year, both men and women. When they go abroad riding or travelling, they don their best clothes, contrary to the practice of other nations ....'[34] He too believed that the wealth came from sheep, rather than from hard labour. He noted that people did not have to work as hard as in other nations; 'the people are not so laborious and industrious as the Netherlanders or French, as they lead for the most part an indolent life .... They keep many lazy servants, and also many wild animals for their pleasure, rather than trouble themselves to cultivate the land.'[35] He also observed

[30]Ibid., pp. 25-6.
[31]Ibid., p. 7.
[32]Ibid., pp. 109-111.
[33]Ibid., pp. 110-111.
[34]Ibid., pp. 70-1.
[35]Ibid., p. 70.

that temperamentally they were independent and individualistic and scornful of foreigners: 'the people are bold, courageous, ardent, and cruel in war, fiery in attack, and having little fear of death; they are not vindictive, but very inconstant, rash, vainglorious, light, and deceiving, and very suspicious, especially of foreigners, whom they despise . . . .'[36] The idea of 'perfidious Albion' was clearly developed. A Dutch physician, Levinus Lemnius, visited England in 1560 and gives an account which agrees with Meteren's description of affluence. He describes how he travelled into 'that flourishing Iland,' partly to see the fashions of that 'wealthy Country.' He met with 'incredible courtesy and friendliness in speech and affability,' perhaps to be explained by the fact that he came from Zealand which of all the continent was perhaps the closest to England. He was impressed by 'the neat cleanliness, the exquisite fineness, the pleasant and delightful furniture in every point of the household,' and the 'wholesome and exquisite meat.'[37] Lemnius described them as honest and straightforward, not obsequious or flattering; 'not bombasted with any unseemly terms or infarced with any clawing flatteries or allurements.'[38] He continued with an allusion to 'their populous and great haunted cities, the fruitfulness of their ground and soil, their lively springs and mighty rivers, their great herds and flocks of cattle, their mysteries and art of weaving and clothmaking . . . the multitude of merchants exercising the traffic and art of merchandise among them . . . .'[39] Finally, he noted that they were obstinate, especially when angered, 'they will not easily be pacified, neither can their high and haughty stomach lightly be conquered, otherwise than by submission, and yielding to their mind and appetite.'[40] In other words, only by agreeing with them could an argument be ended. Points from these general descriptions are echoed in many other visitor's accounts. An Italian physician, Cardano, who visited the country in 1552 noted that 'they are quickly angered, and are in that state to be dreaded.'[41] Another Italian in his description in 1548 also commented on the arrogance of the English, who thought their country the best in the world, and different from all others. 'The English are commonly destitute of good breeding, and are despisers of Foreigners, since they esteem him a wretched being and but half a man (semihominem) who may be born elsewhere than in Britain, and far more miserable him whose fate it should be to leave his breath and his bones in a foreign land . . . .'[42]

[36]*Idem.*
[37]Ibid., pp. 78, 79.
[38]Ibid., p. 79.
[39]*Idem.*
[40]Ibid., p. 80.
[41]Ibid., p. xlix.
[42]Ibid., p. 186.

All these writers clearly felt that there was something different not only about the economy, but also the personality of the English. It could conceivably be argued that this had sprung up mysteriously and rapidly in the first half of the sixteenth century as a result of the Protestant Reformation and the profound agricultural revolution which Weber and Marx suggest occurred. It is therefore particularly interesting to look at the account of an Italian visitor who wrote a report on England for his government, describing a visit in 1497, almost thirty years before the English Reformation and before the new 'capitalism' could have had any deep effects. We may wonder whether he felt he was visiting a nation already different from the Continent, or an island whose basic economy and society mirrored the European tradition.

The 'Relation, or rather a true account, of the island of England' was written in connection with the embassy of Andrea Trevisano to the court of King Henry VII, as a report to the ambassador's government.[43] It was not written as either propaganda or for a literary market, and there is no particular reason to believe that it exaggerates. The author was struck by the great wealth of the country: 'the riches of England are greater than those of any other country in Europe, as I have been told by one of the oldest and most experienced merchants, and also as I myself can vouch from what I have seen.'[44] He thought that this was due to the 'great fertility of the soil,' the 'sale of their valuable tin,' and 'from their extraordinary abundance of wool.' Whatever the cause 'everyone who makes a tour in the island will soon become aware of this great wealth' — high praise from a Venetian visitor at the end of the fifteenth century. The wealth was widely distributed: 'there is no small innkeeper, however poor and humble he may be, who does not serve his table with silver dishes and drinking cups; and no one, who has not in his house silver plate to the amount of at least £100 sterling, which is equivalent to 500 golden crowns with us, is considered by the English to be a person of any consequence. But above all are their riches displayed in the church treasures . . . .'[45] They also 'all from time immemorial wear very fine clothes.'[46] Even when engaged on a military campaign they liked to live well for 'when the war is raging most furiously, they will seek for good eating, and all their other comforts, without thinking of what harm might befall them.'[47] The author noted that money and trade were widespread. 'The common people apply themselves to trade, or to fishing, or

[43] According to Rye, ibid., p. 43. The exact date was not established when the text was published as *A Relation, or rather a true account of the Islands of England, . . . About the year 1500*, translated by C. A. Sneyd (Camden Society, 1848).
[44] Ibid., p. 28.
[45] Ibid., pp. 28-9.
[46] Ibid., p. 22.
[47] Ibid., p. 23.

else they practice navigation; and they are so diligent in mercantile pursuits, that they do not fear to make contracts on usury.'[48] He believed that 'there is no injury that can be committed against the lower orders of the English, that may not be atoned for by money.'[49] He also noted that they were very arrogant, self-assured and suspicious of foreigners. 'They have an antipathy to foreigners, and imagine that they never come into their island, but to make masters of it.'[50] This was related to the fact that 'the English are great lovers of themselves, and of everything belonging to them; they think that there are no other men than themselves, and no other world but England; and whenever they see a handsome foreigner, they say that "he looks like an Englishman" and that "it is a great pity that he should not be an Englishman"; and when they partake of any delicacy with a foreigner, they ask him, "whether such a thing is made in *their* country?"'[51] This is a self-awareness and confidence in the late fifteenth century which we may be surprised to find.

The author is especially interesting on the personality and social character of the English. Combined with their self-confidence and arrogance went a mutual suspiciousness; each individual was out for himself and trusted no-one else. As compared to Italian society, it seemed that the English had no 'sincere and solid friendships amongst themselves, insomuch that they do not trust each other to discuss either public or private affairs together, in the confidential manner we do in Italy.'[52] This lack of trust was shown, and we might suggest partly caused by, the family system and upbringing which the visitor found so odd. He remarked that 'the want of affection in the English is strongly manifested towards their children; for after having kept them at home till they arrive at the age of 7 or 9 years at the utmost, they put them out, both males and females, to hard service in the houses of other people, binding them generally for another 7 to 9 years. And these are called apprentices . . . .'[53] The author dismissed the native's explanation that it was 'in order that their children might learn better manners,' believing that it was because the parents 'like to enjoy all their comforts themselves, and that they are better served by strangers than they would be by their own children . . . . if they had their own children at home, they would be obliged to give them the same food they made use of for themselves.'[54] The author found this shedding of the young repulsive. If

[48]*Idem.*
[49]Ibid., p. 26.
[50]Ibid., pp. 23-4.
[51]Ibid., pp. 20-1.
[52]Ibid., p. 24.
[53]*Idem.*
[54]Ibid., p. 25.

the parents had taken them back when their apprenticeship was over 'they might, perhaps, be excused' but 'they never return.' Instead, they have to make their own way, 'assisted by their patrons, not by their fathers, they also open a house and strive diligently by this means to make some fortune for themselves.'[55] The author perceptively noted that this meritocratic system, so different from a 'domestic mode of production' where the family form one economic unit, leads to insecurity and the desire for constant accumulation. He wrote, 'whence it proceeds that, having no hope of their paternal inheritance, they all become so greedy of gain, that they feel no shame in asking, almost "for the love of God," for the smallest sum of money.'[56] Yet he also conceded that such a system allows very considerable social mobility, describing at great length how apprentices amass a fortune later in their life, for instance by marrying the mistress of the house. To illustrate this he told a story of how the brother of the Duke of Suffolk, poor but noble, married the rich old woman with whom he was boarded.[57] This individualistic, self-help, social system was also shown not merely in national character and economics, but also in religion. The author noted that though nominally good Catholics, 'there are however, many who have various opinions concerning religion.'[58]

If we compare this description of England in 1497 with the later ones we have quoted, it is difficult to see a fundamental difference. It appears that England was already peculiar in its social and economic structure, and that this difference was not merely a matter of geography and language, but was rooted deep in its laws, customs and kinship system. Although it is unlikely that Englishmen, 'rarely conscious of the quality of the air they breathe' would have been quite so aware of the difference,[59] we may survey briefly the reactions of some of those who by choice or of necessity spent periods on the continent or the Celtic regions and reflected on the differences they found.

It would be possible in a longer survey to show that many Englishmen were aware that their economy, social structure and political system was radically different from that of neighbouring nations. For instance, the wide distribution of wealth and less stratified society of England was noted by Fuller early in the seventeenth century when he

[55]Ibid., pp. 25-6.
[56]Ibid., p. 26.
[57]Ibid., pp. 27-8.
[58]Ibid., p. 23.
[59]R. H. Tawney, *Equality* (1931; Unwin paperback edn., 1964), p. 35, made this remark, adding that 'the course of wisdom, therefore, is to consult observers belonging to other nations.' By taking those who had spent several months or years abroad, it is hoped to avoid the consequences of the observation that 'He little knows of England who only England knows' (Robert Lowie, *Social Organization* (1948)), p. 19.

described the English 'yeomen' as 'an estate of people almost peculiar to England. France and Italy are like a die which hath no points between sink and ace, nobility and peasantry — the yeoman wears russet clothes but makes golden payment, having tin in his buttons and silver in his pocket.'[60] The difference which De Tocqueville had noted was already present. When the English compared themselves to the Irish they found that something about English social structure, particularly the inheritance customs, meant that England had grown immensely more wealthy. Sir John Davies wrote in 1612:

> For, though the Irishry be a Nation of great Antiquity, and wanted neither wit nor valor; and though they had received the Christian Faith, above 1200 years since; and were Lovers of Music, Poetry and all kinds of learning; and possessed a Land abounding with all things necessary for the Civil life of man; yet (which is strange to be related) they did never build any houses of brick or stone (some few poor Religious Houses excepted) before the reign of King *Henry* the Second, though they were Lords of this Island for many hundred years before and since the Conquest attempted by the English . . . . Neither did any of them in all this time, plant any Gardens or Orchards. Inclose or improve their Lands, live together in settled Villages or Towns, nor make any provision for posterity . . . .[61]

Davies believed that this was because the English had primogeniture, and Ireland had partible inheritance.

Sir Thomas Smith's first draft of *De Republica Anglorum* was written in 1565 while he was an Ambassador in France. One of the major differences he noticed was the very one which De Tocqueville had thought was the central key to the peculiarity of England, the fact that there was easy social mobility from the bottom to the top of society:

> as for gentlemen, they be made good cheap in England. For whosoever studieth the laws of the realm, who studieth in the universities, who professeth liberal sciences, and to be short, who can live idly and without manual labour, and will bear the port, charge and countenance of a gentleman, he shall be called master,

---

[60]In the *Holy State*, quoted in Charles Wilson, *England's Apprenticeship* (1965), p. 21; Sir Thomas Overbury at the same time noted a similar independence among the English yeomanry: 'He is lord paramount within himself, though he hold by never so mean a tenure,' quoted in J. Dover Wilson, *Life in Shakespeare's England* (Penguin edn., 1944), p. 30. Another writer who noticed the wide distribution of wealth and described a social structure which showed no sign of a simple dichotomy between 'lord' and 'peasant' was William Harrison. He stated that 'We in England divide our people into four sorts, as gentlemen, citizens or burgesses, yeoman, and artificers or labourers.' *The Description of England* (1583; Folger Shakespeare Library edn., 1968), ed. Georges Edelen, p. 94. His description of the 'yeoman' (p. 117) is very far in every respect from the model 'peasant' described in chapter one.
[61]Quoted in Pocock, *Ancient Constitution*, p. 60. For a further recent discussion of the very great differences between England and Celtic countries at this period, see Perry Anderson, *Lineages of the Absolutist State* (1974), pp. 130-1, 135-6.

for that is the title which men give to esquires and other gentlemen, and shall be taken for a gentleman.[62]

Smith then proceeded to give a most interesting description of the same wealthy middling yeomanry which Fuller had considered to be peculiar to England, providing a necessary step in the ladder between labourers and gentry. Such yeomen worked hard to place their children one step higher up the ladder, turning their growing wealth into social honour. The passage again indicates the accumulative drive, a wide distribution of wealth, and easy social mobility, a situation in mid sixteenth-century England which Smith was consciously comparing with his experience in France. The yeomanry,

confess themselves to be no gentlemen, but give the honour to all which be or take upon them to be gentlemen, and yet they have a certain preeminence and more estimation than labourers and artificers, and commonly live wealthily, keep good houses, and do their business, and travail to acquire riches; these be (for the most part) farmers unto gentlemen, which with grazing, frequenting of markets, and keeping servants not idle as the gentleman doth, but sich as get both their own living and part of their masters, by these means do come to such wealth, that they are able and daily do buy the lands of unthrifty gentlemen, and after setting their sons to the school at the Universities, to the law of the Realm, or otherwise leaving them sufficient lands whereon they may live without labour, do make their said sons by those means gentlemen.[63]

Smith discusses the history of this strata, arguing that well back into the medieval period the 'yeomen of England' had been famous, in opposition to the nobility of France: in battles, the French kings fought with their noble horsemen, the English with their yeomen on foot.[64] What Smith considered to be an ancient difference in social structure might, he realized, be criticized. He therefore considered the question of 'whether the manner of England in making gentlemen so easily is to be allowed.'[65] He replied that it should, for whereas in France the King would lose revenue thereby, since the nobility were less heavily taxed, this was not the case in England — again a point made by De Tocqueville. Finally, Smith stressed that when considering the Commonwealth of England, one was dealing with a land filled with free men, who had of their own free will agreed to live together. It was an association of equals based on contract, not a kingdom of subjects ruled

---

[62]Sir Thomas Smith, *De Republica Anglorum: The maner of Government or policie of the Realme of England* . . . (1583; reprinted by the Scolar Press, 1970), p. 27. This passage is copied almost verbatim from Harrison, *Description of England*, pp. 113-4.
[63]Ibid., p. 30. This passage is likewise based on Harrison, *Description of England*, pp. 117-8.
[64]Ibid., pp. 31-2.
[65]Ibid., p. 28.

by a superior monarch: 'a common wealth is called a society or common doing of a multitude of free men collected together and united by common accord and covenants among themselves, for the conservation of themselves . . . .'[66] Here we have the stress on liberty and equality.

About ten years before Smith wrote, another Englishman, John Aylmer, later Bishop of London, was living in exile on the continent. In 1559 he published a pamphlet entitled *An Harborowe for Faithfull and Trewe Subjects* in which he exhorted his fellow countrymen to defend their land against Continental invaders. Although it is clear that this description of the comparative position of the Englishman and his Continental counterparts is heightened for effect, the previous descriptions by foreigners themselves gives it a support. Furthermore, it is interesting as a self-view by an intelligent Englishman, and some of the minor details, which we can check, ring true. Since it is a particularly lively account it is worth quoting fairly extensively. He urged his fellow countrymen to pay taxes towards the raising of defences.

Oh England, England, thou knowest not thine own wealth: because thou seest not other countries penury. Oh if thou sawest the peasants of France, how they are scraped to the bones, and what extremeties they suffer: thou wouldest think thy self blessed (as indeed thou art) which hast rather fathers and mothers to thy governors, than Kings or Queens. The husbandman in France, all that he hath gotten in his whole life, loseth it upon one day. For when so ever they have war (as they are never without it) the kings soldiers enter into the poor mans house, eateth and drinketh up all that ever he hath . . . the poor man never goeth to the market, to sell anything: but he payeth a toll, almost the half of that he selleth: he eateth neither pig, goose, capon, nor hen: but he must pay as much for the tribute of it there, as it might be bought for her: O unhappy and miserable men that live under this yoke. In Italy they say it is not much better, the husbandmen be there so rich: that the best coat he weareth is sacking, his nether stocks of his hose, be his own skin, his diet and fare not very costly, for he cometh to the market with a hen or two in one hand, and a dozen eggs in a net in the other, which being sold and told, he buyeth and carrieth home with him, no Beef or Mutton, Veal or sea fish, as you do: but a quart of oil to make salads of herbs, wherewith he liveth all the week following. And in Germany though they be in some better case than the other: yet eat they more roots than flesh . . . Now compare them with thee: and thou shalt see how happy thou art. They eat herbs: and thou Beef and Mutton. They roots: and thou butter, cheese, and eggs. They drink commonly water: and thou good ale and beer. They go from the market with a salad: and thou with good flesh fill thy wallet. They lightly never see any sea fish: and thou hast they belly full of it. They pay till their bones rattle in their skin: and thou layest up for thy son and heir. Thou are twice or thrice in thy lifetime called upon to help thy Country, with a subsidy or contribution: and they daily pay and never cease. Thou livest like a Lord, and they like dogs

[66] Ibid., p. 10.

. . . We live in paradise. England is the paradise and not Italy, as commonly they call it. For they have figs, oranges, pomegranites, grapes, peppers, oil and herbs; and we have sheep, oxen, cows, calves, conies, fish, wool, lead, cloth, tin, leather, and infinite treasure more, which they lack. We have plenty of all things: and they scarcity of all things. Oh if thou knewest thou English man in what wealth thou livest, and in how plentiful a Country: Thou wouldest vii times of the day fall flat on thy face before God, and give him thanks, that thou wert born an English man, and not a French peasant, nor an Italian, nor German.[67]

Aylmer further urged his countrymen that 'you have God, and all his army on your side,' adding a marginal phrase beside the passage which beautifully epitomizes, when slightly misconstrued, the arrogance which foreigners found so distasteful: 'God is English.' Even if we discount much of the rhetoric, it is based on the experience of a learned and intelligent man, sometime tutor to the Lady Jane Grey and a leading churchman, who had seen all the countries he spoke about, except Italy.

That basic differences in standard of living, liberty of the subject and social mobility, as well as other aspects, were very visible when England was compared with the rest of the continent by the middle of the sixteenth century, appears plain. But in order to prove our argument that these peculiarities were much older than the Reformation and supposed emergence of capitalism at the end of the fifteenth century, it is necessary to find an Englishman who wrote about the differences between England and the continent before 1500. We need the equivalent of the Italian quoted who visited England in 1497. Fortunately such a man exists in Sir John Fortescue, Lord Chancellor to King Henry VI. He fled into France with Henry in 1461 and during the next ten years of exile wrote his *Learned Commendation of the Politique Laws of England*. The expanded title of the work clearly shows its nature and bias: 'wherein by most pithy reasons and evident demonstrations they are plainly proved far to excel as well the Civil laws of the Empire, as also all other laws of the world, with a large discourse of the difference between the ii governments of kingdoms, whereof the one is only regal, and the other consisteth of regal and political administration conjoined.' The work was written in the form of a dialogue between the lawyer and the young prince, whom he was trying to teach the principles of English politics and law, illustrated by a comparison between England and France. Again, we must necessarily expect a heightening of effect, yet the broad outline of what were thought to be the contrast seems incontestable.

[67]Part of the pamphlet, from which this quotation is taken, is reprinted in George Orwell and Reginald Reynolds, *British Pamphleteers* (1958), i, pp. 29-33.

Fortescue dwelt mainly on the political and legal differences. The central political one was that France was an absolute monarchy, where all law emanated from the King and where people were subjects. England was a limited monarchy, based on the voluntary acquiescence of the people, and where the King himself was bound by the same laws as his countrymen. England was an association of free men, as Smith later described, held together by mutual contracts. Fortescue argued that 'I do most evidently see that no nation did ever of their own voluntary mind incorporate themselves into a kingdom for any other intent, but only to the end that thereby they might with more safety than before maintain themselves and enjoy their goods from such misfortunes and losses as they stood in fear of . . .'[68]

The major legal differences flowed from the differences between Civil (Roman) law, and English Common Law: the differences in methods of trial, the use of juries, the absence of torture in England, the use of sheriffs in the legal process. Fortescue noted the same oppressions of the rural population by royal troops in France that Aylmer had mentioned; 'so that there is not the least village there free from this miserable calamity, but that it is once or twice every year beggared by this kind of pilling (pillage).'[69] This and other exactions, such as the salt tax, led to the great poverty of the rural inhabitants which Fortescue observed around him.

The people being with these and diverse other calamities plagued and oppressed, do live in great misery, drinking water daily. Neither do the inferior sort taste any other liquor saving only at solemn feasts. Their shamewes (a gown cut in the middle) are made of hemp, much like to sack cloth. Wollen cloth they wear none, except it be very coarse, and that only in their coats under their said upper garments. Neither use they any hosen, but from the knee upwards: the residue of their legs go naked. Their women go bare foot saving on holy days. Neither man nor women eat any flesh there, but only lard or bacon, with a small quantity whereof they fatten their potage and broths. As for roasted or sodden meat of flesh they taste none, except it be of the innards sometimes and heads of beasts that be killed for gentlemen and merchants.[70]

In England, on the other hand, the position of rural inhabitants was very different. The absence of heavy taxation, of billeted soldiers, and of internal taxes, meant that 'every inhabiter of that realm useth and enjoyeth at his pleasure all the fruits that his land or cattle beareth, with all the profits and commodities which by his own travail, or by the

[68] John Fortescue, *A Learned Commendation of the Politique Laws of England* (a facsimile reprint of the 1567 edn., Amsterdam, 1969), fol. 33^v. The similarity of this view to that expressed two hundred years later by Thomas Hobbes is obvious.
[69] Ibid., fol. 80.
[70] Ibid., fols. 81-81^v.

labour of others he gaineth by land or by water.'[71] The result, as Fortescue saw it, was that

the men of that land are rich, having abundance of gold and silver and other things necessary for the maintenance of a mans life. They drink no water, unless it be so that some for devotion, and upon a seal of penance do abstain from other drinks. They eat plentifully of all kinds of fish and flesh. They wear fine woollen cloth in all their apparel. They have also abundance of bed coverings in their houses, and of all other woollen stuff. They have great store of all hustlements (utensils, tools) and implements of husbandry, and all other things that are requisite to the accomplishment of a quiet and wealthy life according to their estates and degrees. Neither are they sued in the law, but only before ordinary judges, whereby the laws of the land they are justly intreated.[72]

These differences, Fortescue argued, lay deep in the structure of a country governed by Common Law as compared to one which suffered from Roman Law and absolute monarchy. So great was the superiority of the English, in their wealth, happiness and legal system, that his royal pupil was forced to ask why the whole world had not developed English law. Fortescue in his reply, took the idea of trial by jury, and showed that such a system depended on a particular form of economic and social structure which was absent in all countries except England.

The basic difference, one which De Tocqueville was later to note, was that the countryside in England was filled with wealthy persons; they did not all migrate to the towns. Thus it was possible to find even in small towns and villages a substantial number of educated, prosperous, inhabitants. In other countries this was not possible. Fortescue argued that the English countryside

is so filled and replenished with landed men, that therein so small a thorpe (village, hamlet) can not be found wherein dwells not a knight, an esquire, or such a householder, as is there commonly called a frankleyn, enriched with great possessions: And also other freeholders and many yeomen able for their livelihoods to make a Jury in form aforementioned. For there be in that land diverse yeomen which are able to dispend by the year above a hundred pounds . . . Wherefore it cannot be thought that such men can be suborned, or that they will be perjured . . . .[73]

whereas,

after this manner . . . none other realms of the world disposed and inhabited. For though there be in them men of great power, of great riches, and possessions, yet they dwell not one nigh to another as such great men do in

[71]Ibid., fols. 84ᵛ-85.
[72]Ibid., fols. 85-85ᵛ.
[73]Ibid., fols. 66ᵛ-67.

England. Neither so many inheritors and possessors of land are elsewhere as in England. For in a whole town of an other country it is hard to find one man which for his livelihood is able to be received into a Jury. For there, except it be in Cities and walled towns, very few that be beside noble men that have any possessions of lands or other immovables.[74]

Fortescue continues by arguing that the nobility in other countries did not live on their land or engage actively in agriculture, as did the English, another difference which Arthur Young and then De Tocqueville were to note for the eighteenth century. The final consequence was that juries of twelve substantial neighbours could not be called, since if they were substantial they would be living far away. The strong polarization between nobles and peasants was clearly present in France, whereas England apparently had a very different social structure.

Fortescue was not in a position to explain this difference, beyond the features concerning heavy taxation, military billeting and the other factors already suggested. His one other argument was that England was by nature richer, and hence her people grew wealthier than elsewhere. This is interesting as it leads him to a very early and glowing account of the wealth of the English countryside, a richness which mean that people 'are scant troubled with any painful labour.' The result of this was that 'they live more spiritually . . . and hereof it cometh that men of this country are more apt and fit to discern in doubtful causes of great examination and trial, than are men wholly given to moyling in the ground: in whom that rural exercise ingendreth rudeness of wit and mind.'[75] If we remember De Tocqueville's description of the illiterate and ignorant villagers of eighteenth century France, we see that the differences between the two countries were very ancient. Although it is implausible to explain them, as contemporaries usually did, by the natural fertility and lack of wild animals in England, it is worth seeing what this particular Englishman in the middle of the fifteenth century wrote when he was describing his homeland to a prince who 'came very young out of England . . . so that the disposition and quality of that land is unknown to you.'[76]

He believed that 'In deed England is so fertile and fruitful, that comparing quantity to quantity, it surmounteth all other lands in fruitfulness. Yea it bringeth forth fruit of it self scant provoked by man's industry and labour.' It is an elegant description of a demi-Eden, where 'the lands, the fields, the groves and the woods do so abundantly spring.

[74] Ibid., fols. 67ᵛ-68.
[75] Ibid., fols. 66-66ᵛ.
[76] Ibid., fol. 65ᵛ.

that the same untilled do commonly yield to their owners more profit than tilled, though else they be most fruitful of corn and grain.' The livestock grazed safely in the absence of wild animals, so that 'their sheep lie night by night in the fields unkept within their folds, wherewith their land is manured.'[77] Again there is a strong impression of England as a land apart in wealth and social structure. Nor did Fortescue imply that this was a new difference. His explanation, a combination of natural fertility, limited monarchy, and Common Law, made him believe that the differences were very ancient. He wrote that 'The customs of England are of most ancient antiquity,' and traced them back through the Normans, Saxons, Danes, Romans to the ancient Britons.[78] He believed that there had been no basic changes in the customs in the preceding thousand years or more; 'in the times of these several nations and of their kings this realm was still ruled with the self same customs that it is now governed withall.'[79] Even if we do not lay any weight on his remarks concerning the period before the Norman invasion, it is interesting that one of the foremost legal minds in England in the middle of the fifteenth century should have considered that there had been little change in the central customs of the country during the previous centuries.

It would be possible to trace this native view of England back before the fifteenth century and it is hoped that medievalists will do so. For example, the fourteenth century *Polychronicon* of Ranulf Higden anticipates the proud account of England in the sixteenth century by William Harrison in his *Description of England*. Thus we are told that Ranulf's 'paeans to British resources remind us that the love of the English for their demiparadise was no Tudor invention.'[80] Moving even further back, the English Franciscan Bartholomaeus Anglicus included a description of England in his massive encyclopaedia written in the middle of the thirteenth century. His brief history of the country completely omitted the Norman conquest, stressing instead the link with the Anglo-Saxons. He believed that England was 'the plenteousest corner of the world, full rich a land that unneth (uncompelled) it needeth help of any land, and every other land needeth help of England. England is full of mirth and of game and men oft-times able to mirth and to game, free men of heart and with tongue . . . .'[81] Again the relative wealth and liberty is stressed.

---

[77] Ibid., fol. 66.
[78] Ibid., fol. 38.
[79] Ibid., fol. 38ᵛ.
[80] Harrison, *Description of England*, introduction by Georges Edelen, p. xviii.
[81] *On the Properties of Things: John Trevisa's translation of Bartholomaeus Anglicus De Proprietatibus Rerum* (Oxford, 1975), ii, p. 734.

This view of the separateness of England was the one which dominated all those who lived in England and wrote about it until the middle of the seventeenth century. J. G. A. Pocock in his work on the *Ancient Constitution and the Feudal Law* has amply documented the views of contemporaries, particularly the Common Lawyers, concerning the originality and peculiarities of England. The author points out that 'Coke . . . does not insist or argue that the Common Law is the only system that has ever prevailed in England, but takes it as much for granted as the air he breathes . . . .'[82] He further states, that in general 'As a key to their past the English knew of one law alone. It was possible for them to believe that as far back as their history extended, the Common Law of the king's courts was the only system of law which had grown up and been of force within the realm.'[83] This view of the 'Ancient Constitution,' which made Coke think that not only was the law immemorial, but that it was so 'purely within the island,' is dismissed by the author as patently false. It is a view of the inhabitants, a native category which 'can expect so little sympathy in the twentieth century.'[84] The historical revolution occurred, Pocock argues, when, in opposition to the great legal minds, certain antiquarians, particularly Spelman, started to compare England to the Continent and discovered that the England of the seventeeth century was descended from a 'feudal' society, basically similar to other 'feudal' societies on the Continent. Although this revolution was crushed and the old views re-asserted themselves in the eighteenth century, it was revived in the nineteenth. Since then we have become accustomed to thinking of English history in three stages: pre-feudal, feudal, post-feudal. Pocock admits there are weaknesses in this, but states that 'it may be doubted whether we have found any more satisfactory set of generalizations to put in its place.'[85] It would be ironic if it turned out that those who lived through the experience, those who did not know that they were merely an offshoot of Europe, who believed that their society was unique and different, turned out to be right, and many modern historians wrong.

[82]Pocock, *Ancient Constitution*, p. 32.
[83]Ibid., p. 30; for another contemporary view, which also saw the Norman invasion as having very little effect on one part of England, Kent, see William Lambarde, *Perambulation of Kent*, (1570; Bath, 1970), pp. 19-21.
[84]Ibid., p. 20: a recent example of the lack of sympathy is given by the summary of English history in Anderson, *Lineages of the Absolutist State*, p. 113; 'the transition from the medieval to the early modern epochs thus corresponded — *despite all local legends of unbroken 'continuity'* — to a deep and radical reversal of many of the most characteristic traits of prior feudal development' (my italics). For another attack on the 'cherished ideological motifs of England's inviolate "continuity" ' from the tenth to the twentieth century', see the same author's *Passages from Antiquity to Feudalism* (1974), pp. 159-60 note.
[85]Pocock, *Ancient Constitution*, p. 119.

If it should turn out to be the case, after further research, that contemporaries were right, it will be noted that the fact was already indirectly recognized in the very use of the word 'peasant'. Modern historians use the word freely about medieval and early modern England, inventing phrases such as 'The Peasant's Revolt' which were not used at the time.[86] Contemporaries were more careful. The word is by derivation a French one, and, according to the Oxford English Dictionary, was 'in early use, properly used only of foreign countries.' Through the centuries supposedly dominated by peasantry, no Englishman thought to use the word in English to describe his society, either when people 'revolted' or at any other time. When the word was used before 1500 it was used to describe foreigners, as we saw Fortescue using it, or in 1475 when describing 'the poor commons, labourers, paisaunts of the said duchy of Normandy.'[87] The only occasions on which it was used of English dwellers was when lawyers imposed the French language and concepts onto English material. Thus Hilton cites an example of 1313 which refers to 'les peisauntz' and the Year Books of 1341-2 speak of 'des paisantz et villeyns.'[88] Of course it is not the word that is at issue, but it is tempting to believe that Englismen did not need to use the term, and that it had no equivalent in English, they knew they were dealing with a social and economic structure which it would be misleading to equate with that in France or the rest of Europe.

In order to prove the argument it would be necessary to undertake an extensive comparative study of England and at least one Continental country in the Middle Ages. This cannot be attempted here. Instead we may briefly turn to the work of a class of historians and lawyers who were interested in comparing social and legal systems by the 'comparative method' and hence saw England in perspective. One of these, F. W. Maitland, has already been cited in support of the argument we are pursuing. It is clear that he realized that English law and society were different from the Continent. A second historian who compared countries, and particularly England and his native France,

[86]It is mildly referred to in contemporary documents as 'the time of rumours' (Richard Smith, personal communication); it would be interesting to know when it was first given its modern name. To anyone familiar with revolts in real peasant societies, the English rising appears different in many respects. Thorner has written that 'Almost always peasant uprisings have been marked by fury, desperation, and brutality' (Thorner, *Peasantry*, p. 508), but the English affair appears to have been orderly and restrained, with very little violence or bloodshed when compared to the German or French or Russian risings of the fifteenth to seventeenth centuries. Nor does it seemed to have been caused by peasant desperation. It was not a purely rural phenomenon and its centre was in areas with widespread freeholding, rather than areas with oppressive villeinage. Postan has noted these difficulties and admits that it 'possessed a number of features difficult to fit into the conventional picture of villeins rising against oppression' (Postan, *England*, p. 609).
[87]*Oxford English Dictionary*, s.v.
[88]Hilton, *Peasantry*, p. 3; *Oxford English Dictionary*, s.v. 'peasant.'

was Marc Bloch. In many places he noted that from at least the second half of the thirteenth century, England's agrarian structure seemed strange when compared to that of France. For example, there was a difference in the relations between the lords and the peasants;[89] in the 'England of the Norman Kings there were no peasant allods,' whereas these were present in France;[90] there was a 'premature decay' in England of 'the old framework of the kindred.'[91] In his essay entitled 'A Contribution Towards a Comparative History of European Societies' Bloch summarized many of the differences.

English agriculture became 'individualistic' while French agriculture remained 'communal';[92] English villeinage was entirely different from French *servage*: 'Villeinage is in fact a specifically English institution.' This is because from at least the second half of the twelfth century the whole system of centralized royal justice and the Common Law set the English agrarian structure on a different course of development to that in France.[93] As a result, 'The French serf of the 14th century and the English Serf or villein of the same period belonged to two totally dissimilar classes.'[94] Bloch realized that he was dealing with two different systems. It seems very likely that if he were alive today and had available the many intensive studies which his work helped to encourage, he would go even further than to say that 'the progress and results of this development' in different countries, 'reveal such pronounced differences of degree that they are almost equivalent to a difference in kind.'[95]

The third major figure we may cite is Sir Henry Maine. During the second half of the nineteenth century his mind ranged across the English, Celtic, Continental and Asiatic legal systems and speculated on their similarities and differences. Clearly, he too believed that English land law was entirely different from that of the Continent and that the difference dated back to at least the first half of the thirteenth century. He wrote that long ago 'the great mass of English landed property had assumed certain characteristics which strongly distinguished it from the peasant property of the Continent as it existed before it was affected by the French Codes, and as it is still found in some countries.'[96] This difference consisted of two major features, ease of

---

[89]*French Rural Structure: An Essay on its Basic Characteristics* (1931; 1966), trans. J. Sondheimer, p. 126.
[90]*Feudal Society* (2nd edn., 1962), trans. L. A. Manyon, i, p. 248.
[91]Ibid., i, p. 140.
[92]Reprinted in Bloch, *Land*, p. 49.
[93]Ibid., p. 59; see also pp. 59-61.
[94]Ibid., pp. 61-2.
[95]Ibid., p. 66.
[96]*Lectures on the Early History of Institutions* (1875), pp. 125-6.

transfer and impartible inheritance. The relative ease with which land could be transferred by individuals, in other words the absence of restrictions placed by a wider group, struck him very forcefully. He wrote that 'Our land law is much more complex than the land law of Continental countries . . . and English real-property law has been still further complicated by the liberty of transfer and devise which we here enjoyed from a comparatively early period.'[97] This freedom was based on premises which were totally contrary to Continental and Asiatic law. One was the idea that all property was purchasable and had, indeed, arisen from an original sale. 'It will be found that English political economy and English popular notions are very deeply and extensively pervaded by the assumption that all property has been acquired through an original transaction of purchase,' a view which Maine thought was 'true' to the facts of the situation.[98] The second premise was that the relationship between people was based on contract, rather than on status from very early on in England. Maine wrote that the 'title of the Lord of the Manor and the title of the Copyholder were then, as now, far more deeply rooted in agreement than in any other deeply feudalized country.'[99] He even went as far as citing Bracton to show that the supposedly central status of 'villein' or serf was not a personal status at all, but a form of tenure; a villein could be a landed proprietor.[100] Thus England had changed from a society based on status to one based on contract by at least the thirteenth century.

The other major difference, as he saw it, was between systems of divisible and indivisible property, or, in other words, partible and impartible inheritance. He argued that from at least the thirteenth century there was a basic difference in this respect between England and France. Although he could not satisfactorily account for the fact that English property was treated as indivisible, and often went to the oldest son, he believed that the introduction of a major feature of this new attitude, primogeniture, could be dated to the period between Glanvill and Bracton, in other words approximately between 1187 and 1268.[101] This was 'the time when the most widely diffused of English tenures — socage — was just putting off the characteristics of the allod, and putting on those of the feud . . . . which is that, when held in individual enjoyment, (land) is primarily impartible or indivisible.'[102] In changing from one system to another 'you find yourself among a new order of legal ideas,' a world where 'a wholly new conception of landed

[97]*Dissertations on Early Law and Custom* (1883), pp. 354-5.
[98]Ibid., p. 325.
[99]Ibid., p. 324.
[100]Ibid., p. 305 note.
[101]*Lectures on . . . Institutions*, p. 126.
[102]*Dissertations on . . . Customs*, p. 341.

property had arisen.'[103] This strange and unique system of highly individual, impartible, property was unknown in the world before the twelfth century, Maine argued.[104] For mysterious reasons it emerged in England alone. The consequences were immense; 'from very early times landed property changed hands by purchase and sale more frequently in England than elsewhere.'[105] Furthermore, 'we are indebted to the peculiarly absolute English form of ownership for such an achievement as the cultivation of the soil of North America.'[106] Elsewhere the effects were often disastrous, as Maine admitted in relation to India. But there was no doubt as to their magnitude. Thus he wrote that 'the greatest change which has come over the people of India (is) . . . the growth on all sides of the sense of individual legal right.'[107] This occurred through the introduction of English law, an alien system which had evolved into one of individual rights and ownership by the thirteenth century.[108] The change was very early and very great. Though to the superficial observer it might, for example, look as if French and English tenures were roughly similar in, say the eighteenth century they were, as we have seen, very different. Given this fact, it is not surprising that surveys of landholding systems throughout Europe conducted in the nineteenth century should find that the English situation was 'wholly exceptional in Europe.'[109] The difference had been present, though disguised, for some six centuries at least.

---

[103]Ibid., pp. 342, 344.
[104]*Lectures on . . . Institutions*, p. 198.
[105]*Dissertations on . . . Custom*, p. 323.
[106]*Lectures on . . . Institutions*, p. 126.
[107]*Village-Communities in the East and West* (3rd edn., 1876), p. 73; also pp. 157-8, 160.
[108]*Dissertations on . . . Custom*, pp. 341-7.
[109]George C. Broderick, *English Land and English Landlords* (1881), p. 90; the survey is in ch. 3 of part III.

8
Some Implications

One implication of the preceding argument is that both historians and sociologists have largely misinterpreted the basic nature of English social structure between the thirteenth and eighteenth centuries. This is a serious charge, and some explanation of the reasons for this apparent misapprehension, particularly by medievalists, needs to be given. For, if the argument is correct, one of the 'most thoroughly investigated of all peasantries in history,' turns out not to be a peasantry at all.[1]

One cause leading to the very considerable error lies in the distorting effect of historical records, particularly those before the mid-sixteenth century. Manor court rolls, accounts, surveys and extents, and taxation records, which constitute over nine tenths of the evidence for rural inhabitants before the Black Death, are bound to give a distorted picture of the world. This is well known to medievalists, at least in theory. For instance, it has recently been shown that labourers and servants are present in large numbers in the later fourteenth century, but not prominent in manorial records. It is easiest to show this fact in a period when such records persist in quantity, but may be tested against other sources, as in the sixteenth century. Suppose we were merely to look at the manorial records and lay subsidies for sixteenth and seventeenth century English villages, we may wonder what impression we would obtain as to stability, the structure of the family, and rights in land, if we did not also use parish registers, wills, listings and other records. These documents were not used by R. H. Tawney in his *Agrarian Problem of the Sixteenth Century* published in 1912. He used the same records as those employed by medievalists and imposed the same models. He consequently paints a picture of large and complex, peasant-style households, and of geographical immobility. Though he admits that

---

[1] Hilton, *Bond Men*, p. 10.

the countryside was being penetrated by cash, the market, and 'capitalism' generally, he sees this as an external force disrupting a traditional 'peasantry.' Thus it is only the recent discovery and extensive use of listings of inhabitants, wills and inventories, court records, and parish registers, which have shaken historians of the sixteenth century from belief in a picture that in many ways resembled that painted by those of the thirteenth. Again, it is not at all difficult to see that if Homans had applied his model to the manorial records of later sixteenth century Essex or later seventeenth century Cumbria, he would have found that the evidence permitted him to make the interpretation he adopts for the thirteenth century. Yet we know that such a model would be totally incorrect for this later period and can prove this to be the case from other sources. The real problem when looking at the situation before the Black Death is how to use the documents to bear witness *against* themselves.[2] We are supported in our task by occasional references even within these sources, as well as the chance survival of certain manuscripts, a unique list of villein families in the thirteenth century or the discovery of peasant land charters. Such documents do not fit into the predicted mould at all well.

In the absence of direct evidence bearing on many of the crucial issues, writers have been tempted to draw on evidence from elsewhere — particularly from continental Europe in the same period, from nineteenth and early twentieth century 'surviving' peasantries in France and Ireland or from modern Third World peasantries. Believing that England in the middle ages was basically similar to other 'peasant' societies, it was considered entirely legitimate as a method of proceeding to fill in gaps in the sources by reference to what was known concerning peasants in other parts of medieval Europe or the modern world. Not only could one construct a general picture of England using shreds of evidence from all over Europe, as Coulton did in the *Medieval Village* and most of his other works, but one could use studies of Russia before the revolution, nineteenth century France or Ireland, China and elsewhere since they were all basically similar. For example, Bennett points out that it is impossible to know much about the daily life and routine of ordinary people: 'the nearest we can hope to get to such condi-

---

[2]Marc Bloch was making the same point when he wrote that 'even when most anxious to bear witness, that which the text tells us expressly has ceased to be the primary object of our attention today. Ordinarily, we prick up our ears far more eagerly when we are permitted to overhear what was never intended to be said.' He also spoke of forcing documents 'to speak, even against their will ....' (*The Historian's Craft* (Manchester, 1954), pp. 63, 64). Elsewhere he wrote that 'A document is a witness; and like most witnesses, it does not say much except under cross-examination. The real difficulty lies in putting the right questions' (*Land*, p. 48).

tions, perhaps, is when we have a few minutes inside the dwelling of a peasant family, not in England, for things have changed radically here, but in some tiny French or Swiss hamlet, where medieval ways and customs are only of yesterday.'³ This use of analogies continues up to the present among medievalists. For instance Krause used census data from sixteenth century Italy and Sweden to fill in gaps concerning England;⁴ Raftis, speaking of peasants being 'rooted' in the village, remarks that in this basic respect the 'villager was one of the traditional peasant type of Western Europe.'⁵

Perhaps the most sustained use of analogies, which is central to the whole argument of the work, is in Homans' *English Villagers of the Thirteenth Century*. At first he appears to leave the question of the similarity between the 'peasants' of the thirteenth century and the rest of the world an open one. We are told that 'if what happened in England in the thirteenth century was like what happens in the parts of Europe where the old peasant culture is still established,' then a certain type of behaviour can be expected in the thirteenth century.⁶ But elsewhere the 'if' is forgotten, and Homans confidently draws on analogies with other parts of Europe in more modern times, for example France and Russia, in order to confirm some otherwise unprovable points.⁷ The most explicit justification of this method occurs when he admits that 'in reconstructing any ancient society, our knowledge of what happens today must give flesh and blood to the dry bones of records,'⁸ and puts this forward as a justification for drawing on a picture of nineteenth century Ireland in order to support his ideas concerning the treatment of the old. In Homans' work, as in that of the others referred to above, there appears to be a strong, self-confirming, and circular hypothesis. It is thought to be self-evident that the rural inhabitants of England between the Norman invasion and the sixteenth century were basically like 'peasants' elsewhere in time and space. These writers therefore hold that it is justifiable to fill in the vast gaps in our records and our knowledge by drawing information from studies of peasants elsewhere. The picture of medieval society which emerges then seems to show that there really were peasants, who acted and felt like Russian, Chinese, Indian and Polish peasants or at least like medieval French, Italian, and

---

³*Medieval Manor*, pp. 237-8.
⁴J. T. Krause, 'The Medieval Household; Large or Small?', *Ec.H.R.*, ix, no. 3 (1957), pp. 423-5.
⁵Raftis, *Tenure*, p. 33. The assumption that the 'basic' social structure of England in the middle ages was the same as that of Europe as a whole is present in writers from Marx and Engels (*Capital*, iii, pp. 885 note, 897), to Hilton (*Bond Men*, pp. 26, 33).
⁶*Villagers*, p. 140.
⁷Ibid., pp. 112-3, 207.
⁸Ibid., p. 157; see also p. 5 for a similar argument.

German ones. Since this is taken as proved, we may look to studies of these other societies in order to fill in further gaps — and so on in an apparently endless spiral of self-fulfilling confirmation. The same fault could also easily be detected in historians writing on later periods.

The attraction of the 'from peasant to industrial' theory lies very deep in our hearts, since it also appeals to the still strong nineteenth century evolutionary mode of thought, with its idea of gradual growth from small, closed, immobile, technologically simple, subsistence economies where life was 'nasty, brutish and short,' towards the humane, mobile, affluent society of modern western Europe and North America. It is, furthermore, attractive to think of this 'progress' from 'lower' to 'higher' as a more-or-less continuous line. Such an evolutionary, or, as it is sometimes known 'whig,' interpretation of history has frequently been unmasked.[9] F. W. Maitland for instance, wrote concerning the legal status of women in the medieval period:

we ought not to enter upon our investigation until we have protested against the common assumption that in this region a great generalization must needs be possible, and that from the age of savagery until the present age every change in marital law has been favourable to the wife.[10]

His warning could be extended to most areas of social history. The spirit which moved Macaulay to see himself on a pinnacle of achievement towards which the past had slowly climbed is still very strong; to find it we need only turn to recent publications in the field of family history, for instance the works of Stone, Shorter and that edited by De Mause.[11] While drawing analogies with other 'peasant' societies as described above, these all agree on the model of evolution from a loveless, harsh, 'peasant-type' situation towards the modern, loving, nuclear family which we now see around us, a framework which again has been superbly exposed by Maitland:

To suppose that the family law of every nation must needs traverse the same route, this is an unwarrantable hypothesis. To construct some fated scheme of successive stages which shall comprise every arrangement that may yet be discovered among backward peoples, that is a hopeless task. A not unnatural inference from their backwardness would be that somehow or another they have wandered away from the road along which the more successful races have made their journey.[12]

[9]For example, in Herbert Butterfield, *The Whig Interpretation of History* (1931).
[10]Maitland, *English Law*, ii, p. 403.
[11]These works were cited in chapter two. The introduction by De Mause and the works of Shorter and Stone would remind anthropologists of much writing in later nineteenth century England, with medieval and early modern men and women replacing the unenlightened 'savages.'
[12]Maitland, *English Law*, ii, p. 255.

There are other explanations for the considerable distortions — one of them being a kind of economic determinism which assumes that because land is the basic factor in production, and England was basically a 'plough' culture, it *must* have had a social structure and ideology similar to other 'plough' cultures such as Russia or China. In fact England is an excellent illustration of the basic fact which both Marx and Weber realized, namely that it is not simply the case that the means of production — the technology and the ecology — determine social relations and ideology, but that there is a mutual interaction. It is far too simple to assume that because the means of producing wealth in thirteenth century England seems to resemble those in nineteenth century Ireland, France or Russia, *therefore* the society was in any basic way similar. It may indeed have been; but this needs to be proved, not assumed.

The combination of this discovery of new sources, particularly for the sixteenth to eighteenth centuries, plus a new interest in local and social history, plus more sophisticated knowledge of what happens in contemporary non-European societies, has made it possible to re-think the whole basic stereotype. Confining ourselves for the moment to the crucial medieval period, and looking with the perspective of an anthropologist and seventeenth century historian, we see that the evidence to contradict almost every one of the supposed characteristics of peasantry has been accumulating rapidly in a number of detailed studies. But lacking any other appropriate model, medievalists have tried to stretch the earlier characterization of medieval society to fit it to the new data without abandoning it entirely. There are a few who rebel openly against a position where 'to all intents and purposes historians have long since disposed of the medieval peasant. He was after all, as we have been told repeatedly, isolated, backward, exploited, and generally unfree.'[13] In general, however, the situation appears to be one which approximates to the final stage before a paradigmatic change.[14] The data does not fit the predictions of the model, yet many historians cling to an outworn stereotype.

Since this may seem an arrogant interpretation, examples should be cited. Some instances are contained in recent work by two of those who have made among the most distinguished contributions to the study of medieval rural England. M. M. Postan's own research, and that stimulated by his work, have been largely responsible for undermining the old consensus. He seems to be aware of this, and yet, protesting too

[13]E. Britton, 'The Peasant Family in Fourteenth-century England,' *Peasant Studies*, v, no. 2 (April, 1976), p. 2.
[14]In the sense defined by Thomas Kuhn in *The Structure of Scientific Revolutions* (Chicago, 1962).

much, attempts to continue to stuff new wine into old bottles. In a short paragraph written in 1968 he proceeds to show that the landlessness, production for the market rather than for use, the employment of hired labour, and other features of medieval society appear to make the medieval English villager very different from other peasantries we know. But he argues that nevertheless 'historians will not fail to recognize in the physiognomy of the medieval villager most of the traits of a true peasantry.'[15] Similarly, Hilton, faced with the fact that Kosminsky had shown for the thirteenth, and Faith for the later four-teenth centuries, that many of the features of peasantry seemed to be absent, can only argue that 'both the market conditions and the extreme population pressure of the second half of the thirteenth century, and the sudden relaxation of population pressure after 1350, covered a relatively short period of time, and took place under peculiar circumstances.'[16] Given the fact that documentary evidence is available only from the second half of the thirteenth century onwards and that we know that the fifteenth century was in many ways similar to the later fourteenth, it would appear that a leading medievalist is close to being forced to argue that the whole of the recorded medieval period in England was 'excep-tional.' In such circumstances we may well wonder whether the underlying model is still appropriate.

It is well known that people do not like altering their basic views. We would therefore expect that those who wish to avoid the consequences of the argument of this book will attempt to show that only a minor terminological re-shuffling is involved. They will ask whether so much fuss should be made over the word 'peasant,' what word can be used instead of it, whether it matters what we call people, and so on. It is necessary to repeat, therefore, that it is not the word which is in debate. It would probably be as well if English historians could abandon it entirely, for it is misleading. Yet it is probably a word that is too deeply ingrained to eradicate. In any case, the avoidance of the word would be of no value if the general model of a 'peasant-like' society, as described in the first chapter, was not modified. It is the associated set of features which is at issue. That more than mere terminology is involved will be apparent if we consider very briefly a few of the effects which the acceptance of the thesis of this work would entail, not only for historical research, but also in the related fields of sociology, anthropology and economics. It is the scale of the alterations which would be necessary in neighbouring disciplines which leads one to believe that paradigmatic shifts are involved.

It is not necessary to spell out the consequences of the argument for

[15]Postan, *Essays*, p. 280.
[16]Hilton, *Bond Men*, p. 39.

the general theories of Marx and Weber. In almost every detail, their views in relation to England in the medieval period appear to be incorrect. They believed that up to the end of the fifteenth century England was basically a 'peasant' social structure in the fullest sense, similar in kind to other European countries. Thus, to challenge medievalists is also to encounter the two most formidable theorists of the development of western society. It is to maintain that when they both chose England as their prime example of the transition from pre-capitalist to capitalist society, they had the misfortune to select a singular and peculiar example. Indeed, one of the major reasons for their choice, the unusually good records produced by a centralized bureaucracy, was one of the products and indexes of this peculiarity. In one sense, at least, this does not matter for Marx. If it is finally proved that he was incorrect about the specific instance, this does not necessarily invalidate his general argument. Yet if we continue to take Marx and Weber as guides to what we should be asking about the origins of modern capitalist and industrial society in the West, we may pose the wrong questions. Furthermore, if we concentrate on the sixteenth century as the watershed, and assume that all the European nations were in essence similar before that time, a range of enquiry is immediately closed to us. We are driven as well to seeing law, social structure and politics as largely a reflection of something else.

To abandon the Marx—Weber chronology may be painful, but hardly shocking. It is not surprising that these two authors, writing a century or more ago, when hardly any detailed work had been undertaken on medieval England, should have assumed that the country was essentially the same as other agrarian nations in Europe and that the differences within Europe really emerged only at the end of the middle ages. Nor is it difficult to see why they should have believed that the basic agrarian structure was very similar to that in other parts of the world. As Ernest Gellner remarks, the Marxian description of the transition from 'feudalism' to 'capitalism' 'may not be true, but it is by no means manifestly or wholly false: no mean achievement for a sociological theory over a century old, concerning issues which are a burning concern to many, and where material is rich and has accumulated at an amazing rate.'[17] The continuing vitality of the hypothesis will no doubt be shown by the reactions to the argument of this book.

It has been argued that if we use the criteria suggested by Marx, Weber and most economic historians, England was as 'capitalist' in 1250 as it was in 1550 or 1750. That is to say, there were already a developed

---

[17]Ernest Gellner, *Thought and Change* (1964), p. 128. As F. J. West has recently pointed out, Marx and Engels had little access to medieval records and they did not even use the major part of the material that was available to them (in Kamenka, *Feudalism*, p. 60).

market and mobility of labour, land was treated as a commodity and full private ownership was established, there was very considerable geographical and social mobility, a complete distinction between farm and family existed, and rational accounting and the profit motive were widespread. This has generally been obscured by an over-emphasis on technology or *per capita* income. But Weber's distinction between the 'spirit' of capitalism and its manifestation in the physical world helps us to see behind the superficial forms. Just as Furnivall could describe Burma as a 'factory without chimneys,'[18] so we could describe thirteenth-century England as a capitalist-market economy without factories. By shifting the origins of capitalism back to well before the Black Death, we alter the nature of a number of other problems.

One of these is the origin of modern individualism. Those who have written on the subject have always accepted the Marx—Weber chronology. For example, David Riesman assumes that modern individualism emerged from an older collectivist, 'tradition-directed' society, in the fifteenth and sixteenth centuries.[19] Its growth was directly related to the Reformation, Renaissance and the break-up of the old feudal world. The 'inner-directed' stage of intense individualism occurred in the period between the sixteenth and nineteenth centuries. Though a recent general survey of historical and philosophical writing on individualism concedes that some of the roots lie deep in classical and biblical times and also in medieval mysticism, still in general it stresses the Renaissance, Reformation and the Enlightenment as the period of great transition. Many of the strands of political, religious, ethical, economic and other types of individualism are traced to Hobbes, Luther, Calvin and other post-1500 writers.[20] Yet, if the present thesis is correct, individualism in economic and social life is much older than this in England. In fact, within the recorded period covered by our documents, it is not possible to find a time when an Englishman did not stand alone. Symbolized and shaped by his ego-centred kinship system, he stood in the centre of his world. This means that it is no longer possible to 'explain' the origins of English individualism in terms of either Protestantism, population change, the development of a market economy at the end of the middle ages, or the other factors suggested by the writers cited. Individualism, however defined, predates sixteenth-century changes and can be said to shape them all. The explanation

[18]In Margaret Mead (ed.), *Cultural Patterns and Technical Change* (New York, 1955), p. 53.
[19]David Riesman, *The Lonely Crowd* (Yale paper edn., 1961), pp. xxv, 6-7, 12-13; *Selected Essays from Individualism Reconsidered* (New York, 1954), p. 13.
[20]Steven Lukes, *Individualism* (Oxford, 1973), pp. 14, 40-1, 47, 53, 62, 67, 74, 80, 89, 95, 99.

must lie elsewhere, but will remain obscure until we trace the origins even further than has been attempted in this work.

Closely related to the question of individualism is that of equality and liberty. One of the major works which consider the supposed origins of the concept of equality is Louis Dumont's *Homo Hierarchicas*.[21] Dumont bases his view of western society on Marx, Weber, Montesquieu and De Tocqueville. He consequently arrives at the same conclusions, particularly of the last named, arguing that individualistic, egalitarian, society with easy social mobility and the strong rights of the person against the group is a relatively recent phenomenon, limited to certain parts of western Europe from the sixteenth century onwards. His aim is to show that Indian caste society, rather than being aberrant in its emphasis on hierarchy and the power of the group, is in fact normal: it is egalitarian individualism which is exceptional, a recent and specialized growth. The argument is less convincing if we come across a large agrarian country with very good records stretching back six hundred years which has always appeared to have had an highly flexible social structure. If since at least the thirteenth century England has been a country where the individual has been more important than the group and the hierarchy of ranks has not been closed, it becomes clear that there is no necessary evolutionary set of stages from hierarchy to equality. They are alternative systems which may co-exist in time. Furthermore, it becomes easier to see that the clash between the Indian and the English systems was between a peasant social structure and a fundamantally non-peasant, individualistic, one.

The same theme can be viewed from the standpoint of the individual and his wider kinship links. We saw that Weber, especially, described a major transition from a kinship-based society, to one based on market, impersonal, relations. There is also a strong tendency to see kinship as gradually playing a smaller and smaller part, to chronicle the 'breakdown' of wider groupings as a consequence of changing technology and economy. One example of this can be seen in the work of social anthropologists who have assumed that the present English family system is the consequence of changes which have occurred in the eighteenth and nineteenth centuries. The modern 'individualistic' system, with its stress on the nuclear family, is spread throughout England and North America, but is generally held to be both peculiar and of recent origin, a reflex reaction to the dislocation caused by the growth of capitalism, industrialization and urbanization. Let us take just three examples.

Radcliffe-Brown argued that romantic love as a basis for marriage

---

[21]Louis Dumont, *Homo Hierarchicus* (Paladin edn., 1972), esp. pp. 35-55.

grew in the eighteenth and nineteenth centuries, out of a previous arranged-marriage society: 'the modern English idea of marriage is recent and decidedly unusual.'[22] More recently, Edmund Leach has written that the nuclear family system 'is a most unusual kind of organization, and I would predict that it is only a transient phase in our society.'[23] A popular sociological survey of English kinship and marriage has also drawn a picture of the eighteenth and nineteenth-century transition from a traditional, extended household, arranged-marriage, kinship-based, 'peasant type' society, to our modern nuclear-family system.[24] But if we are correct in arguing that the English now have roughly the same family system as they had in about 1250, the arguments concerning kinship and marriage as a reflection of economic change become weaker. To have survived the Black Death, the Reformation, the Civil War, the move to the factories and the cities, the system must have been fairly durable and flexible. Indeed, it could be argued that it was its extreme individualism, the simplest form of molecular structure, which enabled it to survive and allowed society to change. Furthermore, if the family system pre-dated, rather than followed on, industrialization, the causal link may have to be reversed, with industrialization as a consequence, rather than a cause, of the basic nature of the family.[25]

We have now begun to bridge the gap between individualism and economic change and may turn to another problem which, appears altered, namely the explanation of the origins of capitalism itself. If it was present in 1250, it is clear that neither the spread of world trade and colonization, nor Protestantism, can have much to do with its origins. Nor is it plausible to argue, as McLelland does,[26] that it was the result of unspecified child rearing changes connected to the religious develop-ments of the sixteenth century. Socialization and the family, especially the apparent absence of 'patriarchal' power and sending children away from home at an early age are clearly very important. But they were part of an English pattern that was probably established by at least the thir-teenth century. Nor can the development of towns have much to do with

[22]In the introduction to A. R. Radcliffe-Brown and Daryll Forde (eds.), *African Systems of Kinship and Marriage* (1950), p. 43; see also pp. 45, 63, on the 'recentness' of the change.
[23]E. R. Leach in Nicholas Pole (ed.), *Environmental Solutions* (Cambridge, 1972), p. 105.
[24]Ronald Fletcher, *The Family and Marriage in Britain* (Penguin, 1962), pp. 45, 47, 69, 166.
[25]Among those who have begun to speculate along these lines are Hajnal, *European Marriage*, pp. 131-3; W. J. Goode, *The Family* (New Jersey, 1964), pp. 108ff and *World Revolution and Family Patterns* (New York, 1963), pp. 10ff. An example of the older view, namely that 'Market capitalism was at the root of the revolution in sentiment' is E. Shorter, *The Making of the Modern Family* (1976), ch. 7.
[26]David C. McLelland, *The Achieving Society* (Paper edn., New York, 1967), pp. 365ff.

the explanation. Like Calvinism and expanding trade, they could be seen as a consequence, rather than as a cause, of the patterns described above. Again we need to take the story further back. Only when it has been established when England really did become capitalist and individualist, or, put in other terms, when it ceased to be, or whether indeed it was ever, a 'peasant' nation, will it be useful to speculate about causes.

What is absolutely clear is that one of the major theories of economic anthropology is incorrect, namely the idea that we witness in England between the sixteenth and nineteenth centuries the 'Great Transformation' from a non-market, peasant society where economics is 'embedded' in social relations, to a modern market, capitalist, system where economy and society have been split apart. This view is most clearly expressed in the work of Karl Polanyi. He depended on Marx, Weber and economic historians for his material, and this led him to conclude that the great change occurred mainly in the seventeenth and eighteenth centuries. Thus he wrote in relation to England and France that 'not before the last decade of the eighteenth century . . . was the establishment of a free labour market even discussed.'[27] Before the sixteenth century land was not a commodity and markets played no important part in the economic system.[28] One implication of this argument, parallel to Dumont's concerning the untypical nature of equality, is that market economies are recent and unusual, so that when Adam Smith founded classical economics on the premise of the rational 'economic' man, believing that he was describing a universal and long-evident type, he was deluded.[29] According to Polanyi, such a man had only just emerged, stripped of his ritual, political and social needs. The implication of the present argument, however, is that it was Smith who was right and Polanyi who was wrong, at least in relation to England. 'Homo economicus' and the market society had been present in England for centuries before Smith wrote. Yet Polanyi's insight that Smith was writing within a peculiar social environment is correct when we realize that in many respects England had probably long been different from almost every other major agrarian civilization we know.

Closely related to the old question of the origins of capitalism is the equally important one concerning the origins of industrialization. Again the terms of the questions we would ask would be altered if the present thesis is correct. It is now very obvious that historians are quite

[27]Karl Polanyi, *The Great Transformation* (1944; Beacon Paper edn., Boston, 1957), p. 70; see also pp. 77, 83.
[28]Ibid., pp. 55, 68-71.
[29]Ibid., p. 43. Adam Smith was, of course, a Scotsman, working in Edinburgh, but his work nevertheless fitted into an anglicized tradition.

unable to explain in purely economic terms why industrialization occurred. However we define the phenomenon and whenever we date its main period, it is extremely difficult to explain why it should have occurred, and, particularly, why it emerged first in England. The most succinct summary of the major explanations that have been put forward in the past, and of the overwhelming objections to each of them, is given by R. M. Hartwell.[30] The factors listed are: capital accumulation; innovations in technology and organization; 'fortunate factor endowments' (coal, iron, resources); *laissez-faire* in philosophy, religion, science and law culminating in the eighteenth-century; market expansion (both foreign trade and the domestic market); a number of miscellaneous factors, including war, autonomous growth of knowledge and 'the English genius.'

After examining all the economic explanations from among these, Hartwell concludes that the theories have 'added little to our understanding of the industrial revolution.'[31] He suggests that the explanation must lie in long-term factors over several centuries: 'industrialization generally was the product of a European civilization long in the making.'[32] He further believes that the solution may lie in the social environment, about which we know 'precious little.'[33] Pursuing these two hints a little way, he argues that there was something special about England before the eighteenth century. It was not industrialized, but nor was it an 'underdeveloped' economy. It fitted into some intermediary category. Asking when it became 'modern,' the author accepts Charles Wilson's conclusion that it was in 1660.[34] Though we agree with Hartwell's summary of the objections to an economic explanation, we have argued that, however we define 'modern,' this is much too late a date. Furthermore, in being like this, England had apparently taken a different course from much of the rest of Europe.[35]

A number of social historians have realized that English property relations were at the heart of much that is special about England, particularly in relation to industrialization. Marc Bloch believed that the growth of individualistic ownership was peculiar to England and was related in some way to the 'two most immediately obvious facts of English Economic History — I mean colonial expansion and the

---

[30]R. M. Hartwell (ed.), *Causes of the Industrial Revolution* (1967), pp. 10 and 58ff. For another recent survey of the causes, which comes to a similar conclusion, see M. W. Flinn, *Origins of the Industrial Revolution* (1966), esp. p. 90.
[31]Hartwell, *Causes of the Industrial Revolution*, p. 77.
[32]Ibid., p. 21; see also pp. 63-4, 78.
[33]Ibid., p. 20.
[34]Ibid., pp. 23-4.
[35]The exact extent to which England differed from Continental countries will only be established by future research.

industrial revolution, for both of which it probably prepared the way.'[36] More recently, Harold Perkin has argued that the major cause of the British industrial revolution was 'the unique nature and structure of English society as it had evolved by the eighteenth century.'[37] The central feature of this social structure was the 'openness of the hierarchy, the freedom of movement up and down the scale, and above all the absence of legal or customary barriers between the landed aristocracy and the rest.' This stemmed, as did everything else, from the individualistic pattern of ownership.[38] But just as Hartwell took the major change to have occurred in the seventeenth century, these authors assume it took place after the Black Death and principally in the sixteenth and seventeenth centuries. We would incorporate their insights into the central contribution of ownership and social mobility, but argue that the change, if change there had been, had already occurred in England by the thirteenth century at least.

In the light of this argument it begins to become clear why England should have been precocious in its economic and social development in the eighteenth and nineteenth centuries, for it had been somewhat different for a very long period. When Kosminsky asked how we were to explain why England, which was 'not the first country to start out on the road of capitalist development' nevertheless 'quickly overtook the countries which had taken that road before her' he was unable to provide an answer.[39] Trapped within a Marxist chronology with its great break at the end of the fifteenth century, he could not account for 'this all-conquering growth of capitalism in a country which apparently occupied a very modest place in the economic life of medieval Europe.' From the information which he cites it is clear that he realized that England in the thirteenth century was a far more sophisticated market economy than did Marx. Yet he was still forced to pose the question in terms which would make it impossible to answer.

England did not set out on the road to capitalism later, nor is it relevant that it played only a modest part in medieval economic life. As Weber has stressed, it is not the splendour of Florence, Agra or Peking that is to be noted, but the social and economic structure and mentality in small market towns and villages. The ethics and organization of England may already have set it apart from the many, more splendid, peasant civilizations which overshadowed it. This should not be taken to imply that other factors such as the absence of marauding armies or

---

[36]Bloch, *Land*, p. 49.
[37]H. J. Perkin, 'The Social Causes of the British Industrial Revolution,' *Trans. Roy. Hist. Soc.*, 5th ser. 18 (1968), p. 127.
[38]Ibid., pp. 136, 135.
[39]Kosminsky, *Studies*, p. 319.

high taxation were unimportant. But all the geographical, technological or other advantages would have been of no account if they had not been associated with a very unusual social, demographic and economic structure.

The origin of this structure is a problem for further investigation. Yet if England's transition was not typical, even within western Europe, it is obvious that to draw parallels between England and currently developing Third World peasantries without taking into account the enormous differences that flow from disparities not only in wealth, but in the social, political and psychological spheres, is a recipe for disaster. If most contemporary countries are trying to move from 'peasantry' to 'urban-industrial' society within a generation, whereas England moved from non-industrial but largely 'capitalist' to 'urban-industrial' society over a period of at least six hundred years, it will be obvious that the trauma and difficulties will not only be very different but probably far more intense.[40] Furthermore, if such countries absorb any form of western industrial technology, they are not merely incorporating a physical or economic product, but a vast set of individualistic attitudes and rights, family structure and patterns of geographical and social mobility which are very old, very durable, and highly idiosyncratic. They therefore need to consider whether the costs in terms of the loneliness, insecurity and family tensions which are associated with the English structure outweigh the economic benefits.

A final test of the theory advanced here is that of the breadth and economy of explanation. Does the hypothesis give a more reasonable explanation than does the generally accepted set of themes, of other features of the past and present, and does it do so with the minimum of re-arranging of the evidence? As an example of width of explanation we may mention the fact that the argument helps to explain the curious effects of English colonization. Englishmen who went abroad took with them a system very different from that present in much of the world. When Daniel Thorner surveyed world peasantries, he noted that the only areas that had never had peasantries at all were those colonized by England: Australia, New Zealand, Canada and North America.[41] It is the argument of this book that this was no accident. Englishmen did not merely shed their traditional social structure as they walked down the gang-plank into the promised land, as at least one writer has disingenuously suggested.[42] When Jefferson wrote, 'We hold these truths to be

---

[40]This is another reason for seeing W. W. Rostow's work as a gross over-simplification of the issues, see, for example, *The Stages of Economic Growth* (Cambridge, 1960), pp. 31-5.
[41]Thorner, *Peasantry*, p. 504.
[42]Shorter, *Making of the Modern Family*, p. 242: 'the colonial settlers seem to have seized privacy and intimacy for themselves as soon as they stepped off the boat.'

sacred and undeniable; that all men are created equal and independent, that from that equal creation they derive rights inherent and inalienable,' he was putting into words a view of the individual and society which had its roots in thirteenth-century England or earlier. It is not, as we know, a view that is either universal or undeniable, but neither is it a view that emerged by chance in Tudor or Stuart England.

One example of the criterion of economy of explanation will end this work. The received theory, that England was like the rest of Europe until the sixteenth-century and then became different, and that it followed roughly the same set of developmental stages, requires rearrangement of most of the evidence we have from the period under examination. Those accepting the conventional wisdom are forced to argue that almost all those who wrote about England up to the nineteenth century, both those who lived there and those who visited the country, were deluded. They are forced to take the view that those who studied their own past and their own present were under a massive misapprehension. We have seen, for example, that Perry Anderson and J. G. A. Pocock dismiss the views of English contemporaries and some later historians as a local and totally inaccurate myth. The dismissal and manipulation of source material seems to me to be hard to defend. Of course contemporaries made mistakes and we have to weigh their words, especially when they were using history for political purposes. Yet it is surely more reasonable to assume that when they argued that England was somehow different, when they used 'peasant' only of foreign countries, and when they minimized the effects of Norman feudalism, they knew, in general, what they were doing.

Postscript

On reconsidering the finished work I am very conscious that there are many arguments which could still be pursued and many types of evidence left unconsidered. Although I have discussed the work of Maine, Marx, Montesquieu, De Tocqueville and Weber, other major sociological thinkers, particularly members of the Scottish Enlightenment, and Durkheim and Tönnies, need consideration. I have omitted them partly because this is primarily intended as a work of history and not a history of sociological theory, partly because I believe that if the argument is proven in relation to Marx and Weber, the implications for the historical views of Durkheim and Tönnies are fairly obvious. Another category of thinkers who deserve further attention are the English political philosophers, particularly Hobbes and Locke, but also medieval writers. Nothing that I have read of or about their work appears to contradict the theses advanced here, but it would be interesting to have an analysis of their writing in the light of this theory.

Another serious gap is the omission of any extended discussion of social and economic structure on the Continent. Although the views of contemporary foreigners such as De Tocqueville and Montesquieu, and of Englishmen who travelled abroad, are cited, the case I have argued will need to be tested with comparative material from French, German, Italian and other archives. All that has been presented here is the viewpoint of a few of the most eminent comparative historians who have thought at the European level, namely Bloch, Maine and Maitland. I have therefore often made assertions which will need to be proved. But I am glad to find support for the general direction of my statements in the recent work of social historians of the stature of H. J. Habakkuk and E. P. Thompson.[1]

[1]H. J. Habakkuk, 'La disparition du paysan anglais,' *Annales*, 20, no. 4 (July-Aug., 1965); E. P. Thompson, 'The Peculiarities of the English,' *The Socialist Register*, eds. Ralph Milliband and John Saville (1965). I am grateful to Keith Thomas for these references.

A further omission concerns the nature of the English evidence used. I have relied heavily on three types of contemporary material: local records, legal textbooks and autobiographical documents. The didactic, artistic and moralistic material in sermons, pamphlets, plays and poems has been little used. Although I am reasonably familiar with such material, it seemed to me that one of the possible reasons for the distortion of English social history has been too heavy a reliance on upper class literature and on writing which stated what *ought* to happen. It has been too easily assumed that this is what *did* happen, at all levels of society. Yet the relative neglect of such sources in this work has at least two consequences.

Firstly, it precludes any detailed discussion of sentiment and of the moral order. Secondly, it presents a harsher and more exaggerated picture than that which we might obtain if this source had been more extensively used. For example, as Keith Thomas reminded me, there is a good deal in the pamphlets and sermons of the time to say that it was a father's duty to leave his property to his children, or that children ought to support their parents financially if they were poor. To cite just one instance, Thomas Becon in the sixteenth century wrote that 'if their parents be aged and fallen into poverty . . . then ought the children, if they will truly honour their parents, to labour for them, to see unto their necessities, to provide necessaries for them . . . .'[2] Yet even such encouragement to give to children or to support the old can be interpreted in two ways — either as evidence that there was a widespread sentiment that this was right, or as proof that moralists were aware that many people needed to be reminded that the way they were behaving was unethical. The difficulties of using such evidence, combined with the desire to keep the argument relatively simple in a first presentation, has led to a decision to reserve a discussion of sentiments to a subsequent work. This will deal with two of the problems briefly alluded to in the text, namely the attitudes to children and the status and role of women. It will explore the consequences of the arguments presented above in these areas and will utilize the moralistic literature largely omitted here.

Another bias which will be clear to readers is in the occupational and class bias of this work. It will be obvious that I have concentrated almost

[2]Thomas Becon, *Works* (reprinted Cambridge, 1844), p. 358. The moral duty was only turned into a legal stipulation towards the end of the sicteenth century, in the Elizabethan Poor Law. Even then, it was only a *financial* duty (not housing), which only fell on children and grandchildren, not even siblings, and which was only recognized where the person was 'poor, old, blind, lame and impotent . . . not able to work' and hence likely to fall to the charge of the parish (Richard Burn, *The Justice of the Peace, and Parish Officer* (16th edn., 1788), iii, p. 655.

exclusively on rural, non-gentry, inhabitants of England. Although I feel that this is justified by the fact that they constituted over ninety percent of the population of England thoughout the period under consideration, it is essential to stress that patterns both among artisans and others in the towns, as well as in the upper social strata, may have been very different from those described here. Since a great deal of history has been written from the top downwards, it does not seem inappropriate to redress the balance a little. Yet it is to be hoped that further work among the other groups will show to what extent their patterns differ from the model we have elaborated here.

A further point is that the argument of this book has a number of implications, only a few of which have been noted in the conclusion. One of those omitted is the question of our conception of England as a 'feudal' society. It would have been tempting to launch out on a reconsideration of the whole question of how far England was ever a 'feudal' society, for this work suggests serious doubts in relation to the conventional views. To have simultaneously re-examined feudalism would have complicated the argument very considerably and the temptation was therefore avoided. Yet it will be obvious that, like a number of medievalists such as Bloch and Postan,[3] I have strong doubts as to the extent to which English feudalism fits into the Continental, particularly French, model. This is a theme which medievalists may well pursue further.

There is one further omission. This work is titled 'The Origins of English Individualism.' Yet the search for the origins has been taken back for nearly eight hundred years from the present, to the start of the thirteenth century, without finding the roots of the peculiar set of inter-related features which have been isolated. The present limits of my competence as well as the constraints of space and time have forced me to stop at the point where records of the manorial courts also cease to survive. This makes for an abrupt ending. Some readers who have persevered to this point may be disappointed that the rejected conventional explanation has not been replaced by a full and complete alternative. I have my own suspicions as to where the 'origins' were in time and space and they are similar to those of Montesquieu quoted on page 170 above. It is not, however, worth presenting guesses unsupported by evidence. It will need other works before we can trace the elusive English back to their particular roots. I hope that this book will prompt others to contribute to that search.

[3]Bloch, *Land*, pp. 58-62; Postan, *England*, pp. 605-7.

Manuscript Sources for the Local Studies

Earls Colne, Essex

Over fifteen hundred separate 'documents,' from single wills to lengthy court rolls or archdeaconry 'act' books of more than four hundred pages, have been used to reconstruct the history of this parish between 1400 and 1750. It is possible to list only a few of the most important sources used.

At the Essex Record Office, Chelmsford:	*Reference*
Account book of Richard Harlakenden, elder & younger, 1603-49	Temp. Acc. 897/8
Registers of baptisms, marriages and burials, 1558-1755	D/P/209/1/1-4
Court rolls of Earls Colne Manor, 1400-1753	D/DPr/66-86
Abstract of court rolls, Earls Colne Manor, 1409-1597	D/DPr/91
Court book, containing rentals, 1588, Earls Colne Manor	D/DPr/99
Register of admission fines for both manors, 1610-1759	D/DPr/100
Rentals of Earls Colne Manor, 1395-1678	D/DPr/105-113
Rental connecting 1838 tithe map with 1598 map and survey	D/DPr/118
Court rolls for Colne Priory Manor, 1489-1752 (with gaps)	D/DPr/1-30

Rentals for Colne Priory Manor, c. 1380-1500   D/DPr/5, 10, 11

Abstract of Colne Priory Court Rolls, 1558-
1750   D/DPr/41-3

Rentals of Colne Priory Manor, 1400-1590   D/DPr/58-9

Survey or Terrier of both manors by Israel
Amyce, 1598   Temp. Acc. 897

Rentals of both manors, 1562-1589   D/DU/292/6

Rental of both manors, 1638   D/DU/292/7

Map of both manors made by Israel Amyce in
1598   D/DSm/P1

Miscellaneous deeds for Earls Colne
properties   D/DPr/175-270

Wills of all Earls Colne inhabitants as listed in
F. G. Emmison (ed.).
Wills at Chelmsford, 1400-1619, 1620-1720, 1721-1858:
(Index Library, vols. 78, 79, 84, 1958, 1960, 1969); as well as wills of
inhabitants of inhabitants in other villages holding land in Earls
Colne, a total of 345 wills between 1502-1750. Another 38 wills in the
P.R.O. and London County Record Office (Consistory Court) were also
used.

Archdeaconry of Colchester Act Books
(detections and corrections), 1540-1666   D/ACA/1-55

Public Record Office, London:

Chancery court depositions, 1518-1712   C1-C10

Lay Subsidy Rolls and Hearth Taxes, 1524-
1675   E 179/108-112, 246

Kirkby Lonsdale, Cumbria:

Roughly the same quantity of records exist for this parish, though
detailed documentation does not start until 1538 with the parish
register. Among the sources used for the.discussion in chapter three are
the following.

Record Office, Kendal:

Listings of inhabitants for the nine townships
  of Kirkby Lonsdale, 1695   WD/Ry

Deeds of properties in Kirkby Lonsdale   Underley Estate

Kirkby Lonsdale Church:

Registers of baptisms, marriages and burials,
  1538-1750

Records Office, Carlisle:

Court rolls and rentals of the Manor of
  Lupton, 1598-1750   Musgrave, Lonsdale

Court rolls, surveys and rentals of Kirkby
  Lonsdale, 1605-1750   Lonsdale

Record Office, Preston:

Wills and inventories for the parish of Kirkby Lonsdale, among the
testamentary papers of the Lonsdale Deanery, approximately two
thousand five hundred documents in all, 1500-1720.

Public Library, Lancaster:

Transcript of missing Kirkby Lonsdale court
  book, 1639-1670   Chippendall

Public Record Office, London:

Chancery depositions, 1597-1713   C5-C10

Index